Fourth Wheel

Copyright © 2022 by Abby Millsaps

All rights reserved.

ebook ISBN: 9798986018003
Paperback ISBN: 9798988800378

No portion of this book may be reproduced, distributed, or transmitted in any form without written permission from the author, except by a reviewer who may quote brief passages in a book review.

This book is a work of fiction. Any resemblance to any person, living or dead, or any events or occurrences, is purely coincidental. The characters and story lines are created by the author's imagination and are used fictitiously.

Developmental Editing by Melanie Yu, Made Me Blush Books
Line Editing, Copyediting, and Proofreading by VB Edits
Cover Design © Silver at Bitter Sage Designs

To every girl who's ever been told she's "too much" by a world that would prefer her to be quieter and softer: illegitimi non carborundum.

This story is for you.

Content Warning

Fourth Wheel is a full-length, high-heat romance novel that contains content some may find triggering, including offensive language, verbal threat of sexual assault, death of a parent, and references to alcoholism and addiction. It is a dual POV story featuring characters in their twenties. It ends with a happily ever after.

Chapter 1

Maddie

"Nope. Abso-fucking-lutely not. You might as well turn around and strut right back out that door."

His reaction is one I'd expect, but I'm still caught off guard.

I scoped out the parking lot before shooting my shot at The Oak tonight.

Jake's Jeep wasn't out back, so why the hell is he here?

I immediately pull out my phone and type out a message to Paige.

Maddie: Abort mission. The owner's here, and he knows my brother. He'll take our fakes.

Paige: WTF? I thought you said the coast was clear! We're already in the Lyft!

I silently groan and roll my lips, tasting the strawberry champagne lip gloss I slathered on just before entering the bar.

Maddie: Head to Holt. We probably can't get into Ray's, but I'm sure there's somewhere we can go. I'll meet you there as soon as I can.

"Oh Jakey," I sing-song. I stash my phone, then hop up onto a stool smack in the middle of the raw-edge bar at The Oak. "You wouldn't really kick me out, would you? We're practically family!" I rest my chin on my hand like I don't have a care in the world as I watch him push off the back bar and stalk toward me.

A lesser woman would shudder at the rage behind his glare.

But I've been honing my ability to drive him crazy for years. He's my brother's best friend, and I've known him my whole life. I'm uniquely skilled at getting under his skin.

Jake plants his hands on the bar and leans forward in a clear effort to intimidate me.

"I'm serious, Maddie. I'm not serving you here," he grits out through clenched teeth.

I stick out my lower lip and pout. What is his deal? He could have just poured me a drink and been done with the whole thing—I wouldn't have stuck around for more than half an hour without my friends here anyway.

But now that he picked this fight, I'm going to win.

"You always make my drinks for me at home or at the cabin," I retort, my voice louder than necessary considering his face is just inches from mine.

He whips his head from left to right, his eyes frantically scanning the patrons sitting on either side of us. Once he's satisfied no one is listening to our exchange, he looks back at me and scowls.

I bite down on one side of my lower lip and give him the biggest doe eyes I can manage, feigning an innocence we both know I don't possess. Fury erupts in his gaze when he realizes I'm intentionally goading him, and I swear his jaw ticks just like my brother's does when he's trying to keep his cool.

Good. If he wants to ruin my night, I can dish it right back and return the favor.

We stare at each other in a silent standoff, and seconds drag on as I try not to buckle under the weight of his glare. Jake is usually up for anything and doesn't give two shits about letting me drink. I'm not a kid. I'm twenty years old. Who is he trying to fool with this concerned big brother act?

Finally, someone calls his name from the other end of the bar, and he blinks, breaking our connection.

"You can sit there and pout all night. No one will serve you—I'll make sure of it." He raps his knuckles twice on the bar, then turns away, but not before I have the last word.

"That's okay, Jakey," I taunt.

His curiosity must get the best of him then, because he turns back to me and cocks one eyebrow.

I smirk before I bring the flask to my lips and suck down a mouthful of vodka.

"I brought my own, just in case."

I lift the pink bejeweled flask in mock salute. The thing is tacky as hell, but I wasn't about to meet up with my friends completely unprepared. I've only been back in town for a week, and my sad excuse for a social life has come to this: putzing around my tiny hometown and meeting up with people I only sort of liked in high school.

Pathetic.

At least I have Paige to keep me company during my impromptu stay in Hampton. She's been my best friend since middle school, and she still lives at home with her parents. When I told her my housing plans fell through for summer and that I'd have to hang out in Hampton until my new apartment was ready, she was thrilled.

I don't share the sentiment.

Hampton, Ohio has nothing on Berkeley, California.

I giggle when Jake's eyes practically bug out of his head before he turns and stalks off toward the guy who called him over. I take another swig from the stupid flask and make a mental note to see if Amazon has something less garish I can order for future BYOB needs.

I watch, amused, as Jake fumes about me to his employees. I know the second he starts issuing orders because that damn finger starts working again, pointing in my direction as he looks between two of the guys wearing those deliciously tight black V-neck shirts. Both men glance over at me, then look back at their boss, nodding like bobble heads at him.

Poof. There goes my fun for the night.

I glance at my phone again to find three missed calls and a text from Paige. I read her message and roll my eyes. They're heading to the hookah bar in Holt, which is as lame as it sounds. There's no way I'm making the drive out there to sit around and pretend to enjoy passing a pipe with Paige, Kyle, Travis, and whoever else they invited to come out with us. I'll either die of boredom or catch mono. I don't know which fate would be worse.

I survey the crowd, not because I want to find a familiar face, but because I'd like nothing more than to find an anonymous hookup for the night.

I'm staying at my parents' house for the summer, but they both travel for my dad's job, so they're rarely home. They have some sort of river cruise planned for this summer, too, so I don't expect to see them except on Zoom and FaceTime. My brother and his wife live in Virginia now, and most everyone else I know from high school didn't come back to Hampton this summer because of internships or whatever.

I was lucky enough to score a one-bedroom apartment just minutes from campus, but my unit won't be ready until August first. I thought I had a temporary place to stay this summer, but the girl from my logic class decided shacking up with her boyfriend sounded more fun than subletting the second room in her apartment, so here I am. I've got a solid eleven weeks to bum around this sleepy Ohio town before I can head back to Cali and move all my stuff out of storage and into my new place.

The prospects are slim tonight—everyone here is in a group or already paired up. Maybe I should just head out to Holt. At least there's more than one bar out that way.

I take another swig from my flask as I consider my options. The vibe at The Oak is admittedly not bad—it feels like a local watering hole but with more of an upscale, hipster vibe. I honestly would probably like the place if Jake Fun-Sucker Whitely-Vargo or whatever his name is nowadays wasn't the owner.

Maddie: ETA 30 minutes. I'm calling a car now.

I close out my messages app and scroll through Instagram for a few minutes, delaying the ride share that will take me out to Holt. Heading to the college town doesn't appeal to me, but it looks like my only option.

I give one last glance around the room, resigned to the fact that I'm going to have to work a lot harder than I planned tonight. But before I can open the Lyft app, someone new walks up behind the bar.

I can't make him out at first because his entire upper body is being blocked by the crate of liquor bottles he's holding against his chest. But when he sets the crate down and turns, my heart flutters and my stomach fills with butterflies.

I try to school my expression as I stare down the bar at a man I haven't seen in the flesh for more than a year.

Fielding Haas.

Well over six feet tall. Broad shoulders. Arm veins for fucking days. Straight white teeth behind a blinding smile that's so intense it almost looks predatory.

His hair's shorter than before, and he's got a gorgeous tan, even though summer's just begun. Somehow, he's even hotter than I remember.

And fuck, do I remember.

I may not have seen the guy around lately, but Fielding was a mainstay at just about every party and holiday get together my freshman year of college. He was good friends with my sister-in-law, and practically besties with Jake.

God, it's been too long. Just seeing him across the bar brings back a surge of memories. I miss his flirty banter and cocky attitude. I loved how he'd blatantly hit on me to get on my brother's nerves. He's hot, and he knows it. Just watching him has my body humming with excitement.

I'm not ashamed to admit that Fielding Haas has starred in more than one fantasy I've conjured up while spending quality time with my battery-operated boyfriend. Who could blame me? His eyes are like crystal-clear lagoons, and he's at least six two!

I squeeze my thighs together on the barstool and try to calm my kitten, but it's no use. If he has this sort of effect on me from across the room, I'm cream on a cracker once he makes his way toward me. Which he's doing. Right now.

But as I watch his confident gait, an inkling of disloyalty tugs at my core.

The last time anyone even mentioned Fielding's name was more than a year ago. My older brother, Rhett, insisted I block him from my phone, going as far as to make me swear I would tell him if Fielding ever tried to contact me. Something had gone down—and as per usual, no one would give me any details—but Fielding is officially on the no-fly list. He hasn't been at any of our holiday gatherings over the last year. It's like he ceased to exist.

If I'm not even allowed to accept a text from the guy, there's no way Jake would hire him to work at his bar, right? Unless...

"It looks like you need a drink," he murmurs in this deep, smooth voice that has me leaning forward in hopes of hearing him speak again. He stands opposite of where I sit and eyes me with a mix of intrigue and curiosity.

If his words hadn't just given him away, that look was a definite tell.

This man isn't Fielding.

This must be the other brother.

The sex kitten inside me revs her engine back to life as his eyes trail from my face to my chest, then back again. I'm smiling so hard my cheeks hurt from the effort. I probably look like an idiot—but I'm an idiot whose night just got a hell of a lot more interesting.

Fielding may be off limits. But no one ever told me to stay away from his twin.

Eat your heart out, Dempsey Haas.

We're eye-fucking each other like no one else in this bar exists. His body's illuminated by the funky teal lights that line the bar shelves behind him, giving his form this ethereal glow.

His eyes… goddamn, those eyes. They're impossibly blue. They're so light they're almost clear. It's like I'm standing on the edge of a pier over a lagoon, gazing down into a bottomless sea of baby blues.

The best part? He's staring right back at me with such intensity it looks like he wants to eat me alive.

I don't have time to come up with something clever to say before Jake is stalking toward us, that damn jaw tick working double-time to make itself known.

"I warned you, Fourth Wheel," he hisses, pointing to me like I'm the one who initiated this conversation.

I reluctantly look away from the man I want to climb like a spider-monkey and raise both hands in faux innocence. "He came over here and started talking to me!"

Dempsey tilts his chin up toward Jake, regarding him while keeping those lagoon-blue irises locked on me. If he keeps looking at me like this, I swear my panties are going to float away in a tidal wave of desire.

"What am I missing here?"

Fuckity fuck. This particular Haas brother has no idea who I am, and Jake's about to squash my fun before I can even get this party started.

But the heavens decide to shine down on me at that exact moment, and a shattering sound rings out from the back of the bar. Jake rushes away from us toward one of the big booths that line the back wall before he can answer Dempsey's question.

"*Don't* serve her," he barks over his shoulder as he hustles toward the commotion.

Dempsey chuckles darkly before leaning closer. "What the hell did you do to get that kind of reaction from him?" I bite back a smile as he continues to check me out.

"Honestly? Between you and me?" I hook my heels on the barstool and boost myself up a few inches, silently cheering when he matches my posture and leans in farther.

"I've known Jake for years. He's *always* hot and cold like that with me. I never know what I'm going to get with him."

Dempsey's eyebrows draw together a fraction as he shifts back slightly. "That doesn't really sound like Jake," he challenges.

Shit.

I assumed Jake was just his boss. That was probably the wrong angle if they're actually friends. I have to spin this somehow. I need a diversion, stat.

I pull out my sparkly flask, because as ridiculous as I feel drinking from it, it will absolutely serve its purpose in this situation.

I unscrew the top, then tilt it to my mouth with a flourish, adding in a satisfied moan after I swallow.

"I brought my own for this very reason," I quip, stashing the flask just as quickly as I whipped it out.

Dempsey's eyes widen in surprise.

He schools his expression a moment later, then leans forward until his forearms are resting on the natural wood bar. I chance a peek and squeeze my thighs together when I get visual confirmation of what I had assumed. Yep. Arms like his brother. Long, sinewy muscles sheathed in perfectly tanned skin. Hands that were made for touching, kneading, teasing. Veins for fucking days.

"I can't let you drink that in here, princess."

I scowl at the cutesy nickname.

"Princess? Really?"

He smirks. "That's what it says on your sparkly pink flask, *princess*," he counters with extra emphasis.

Huh. So it does.

Tou-fucking-che, Dempesy Haas.

"You don't miss a thing, do you?" I shift my hips on the bar stool and bring my shoulders together, giving him a perfect peek of my cleavage.

"I don't, thank fuck."

Straightening, I tilt my head in question.

"I wouldn't forgive myself if I missed a single thing when it comes to you."

Once again, I'm grinning like a fool. I can't help it. I thought I was going to have to chase this one down. But it seems like I may have found a willing participant tonight after all.

"Why don't you hand me a glass so I can sit here and drink this properly?"

Dempsey glances to the other end of the bar, and I follow his gaze, only to find Jake's eyes on us.

"Tell you what. Stash that when Jake and the other guys come by. I'll pour you a soda so it looks like you have a reason to be sitting at the bar."

"I do have a reason to be sitting at this bar," I counter as I gaze up at him through my lashes.

Dempsey doesn't respond. Instead, he busies himself with scooping ice into a glass, then filling it to the brim with fizzy soda.

"Are you waiting on someone?" he asks as he slides me the drink.

"Not anymore."

"So are you heading out soon?" he questions, the slightest hint of disappointment in his tone.

"Not anymore," I repeat as I put the stir stick into my mouth and suck.

To my delight, he lets out a quiet scoff while he watches me take a sip of soda.

"Let me take care of my other customers, then I'll be back. Don't go anywhere."

I give him a playful shrug and try to look coy. He doesn't need to worry, though. I'm not moving from this barstool until I'm leaving with him.

Chapter 2

Maddie

I flick my wrist and send another tot flying. It arcs through the air before landing in Dempsey's mouth. His eyes light up in delight, and I raise both hands in victory. We're officially four for seven, which is pretty damn good, if I say so myself.

"You two are getting on surprisingly well," Jake chirps as he brushes past Dempsey and moves to the other end of the bar.

I scowl in his direction, but as expected, he ignores me.

That's the third or fourth comment Jake has made in the last hour that almost blows my cover. What's his freaking deal tonight? Can't he see I'm a woman on a mission?

He's probably just pissed off that I had the brill idea to DoorDash an order of tater tots from his restaurant next door. Not my fault he doesn't serve food at The Oak. He's got a fully functional kitchen twenty feet away, but I wasn't about to lose my seat at the bar: in the middle of the action, in the halo glow of Dempsey's attention.

Whatever. Jake isn't my priority right now.

I don't know if it's the effects of the vodka I polished off half an hour ago or the charms of this man, but I can't take my eyes off Dempsey Haas.

He has a little of that "aww, shucks" Andy Griffith energy that reminds me of my brother, but there's something darker simmering below the surface. He isn't some fuckboy who's all talk and no action. No, he's gorgeous. Charismatic. Enticing without being overly cocky. He's obviously older than me, with an inimitable confidence about him.

He moves with this grace and ease, like he genuinely enjoys refilling drinks and flirting with every single person who hits on him. And believe me—I've been keeping track. Just about every person he talks to acts like they're the moth and he's the flame.

Watching him flirt doesn't bother me. They can try to get his attention all they want.

But he keeps coming back to *me*.

None of the other guys working have even tried to approach me—whether because of Jake's warning, or because Dempsey hasn't gone three minutes without checking on me, I'm not sure.

Jake's been hovering for the last half hour, prowling and scowling. It pisses him off that I stayed after he shut me down—and that Dempsey's paying me more than my share of attention.

Serves him right for trying to dismiss me.

Honestly, I should be grateful Jake tried to shoo me out of the bar. He gave me this opportunity to get Dempsey's attention. I've learned plenty about the other brother over the last few hours.

He is well liked and respected by everyone he works with. They all treat him like he's their big brother or their dad or something. Even Jake talks to him differently than he talks to the other guys.

He is all charm and smiles when he faces the front of the bar, but the second he turns around, he frowns. It's not an angry frown, but he makes this serious expression where his eyebrows pull and his entire forehead wrinkles. The first time I saw it, I was overwhelmed by the urge to run my hand over his face and smooth out the wrinkles. I've been itching to touch him for hours. There's no way I'm leaving here tonight without a taste. Or a feel. Or hell, the full Dempsey Haas experience, if he's up for it.

And most importantly, he absolutely, positively, 100 percent has no idea who I am.

And I'm going to keep it that way. At least until I get what I want.

Chapter 3

Maddie

Last call was twenty minutes ago, and I'm working overtime trying to play this right. There are still a few other patrons milling around, and Jake's been sitting at the far end of the bar, staring at a laptop, paying me no attention.

I slide my key ring around on the bar again, fighting the temptation to carve my initials into this big chunk of wood with my house key. Who would willingly choose something like this for a bar? The thing's not even sanded or varnished.

I've seen less of Dempsey in the last twenty minutes than I have all night. He keeps going from the bar to the little hallway that must lead to a stockroom or offices before coming back again. I just need him to stay here for more than thirty seconds for this to work.

The next time he approaches, he's carrying a few bottles in his arms. I give him a salacious up and down, and he raises one eyebrow when he spots the keys in my hands.

"Heading out?" he asks.

This is probably the best opening I'll get.

I hop off the barstool intentionally fast, legit stumbling a bit as I establish my balance in these heels. I hold up my keys for emphasis, letting them jingle and tempting fate.

"Stop right there."

I fight back a grin as Jake's bossy-ass command rings out across the bar.

"What the hell do you think you're doing?"

When I look over at him, he's already on his feet.

"I'm going home, Jakey. Just like you wanted." I jingle my keys again for emphasis.

No one knows I didn't drive here tonight and that my only option is to call a ride share. Or at least, that *was* my only option, until this totally brill plan took shape.

"You know damn well I'm not going to let you drive," he asserts, coming to stand a few feet from me with his big-ass arms crossed over his chest.

"Why not? You didn't serve me," I mock-scoff, throwing out an arm and gripping the bar with one hand for balance. He tracks my movements as the tension between us rachets up ten degrees.

"Put your damn keys away before I take them, Fourth Wheel. I'll drive you home when I'm done."

I don't dare peek over to see if Dempsey's watching our exchange. I just hope for the best and shoot my shot.

"I'm not interested in waiting for you to count your pennies or whatever it is bar owners do at the end of the night. I'm ready to go now."

I turn on my heel slowly, acutely aware of Jake's eyes on me. If he stops me before Dempsey has a chance to intervene...

"Do you live around here? I'm almost done with my closing tasks. I could give you a ride home."

Yahtzee. Bingo. Bullseye. *Mine*.

I brush the hair out of my eyes and turn to smile at my new knight in shining armor.

"You're sure you don't mind?" I ask at the same time Jake says, "Seriously?"

Dempsey stops where he stands behind the bar, his gaze shifting between Jake and me. He's doing that little brow-scrunch, like he's trying to work out what he's missing. That's the one thing I don't want him to figure out before I get him out of this bar.

"Why not?" he finally levels at Jake. "She's a friend of yours, right?" He turns to me before giving Jake a chance to answer. "Do you live far?"

"I'm staying at my parents' house. It's only a few minutes past the train bridge," I offer before Jake can insert himself again.

Dempsey nods and gives me a little half smile. "I just need to grab my keys."

He moves out from behind the bar, and I hustle to catch up. Partly because I'm eager to see what happens when we don't have a stupid tree trunk between us. But also because I need to get away from Jake. I don't *think* he's figured out that Dempsey doesn't know who I am, but I have absolutely no intention of letting him be the one to spill the beans.

Dempsey makes his way down a dark, narrow hallway, and I follow, although I'm not sure he realizes he isn't alone. We walk past the bathrooms toward a metal cage filled with bottles. He stops abruptly, and I smack right into his back, letting out an *umph* of surprise.

Just as I teeter, he spins around and grasps my forearms.

"Careful, princess."

His hands are big enough to encircle my wrists completely, and even though it's dark, I can feel his eyes boring into mine. We're standing close enough to share breath. He's leaning forward so his chest is almost pressed to my ear. I can practically feel his heartbeat in my own body.

"I'm parked out front," he whispers, his words warm as his aura washes over me.

He's still grasping my arms. I'm still leaning in, desperate to get closer. I feel tiny in his arms. His aftershave smells deliciously expensive. God, he's just my type.

"Okay," I whisper back, willing him to kiss me right here in this dang hallway.

He chuckles darkly at that. I'm being way too obvious, but I don't care. "We're going to have to walk back through the bar and out the front door if you want to be alone with me."

I squeeze my thighs together at his bluntness. There's no way I was imagining our chemistry all night, but it still makes a girl feel good to know she's nailing her target.

"Okay," I repeat, practically panting as his fingers skim up my arms, grip my shoulders, and gently turn me around.

"Lead the way, princess," he croons in my ear.

Chapter 4

Dempsey

"Come on!" she calls over her shoulder as she practically skips into the crosswalk toward the town center.

"Hey! You didn't look both ways!" I holler like an overly concerned dad as she strolls into the street without slowing her pace.

Like a little blond fairy, she flits around, making my brain work overtime as I track her movements and consider all the naughty things I'd like to do to her tonight.

Before I can catch up, she stops in the middle of the crosswalk and spreads her arms wide. She's so fucking pretty standing there in her white skirt and fitted black tank top. I'm overwhelmed by the urge to pull her against me and never let go.

"No one's out in Hampton at this time of night. It's just you and me, Dempsey," she declares, spinning around in a circle with her face tilted toward the sky.

I catch up to her and ensnare her with an arm around her waist, pulling her across the road to safety while relishing the way she melts into my side like she can't possibly get close enough.

I'm only slightly embarrassed I haven't asked her name. She obviously knows mine. She probably heard Jake or one of the guys say it at some point tonight.

Typically, I prefer anonymity out of my one-night stands. But that's not the case tonight. It's strange to immediately and unexpectedly want *more*.

I want to know her name. I want to know her story. I want to know exactly what she sounds like when she's clinging to the edge, seconds away from shattering around my cock. I haven't even had this woman yet, and somehow, I'm already craving more.

Not wanting to break our connection, I move my arm up to rest it on her shoulder and feel her shudder under my hold.

"Cold?" I ask, already shucking off my jacket. I help her slip it on, then watch as she pulls her long blond hair out from under the collar, her loose curls cascading down the center of her back. When she pushes a few strands behind her shoulder, I get a whiff of her scent, and I can't help but inhale again. She smells like sweet strawberries—like summer and sunshine.

"Why don't you park in the back like everyone else?" she asks as we walk along the brick path that cuts through the town green.

Wait, what?

Most of the employees *do* park in the back lot behind The Oak, and some patrons do, too, when all the street spots are taken, but it's weird she noticed and thought to ask.

I shrug off her question as genuine curiosity. "I'm not usually in a rush to get home after work. I'm new to bartending. It's sort of overwhelming to have people clamoring for my attention all night. I like having a few minutes to myself after all the craziness."

I click the auto-start on my Range Rover, lighting up the interior of the car as I guide her toward the vehicle.

"Wait—that's your car?" She cranes her neck to look up at me, that same mischievous expression she's been taunting me with all night dancing on her face.

"It is," I confirm, guiding her toward the passenger door.

"You're a bartender at The Oak, yet you drive a Range Rover?" she deadpans.

I fight back a smirk, instead repeating the line she used on me earlier. "You don't miss a thing, do you?"

Before we make it to the car, the first hushed chime of the clock tower fills the quiet night air. Her body stiffens in my grasp, then she spins out of my hold and grabs me by the hand.

"Come on!" She pulls me in the direction of the red brick structure that keeps time at the corner of the downtown green.

"Dempsey. Hurry!"

I have no idea what the rush is or where she thinks she's going. But I find myself picking up the pace to meet her demand.

We reach the base of the clock tower as another bell chimes quietly, the low tone muted because of the late hour.

She tugs on my arm until I'm standing before her, my back to the structure. It's at least thirty feet tall and is a historic icon in Hampton. The town is obsessed with preserving the original components, muffling the chimes when they ring out during the middle of the night instead of putting it on a digital timer. Hence the low tones we're hearing now as the clock announces that it's one a.m.

"I used to tell the clock tower all my secrets." She's winded from running, and her voice is breathy because of it. Her hands find my chest, smoothing over my pecs as she pushes me against the brick and mortar. She keeps her hands in place, but takes two big steps away from me, then uses her body weight to push me against the bricks.

"What are you—" I question.

"I want you to feel it," she insists as she keeps me pinned in place. I don't have time to question her, because the clock chimes again, and I instantly feel the vibrations from the crown of my head to the tips of my toes.

I hold my breath in surprise as the low humming courses through my body. The sound radiates through my limbs, and there's an ebb and flow to the way the vibration grows. It peaks before it backs off slightly. That's the only warning I get before it rings out again.

"Do you feel it?" she whispers in wonder.

I nod my confirmation and hold my breath again, waiting for the next toll to ring out and light up my insides.

"I want to feel it, too."

That's the last thing I hear before the bricks tremble behind my back and her lips press into mine. Her hands move up my neck to cup my face as her sweet, greedy tongue begs for entrance.

I willingly let her in and wrap her in my arms. She tastes just like she smells: strawberries, sugar, and the sharp tang of vodka. Her kiss is bold and confident, her lips relentless as she hypnotizes me with her mouth. Her hands are everywhere—skimming down my sides, teasing along the hem of my jeans. She even squeezes my ass, the little spitfire.

Every time the clock strikes a chord, her tongue enters my mouth and dances with mine. I'm consumed by the vibrations at my back and the ministrations of her hands. I crave each resounding toll, desperate to feel the depth of her wanting as I'm deprived of most of my senses.

When the next chime rings out, I pull her tighter against my chest. We moan in unison as the vibrations roll through us, inspiring a wave of desire that has my dick hardening in anticipation.

We make out in the middle of downtown Hampton until the clock tower grows quiet. Her hands are still cupping my jaw, and I feel her smile against my mouth before she finally stops kissing me. She tilts her head back to meet my gaze.

"I have the house to myself tonight. Please take me home."

From the look in her eyes, it's clear she's asking for so much more than just a ride. I push off the clock tower and link our hands as I guide her back to my still-running car. I open the passenger door for her and swat her butt as she climbs in. She yelps but then gives me the sauciest look as she buckles her seat belt.

I knew it in the bar, but now I feel it in my bones. This girl is something special, and I'm going to make the most out of tonight.

Chapter 5

Maddie

I only broke off our kiss because I could feel my pulse in my pussy. If I hadn't stopped, things would have absolutely gone too far. I'm not about to get arrested for indecent exposure in the middle of downtown Hampton when I've got an empty house waiting for us just down the road.

Dempsey pats his pockets before climbing in the driver's seat, then sticks his hand in both cupholders, coming up empty.

"Looking for this?"

I hold up his phone as his head snaps up to attention. I swiped it out of his back pocket while we were swapping spit against the clock tower. Partly because I wanted to make sure I got his number. But also because I didn't want him to put my address into the GPS, just in case it was linked to my brother's contact information somehow.

His eyes widen in shock as he stares at my outstretched hand. He gives his head a little shake and puts the Range Rover in drive.

"I didn't want you to disappear in the morning without getting my number," I explain, crossing my legs as he pulls out of his parking spot. "Head out past the train bridge, then I'll tell you where to turn."

He doesn't argue, instead muttering under his breath like a put-out grump.

"What's your passcode?"

He scoffs. "I'm not telling you my passcode, princess. Give that here." He reaches for the device without taking his eyes off the road, but instead of giving him what he wants, I give him something better.

I grasp his extended arm at the wrist, then lick from the center of his palm to the tip of his middle finger. I pause at the tip, and he lets out a quiet grunt while shifting his hips in his seat. I push his middle finger into my mouth, close my lips around his top knuckle, and swirl my tongue around him.

"Fuck," he hisses.

"Exactly," I retort, pulling his finger from my mouth and dropping his hand. "Now tell me your passcode so we can exchange numbers. We're going to be way too distracted once we get to my house."

He doesn't bother arguing this time and rattles off the four-digit passcode. I add my number and contemplate what name to use, finally settling on Clock Tower Girl before sending myself a text.

"There," I announce with a flourish, placing his phone into one of the cupholders between us. "Turn left at the next light," I add once I realize we're close to my street.

Dempsey coasts his fancy-ass Range Rover down Willow Drive while I fantasize about all the dirty things I want to do to him tonight. I felt his cock through his pants when I pushed him into that clock tower. He's big, just like I knew he'd be. Thankfully, I don't have any other plans this weekend, and I always did like a good challenge.

I pull out my phone as I glance up to see where we are. "Oh, we're almost here. It's the third house on the left after the flag-pole," I tell him mindlessly as I save his number.

The car slows, then I feel his eyes on me.

"This is your house?" he murmurs.

Something about his tone stops my heart right in my damn chest. When I look over to meet his gaze, the man I flirted with all night and made out with just minutes ago is gone.

Instead, all I see is loathing.

Shit.

"Yep," I quip, my voice high-pitched and shaky. "Just pull in the driveway and park on the left. I've got the place to myself all summer."

He frowns as he pulls into the driveway and slams the gearshift into park, focused intently on the closed garage door.

"Have you lived here long?" he grits out without turning his head to look at me.

Damn. I can't lie to him. Well, I guess that's not entirely true since I've been lying by omission all night, but for some inexplicable reason, I feel compelled to answer honestly.

"I've lived in this house my whole life," I confirm, unlatching my seatbelt to give myself an excuse not to meet his gaze.

"And you know Jake how, exactly?"

Fuckity fuck. The jig is up.

Had I suspected he'd been here before, I would have insisted we go to his place. I never expected him to recognize my damn house. When the hell would he have been here?

Evading the truth is futile. He knows who I am. Or he's pretty damn sure. And he's really fucking pissed, based on the vibes he's throwing my way.

I huff out a sigh and grab the door handle before answering. I don't know what's more disappointing: that I didn't foresee this snag in my plan, or that I won't get to see his dick.

"I've known Jake my whole life," I admit. "He's been best friends with my brother since before I was born."

I sneak a glance at him to gauge his reaction and am shocked as shit when he reaches a hand out, grips my chin, and turns my head so I'm facing him.

He's leaning in so close I can see the gold flecks in his irises. If I wasn't sure he was pissed, this would be so fucking hot. He squeezes my chin a fraction tighter.

"So that means your brother is—"

I don't give him a chance to finish that statement.

"Rhett," I spit out in frustration. "My brother is Rhett Wheeler."

Chapter 6

Dempsey

No. No fucking way.

This can't be her house.

I've been here before. Relaxed in the hot tub out back. Played beer pong in the sunroom. Crashed on the living room couch.

I've raced down this street going fifty miles an hour. I've left my car running in this driveway as Jake and I frantically ran around back. I've pulled my brother away from this yard and wrestled his drunk ass into my car.

I know this house. This *can't* be her house. Because if it is, that means the girl I almost slept with tonight is related to none other than...

"Rhett. My brother is Rhett Wheeler."

Jesus fucking Christ.

I drop my hand from her face and lean back in a desperate attempt to put distance between us. I ball both hands into fists and will myself to keep it together as the truth taints the chemistry between us.

How could I not have put two and two together? I'm shocked Jake didn't call me out for what was clearly about to go down.

But the true root of my rage lies with her.

There's no way she doesn't know who I am. Fielding spent Christmas with her family two years ago, for crying out loud. Is emotional catfishing a thing? I don't know what she's playing at, but she's definitely playing.

"Out," I bark when I finally manage to form a coherent thought. I grip the steering wheel with both hands and stare straight ahead, silently counting down the seconds until she's out of this car and out of my life forever.

When she doesn't respond or make any move to leave, I turn my head and glare.

The girl has the audacity to look me in the eye and pout.

"Seriously? That's it? You're not going to walk me to the door?"

"Get out of my fucking car!"

The volume of my fury surprises me, but my outburst has its intended effect. Her bratty smile is replaced with a surly scowl.

"Sheesh, Haas. I was just teasing." She shifts forward and opens the door.

I should let her go. That's what I want, right? To get her out of my car and to erase the memory of this entire night from my mind?

But curiosity gets the best of me. "So you *do* know who I am?"

She gets out of the car but turns to me and nods.

"And you know who my brother is?" I push.

She shifts her weight from foot to foot.

"Of course I know who he is. He looks just like you." She pops one hip and crosses her arms over her chest.

I find my eyes wandering in search of that hint of cleavage she's been teasing me with all night but avert my gaze quickly when I remember what's happening here.

"So given everything you know about my brother... and about what happened last spring..."

She's regarding me with a less-hostile, almost confused expression now. I don't know what I'm trying to accomplish by lecturing her in her own damn driveway, but I feel compelled to put her in her place.

"You knew who I was when we started talking at The Oak tonight. And I think it's safe to assume you knew I didn't know who you were. So you were what—looking for trouble? Provoking me? Stirring the pot?"

She shrugs and glances toward the house for a few seconds before answering. "I don't see what the big deal is. I'm not my brother..."

"Obviously," I deadpan.

"And you're not *your* brother," she snaps.

Interesting.

Little miss spitfire can dish it out, but she doesn't know how to take it.

We stand there for a beat, glaring at each other. I say nothing, because there's nothing left to say.

Pulling one over on me didn't work. She's not sorry; she's just sorry she got caught. She can stomp and pout all she wants. We're done here.

"Close the door, please," I instruct, trying to sound cordial as I put the car in reverse. But instead of doing as I ask, she swings the door open farther, plants her feet, and brings both hands to her hips.

"What the fuck is your problem? I thought we were having a good time. There's no reason you can't come in and do what we were planning to do, Dempsey."

I scoff at her boldness and the absurdity of what she's implying. But what did I expect? She's a child. A little girl. A spoiled princess who's used to getting her way.

"No can do, princess. It's been real. Don't ever talk to me again."

I let the car ease back a few inches so she knows I'm serious about leaving. She finally takes a step back to prevent the door from hitting her. Once she's out of my way, I whip out of the driveway so fast the passenger door closes on its own.

Good fucking riddance.

Chapter 7

Dempsey

I use my key to let myself in the front door, then call out his name to make my presence known so I don't startle him this late at night.

"Jake!"

I don't have to wander far—he's still perched at the end of the bar, focused on his laptop.

He gives me a nod as I approach, then holds a finger up in my direction, his gaze shifting from the computer screen to the phone in his other hand.

"Dammit, Jake. I need to talk to you *now*."

I don't want to be here any longer than I have to be. I just need to know I'm not going crazy before I take my sorry ass home and put this whole night to rest.

"Just *hold on*," he grits out without looking up from his phone.

I grip the edge of the bar to stop myself from pacing as he types out a message and sends it off before finally giving me his full attention.

"I wasn't trying to brush you off, bro. I just had to let Cory know I might be later than planned."

Okay, fair. But I need answers. And I'm fading fast. I shift closer and lean my forearms on the back of a barstool rather than take a seat beside him.

"That girl tonight... that girl was Wheeler's sister."

I don't pose it as a question. I'm honestly embarrassed I didn't connect the dots sooner.

Jake runs a hand through his hair and looks at me like I'm dense. "Um, yes. You heard me call her Fourth Wheel, didn't you?"

I hang my head in shame. I heard it. I even wondered what it meant. But I never dreamed the "Wheel" stood for Wheeler.

I drop my chin to my chest and shake my head, eventually glancing up at my friend when he clears his throat.

"I had no idea she was Rhett's sister."

Jake's eyes grow wide as he stares at me, unblinking, then his face morphs from shock to confusion before it finally settles on disbelief.

"How have you never met Maddie?"

Hearing her name spoken out loud for the first time breaks something inside me. I'm at war with how I feel right now—I'm at war with how she *made* me feel tonight.

"Fuck. I don't know," I snap. "I've been a little busy picking up the pieces of my brother's shattered heart after he was fucking destroyed by that girl's family last year. I guess I haven't had time to study the Wheeler family tree."

Jake cocks one eyebrow and regards me, but he holds his tongue. Fielding and his infatuation with Maddie's sister-in-law aren't topics we talk about, and for good reason. The whole thing was a mess, and a lot of people got hurt because of it.

One person is *still* hurting because of it.

My brother's face flashes in my mind, and guilt rolls through me when I think about what almost happened tonight. How Maddie *knew* who I was, yet she pursued me anyway...

I shake my head and blow out a long breath. "I'm sorry, man. This whole night's got me all twisted up. I didn't mean to take it out on you. I just can't believe she almost got me like that. I can't fucking believe I almost..."

"You're good," Jake reassures me. "Between you and me, I'm *not* surprised she tried to pull something. Maddie's a piece of work. She's *always* been a troublemaker, yet she *always* gets away with it. But I am surprised you've never met her. You and Rhett played lacrosse together all four years at Arch, right? I'm sure she was at those games."

I nod absentmindedly as I try to recall any memory I might have of the girl I almost hooked up with tonight.

"Wait," I mutter as information clicks into place. "You told me not to serve her. I assumed she was younger than us, but is she actually... Fuck. She's underage, isn't she?"

Jake squints one eye and screws up his face in a grimace.

"Maddie's twenty."

For fuck's sake.

"Well, that answers your question, then. She would have been eleven fucking years old when I graduated from Arch."

The admission tastes vile on my tongue. The gravity of my poor judgment is overwhelmingly heavy. I bow my head again and just let it hang.

When I finally look up, Jake is watching me, his expression a mix of pity and understanding.

I swallow past the lump in my throat before I speak again.

"He can never know."

"Which one?"

"Neither," I insist without hesitation.

He cocks his head to the side like he wants to argue, but this isn't his call to make. I'm not bending on this. After a tense moment, he concedes. "Yeah, okay. They won't hear a word about this from me."

I let out a sigh of relief, then glance around the empty bar. There's something peaceful about being at The Oak after last call. The juxtaposition between this moment and the usual hustle makes the quiet that much sweeter.

"Need any help closing up?" I ask. I'm dead on my feet, but I'm not in any hurry to go home.

"Nope," he says, hopping off the barstool, then turning to gather his things. "I'll finish up and lock the back door. Just go out the way you came and lock the door behind you."

I nod and lift a hand before walking out the front door and coming face to face with the clock tower on the corner of the green.

I'm never going to look at that damn brick structure the same way again.

A muffled chime rings out through the night as I pull open the car door, and I can't help but look up one more time as the clock strikes two.

Fuck. I made out with Wheeler's underage sister tonight.

And as much as I hate to admit it, I loved every fucking second of it.

I slink into the house through the garage door, surprised to hear a familiar song being plucked on the acoustic guitar as I make my way through the foyer.

Mom must be settled for the night if my brother's messing around with his guitar.

Thank God.

The last week has been a total dumpster fire. An unexpected, uncontrollable dumpster fire.

My brother and I live at home, and we share the responsibility of taking care of our mom. We've always been able to count on her regular "wellness retreats" to cut us a break. The fancy rehab facilities she frequents are designed to be a detox and reset under the guise of an extended spa experience. More than that, they guarantee respite for my brother and me.

But last week she left for one of her favorite facilities in Arizona, only to show up at home two days later.

Two days.

She was supposed to be gone for three weeks.

Three weeks away, followed by at least a month of sobriety. That's what I was expecting. Instead, I'm frantically trying to rearrange my work schedule and figure out what the hell happened.

She won't talk about it—every time I ask, her eyes get watery, and she apologizes for being such a burden.

I can barely hold it together when she gets like that, so the conversation never goes any further. It is what it is. I accepted a long time ago that this is how it has to be.

There's not a single overhead light or lamp on, the only source of illumination the nearly full moon filtering in through the floor-to-ceiling windows.

I hop over the steps that lead into the sunken living room, then flop onto the oversized couch with enough force to elicit a grunt from my brother.

He's flat on his back with his long, jean-clad legs hanging off the side, his guitar resting against his bare chest. I mirror his position, scooting back until the crowns of our heads touch.

"How was she?" I ask as I close my eyes and let the chorus of "Gravity" by John Mayer expunge the racing thoughts from my mind.

Fielding shifts, forcing my head to the side as he fidgets to get closer. I'm not sure if he's aware he's doing it, or if it's instinct, but there's comfort in the way he unconsciously tries to get as close as possible after we've been apart all day. I crave the connection just as deeply as he does.

"Sad and sober," he murmurs once he gets comfortable. He exhales before he starts the chorus again.

Our mom's an addict. An alcoholic. A pill popper. She's been like this for years.

And yet, no matter the label—no matter how accepting or detached we try to be about the reality of the situation—there's one hard truth that reels us both in time and time again. It's the reason we're twenty-seven years old with Ivy League educations but living at home. It's the reason neither one of us feels like we can leave this town.

She's our mom.

I guess sad and sober is the best I can expect. The forthcoming relapse is inevitable. I should be grateful it didn't happen tonight.

"And you?" I ask out of obligation. I stretch my legs out on the end of the couch until my knees and ankles pop, waiting for whatever version of the truth he's willing to share.

I don't need to ask to know my brother's a fucking mess. A few years ago, he fell for a girl who wasn't his to love, and he hasn't been the same since.

He's heartbroken. He has been for over a year. And I don't know how to fix him.

"Sad and sober," he sings as he strums the same two chords again.

The stink of weed clings to his blond curls, but I don't call him out on it. I'd much rather he get stoned than drink or hit something harder when he's home alone with her.

"Why are you down here?" he asks, rubbing his head against mine until he's essentially noogying me with his thick skull.

It's a fair question. On nights I work at The Oak, I usually bring someone home. When I do, I usher them up the flight of stairs off the garage to my wing of the house, then I make sure they're gone by morning.

"Quit it." I smack a hand in his direction, and he grunts when I slap him in the face. I'm too tired to wrestle with him right now, and thankfully he seems too out of it to start shit.

"I had a rough night. I just wanted to come home and sleep. Figured I could make breakfast for us in the morning."

"Ohh... breakfast," he croons without missing a single chord of the song.

I knew that would appease him. The guy's a sucker for waffles.

"So what you're not saying is that you struck out with the ladies tonight? Maybe you're losing your touch, brother."

I scoff at his goading, then let out a sigh when I picture her face. I'm still thinking about her full, glossy lips. Her defined cheekbones. That mischievous glint in her deep brown eyes and the way she tracked my every movement all night long.

"There was almost a girl," I admit.

Just because he can't ever know about Maddie doesn't mean I'm forbidden from thinking about her again. Which is good, because it'll be a long-ass time before I can forget that kiss.

"Tell me about the girl," he prods, strumming softer now.

"She had big doe eyes and an endless supply of sass. Blond hair, perfect, perky tits. She smelled like strawberries and sugar. She was a little bit wild. She was beautifully free."

My brother sighs before his guitar goes silent.

Fuck.

Too far.

I knew better. But I'm too tired to think straight. I know it's not my fault—I could have described Maddie as a six-foot-tall bright green alien with two heads, and somehow, it would still remind him of *her*.

We both fester in the heaviness of his heartache, but he doesn't let the moment linger.

"So there was a girl. And she was hot as fuck. And yet you came home alone?"

"And yet I came home alone."

I don't have to feign disappointment. Had she been anyone else—anyone else in the whole goddamn world—I would be making her scream my name at this very moment. Just because I can't have her doesn't mean I didn't want her.

"Don't worry, Dumpy. You'll get her next time."

I smile sadly and mentally accept the truth my brother can never know. Maddie Wheeler will never be mine. Despite how much I wanted her tonight... despite the connection I felt when she shoved me up against that clock tower and kissed the shit out of me...

I won't get her next time because there can't be a next time.

I peel myself off the couch, stand, and offer my brother a hand. He stares at it sleepily, then meets my gaze before shaking his head in dismissal.

"I'm good out here," he insists through a yawn as he strums his guitar again.

I yawn in reply, then duck to kiss his forehead and ruffle his hair.

"Love you, bro," I call over my shoulder as I head to my wing of the house.

"Love you more," he replies. Like he always does. Like I know he always will.

Chapter 8

Maddie

I adjust the strings on my bathing suit bottoms and glance up to see what the hell the boys are doing now. They're so obnoxiously loud I've given up on trying to listen to music or take a nap. Paige is on the lounger next to me. We've been out here all afternoon tanning and taking periodic dips in the pool to cool off.

Of course, she invited the boys, too, which is not my idea of a good time.

Travis and Kyle showed up half-drunk, even though it's only two in the afternoon. They pulled my brother's old paddleboards out of the garage, and they've invented some sort of jousting game where they try to smack each other off balance. I swear there's more water out of the pool than in it at this point.

"Kyle looks so fucking hot in those white swim trunks," Paige groans as she sits up and adjusts her chair.

I'm grateful my oversized sunglasses hide my eye roll. She's been into Kyle since our sophomore year of high school. You'd think she would be tired of being led on after five years, but my best friend just doesn't know how to quit. She's a catch, and she could do so much better than Kyle Slater. The guy's destined to be an insurance salesman.

I was sure she'd get over him when we all went our separate ways for college. Kyle and Travis both ended up a solid four hours from here at Easton. Paige goes to Holt, which is only about twenty minutes from Hampton, but she lives on campus during the school year. She could have her pick. She's just really bad at picking.

"Meh," I finally reply. "I've seen better."

"Oh, come on. Don't tell me Hampton guys aren't good enough for you anymore."

"*Those* aren't guys." I jut my chin in the direction of the pool as Travis tries to stand on top of Kyle's shoulders while the latter is fully submerged under water. "Those are boys."

"I mean, I guess," she relents. "But it's not like we've got better options this summer."

I almost did.

My mind goes to him again, just like it has all weekend. Visions of the tall, broad man I made out with on Friday night invade my consciousness. I've replayed that moment so many times. I'm still mad at myself for fucking it up by bringing him here. I almost had him, dammit. Only two days have passed, but I won't be over him anytime soon.

Which is fine. Dempsey Haas has most definitely not seen the last of me.

As soon as I walked into the house alone on Friday night, I realized I was still wearing his jacket. Plus, I have his cell phone number. He's not getting off the hook that easily. I'm just trying to figure out my next move. Maybe there's something I can do to get back in his good graces or to change his mind about not following through with what we both so clearly wanted two nights ago.

"Do you think you'll hook up again?"

"Wait, what?"

I haven't been paying attention to a word Paige is saying—I don't know what she's even talking about right now.

"Trav-is," she says, emphasizing each syllable like I need her to slow down. "Do you think you'll hook up again this summer?"

Ugh.

Travis.

I guess not full-blown *ugh*. But a mini *ugh*, for sure.

We dated for a few months in high school. We went to senior prom together. And then we went off to different colleges and things fizzled. But when we're both back in town, and when I'm exceptionally bored, I seem to end up in bed with him.

He's objectively attractive. And he's sort of funny—if I'm drunk. He's okay-ish in bed. Or maybe I've just learned to manage my expectations when it comes to him.

Note to self: if you fake it the first time you hook up with someone, be prepared to fake it again... and again... and again... *every time you make that same mistake.*

More than anything, Travis is convenient. Neither one of us is interested in taking things further. So when I'm home, he'll do.

I don't dislike the guy. But I get annoyed with myself when we hook up nowadays. Like, *come on, Madison. You can pull better, girl!*

"We'll see." I shrug.

Paige gives me the biggest smile and lets out a little squeal before pinching my thigh. She'd love nothing more than for us to end up paired off with these guys, or some version of them, living in Hampton and pregnant by the time we're twenty-five.

If that's her version of happily ever after, I want that for her. But that's so far from the vision I have for my own life. I don't want to hurt her feelings, though, and it would be a pretty lonely summer if I didn't have her to hang out with. So I return her smile and ignore the buffoons who have dislodged so much water from my parents' pool it's down a solid three inches.

Needing to cool off, I sit up and make my way over to the water. Paige follows, and we perch on the edge of the pool and let our legs hang down while splashing water up and down our arms. It's only mid-May, but the high today is ninety-two. I'm glad my parents were home a few weeks ago to get the pool opened up for the season.

Travis pops his head out of the water inches from where we sit.

"Hey ladies." He grins, raising his eyebrows behind his aviators—yes, he's still wearing them, even underwater. He's somehow trying way too hard, and also not hard enough.

"Can I take you to a party next weekend, Maddie girl?"

I inwardly cringe at the nickname. Only my brother's allowed to call me that. The faking it lesson applies here, too. I should have never let him get away with it once, because now it's too late to course correct.

"That depends," I hedge. "Are Paige and Kyle going?"

Travis spins around to call out to his buddy. "Yo. Ky! We're taking the girls to that party at Adley's house on Saturday night. Cool?"

Kyle grunts something that sounds like agreement, and Paige squeezes my arm appreciatively. Travis gives me an obnoxiously unsubtle up and down and swims a few inches closer, then grips both my knees and uses them as leverage to raise himself out of the water until we're eye to eye.

"Looks like it's a date," he whispers in what I'm sure he thinks is an attempt at being sexy. I muster up a half smile before shaking him off, standing up, and heading to the sunroom for a drink.

Well, it looks like I'm going to a party.

"Maddie! Wait!" Paige calls as I make my way across the backyard. "We need to go shopping!"

I wonder if my sister-in-law has any job openings at her non-profit. Apparently, I'm exceptionally good at charity work.

Chapter 9

Maddie

I get out of the shower with five minutes to spare before our Sunday night Wheeler family Zoom call. Why we have to sit awkwardly in front of our computers like we're in a board meeting once a week is beyond me. We have a family group chat. I text my brother almost every day. I talk to my mom on the phone multiple times a week.

But alas. Family Zoom calls started at the beginning of my sophomore year at Berkeley, and they've been going strong ever since.

I grab a hairbrush and work through my tangles as the call connects on my end. Rhett's already logged in, because of course he is. I do the awkward Zoom wave when he and Tori pop up at the top of my screen.

"Hold on," I mutter as I hop up to find a hair tie. I wrestle my hair into a messy bun and pull it tight as I sit back down in front of my vanity.

My parents are both on the call now, so I wave to them as well.

"Hi kids! You all look so good! I love seeing your smiling faces like this," my mom croons. "How are things at home, Maddie?"

"Things are good. Quiet, mostly. It was hot today, so I had a few friends over and we used the pool. Other than that, nothing to report."

"Are you just going to lay out by the pool all summer, Maddie girl?" Rhett teases. "Why don't you go get a job?"

I scoff at his comment but hold my tongue. Tori play-punches him, and my mom starts in on him right away.

"Maddie worked hard all school year to maintain her grades and make the dean's list, Everhett. She has her whole life ahead of her to work. She's allowed to just relax and hang out at home this summer."

"Yeah, Rhett," I pile on. "Not everyone wants to grow up and be a workaholic."

My brother rolls his eyes but doesn't back down. "I'm just saying. We don't have any plans to come up that way until Labor Day, and even then, we'll probably just go to the cabin. You're gonna be bored sitting around Hampton all summer, and boredom usually means *trouble* for you."

The way he says "trouble" makes the hairs on the back of my damp neck stand at attention.

I glare at my brother through the screen, searching his face for some sort of tell. There's no way he knows I was at The Oak on Friday night, right?

I wouldn't put it past Jake to call Rhett and tattle. But my brother's direct, and he doesn't bullshit with me. It's not his style to make off-handed comments just to see if he can get a rise out of someone. If he knows something, he'd call me out privately. Wouldn't he?

I stare at the screen for a few more seconds as my mom yammers on about the river boat cruise they booked for later this summer. My brother's listening intently, smiling and rubbing his wife's leg.

No, I decide. He doesn't know. And I intend to keep it that way.

I slip my phone under the vanity and send off a text.

Maddie: Jakey! Do you have any days off this week? I'm working on a surprise for Tori and Rhett's anniversary, and I need your help.

My phone vibrates in my hand, and I have to fight back a grin. That was almost too easy.

Tori's telling us all about the new location site for Camp New Hope-Norfolk, so I smile and nod every few seconds like I'm listening.

I glance down at my phone between all the smiling and nodding.

Jake: I'm off Wednesday and Thursday. Just let me know what you need.

I can't help but smirk this time. *Sucker*.

I make a mental note to stop at the drugstore and pick out a cheesy card about true love to send to my brother and sister-in-law. That's the extent of my anniversary celebration plans for those two, but Jake doesn't need to know that.

And now I know which nights he *won't* be at The Oak this week.

I have every intention of persuading Dempsey Haas to jump into bed with me. In fact, it's my new personal mission. I'm even more optimistic now that I know Jake won't be there to interfere with my plan.

Rhett thinks I'll be bored sitting around all summer. Little does he know that I've just set an audacious goal and kicked off a massive project for myself.

Operation: Hot Haas Summer is officially a go.

Chapter 10

Dempsey

The shit talking on the courts has already begun when I swipe into the rec. I peek over the ledge and grin.

Our court reservation doesn't start for twenty minutes. But since most of the guys in my league are retired or work for themselves, they're always here early, staking it out and "warming up," as they like to say, sweatbands and knee braces securely in place as they heckle the college-age players.

I hit the locker room and change quickly, stashing my phone, towel, and water bottle in the bag I'll take to the bench.

My brother's already sent me two selfies in full gear. One of the reasons I still participate in these basketball games with my dad's old buddies is because I can usually convince Field to come up to Holt with me. I drop him off at the ice rink where he shows off during open skate or joins a pickup hockey game, then I spend two hours sweating it out and not worrying about anything except what's happening on the court.

"Ready to kick some ass today, hot stuff?" Richard claps me on the shoulder when I scoot down the bench to join him.

As the youngest player by at least thirty years, I'm a highly sought-after floater. I don't bother keeping track of whose team I'm on each week anymore. Richard and Marty make sure to let me know.

"I don't know, Rich. I've been feeling a little rough this week." I feign a grimace as I roll out my shoulders and fight back a smirk at the righteous indignation on his face.

"Dammit, Martin. You played the kid too hard last week. That's hostile sabotage," Richard admonishes.

I chuckle but intervene before things get too heated.

"I'm fine. Just let me get out there, and I'm sure I'll loosen up quick."

Harold's standing next to the facility supervisor, confirming that our court reservation starts at two like it always has. Really, he just wants to make sure the young guys on the court clear out as soon as we're up.

The first game is always full court.

The subsequent games are almost always half court.

That's the nature of the beast when half the players have undergone at least one knee or hip replacement.

"Heard from your old man lately?" Marty pants as he takes a break beside me after the first game.

He always asks about our father. And the theme of every response I give is the same.

"His secretary forwarded me a press release about the new Columbus build. So yeah, I guess you can say I've heard from him."

Marty gripes under his breath, far more put out about the state of my relationship with George Haas than I am.

The lack of communication doesn't bother me. My father is not a good person.

He was decent enough when we were little, showing occasional interest in Fielding and me when it came to academics and sports. For the most part, he was like the other billionaire dads I knew: distant, aloof, and put out by any situation or need that he couldn't ask his secretary to handle.

I lost all respect for him when he moved our family to Hampton. Fielding and I had our pick of the top private schools in the country, and we were prepared to enroll as boarding students at Archway Preparatory Academy.

But the summer before we were set to leave, our mom's drinking became noticeably worse. Our dad took matters into his own hands, and the rest is history. He said our mom would be better out of the city. He said it was the right decision for our family.

He moved us into a mansion on the outskirts of Hampton, overlooking the Cuyahoga Valley National Park.

It turns out he just wanted a place to dump her so she was out of his hair.

Our parents divorced when we were in high school. My dad hasn't been back to Hampton since we graduated from Arch.

Neither Fielding nor I want anything to do with the man. We chose alternate career paths on purpose, neither interested in working for him nor with him in real estate development.

Not that it matters. Between the trusts from our grandparents and our mom's money, I'm almost certain our net worth is as much, if not more than his.

The best way to describe our relationship now is strained but civil. He's never been interested in being a parent. We don't need his money or business connections. And now that we're adults, we see his choices for what they were: abandonment and neglect.

It's an impasse I grappled with for years.

But he made his choice. Even if it doesn't make sense, I'm man enough to accept that the responsibilities he shucked off are mine to bear.

"I'm glad you still make it to these games, son," Marty mutters as he uses my shoulder to push to his feet.

I don't bother replying, just guzzle down a mouthful of water and wipe at the sweat dripping down my face as I follow him onto the court for the next game.

Chapter 11

Maddie

I pull open the front door with more force than intended and stumble back before gaining my composure. Blowing out a long breath, I fluff my curls and stand up straighter.

The Oak is surprisingly crowded for a Wednesday night. Some old dude is blasting through the sound system—Bruce Springsteen, maybe? Along with the guy from Fun.? I don't know why Jake insists on only playing songs that were popular at least two decades ago.

I could claim a table in the back and bide my time. Order a soda. Scope out the scene. I didn't exactly think through what I was going to do when I arrived here tonight. But one glance at the bar has me halting in my wedges in the middle of the dang room.

I'm frozen in place, held captive by cerulean-blue eyes and a disapproving glare. Fuck. That's hot. My cheeks heat under his stare. I squeeze my legs together and bite down on my lip. But I don't dare turn my head or look away: I stare right back into the eyes of Dempsey Haas.

What is it about pissing this man off that makes me want him even more?

I'm a moth. He's the flame. I'm the moon. He's the sun. It's like he's pulling me to him with the force of his gaze.

I walk on trembling legs to the end of the bar. He meets me on the other side.

"What are you doing here?" he demands in a whisper I barely hear over the music and the chatter of the people around us.

"Hmm?" I ask innocently, hopping up onto a barstool and leaning forward so he has a clear shot of my cleavage in my white tank top.

I've gotta hand it to the man. He doesn't break eye contact as he leans in closer to repeat himself.

"I said, what are you doing here? There's no reason for you to be here right now."

Oh yes, there is.

"I come in peace," I insist, letting a small smile grace my lips. "I just wanted to return your jacket." I shrug nonchalantly, then do an internal happy dance when he narrows his eyes and his brows wrinkle together.

Maddie 1, Dempsey 0.

He crosses his arms over his chest and turns away from me, surveying the rest of the bar. God, he has the best arms. His forearms are lean and lickable, but his biceps deserve their own area code. They're just so wide and beefy. I don't think my fingers could touch if I tried to circle one of them with both hands. I bet he could hold himself in a plank position for hours with those puppies—

"So where is it?" he demands without looking at me.

Wait, what?

When I don't answer, he turns back to me and smirks.

"Where's my jacket, Maddie?"

Maddie? Shit. Is it hot in here? Dempsey Haas knows my name. Dempsey Haas just *said* my name, and he made it sound so damn fine.

"Maddie. Seriously."

I shake myself out of my stupor to find him turned back to me now, his arms spread long on his side of the raw-edge bar. I clear my throat and sit up a bit straighter.

"It's in my car. I didn't bring it in because I didn't know if you were working," I explain.

"You could have texted me," he counters.

Oh. I could have? Good to know.

"After the way things ended last Friday..." I intentionally trail off and peek up at him through my lashes. "I didn't even think to try. I figured you had probably blocked my number."

His eyebrows pull together again, forming that squishy little wrinkle above his nose. I wiggle my toes in my wedges as I fight the urge to stand up and smooth it out. Gah. Why am I such a sucker for that grumpy forehead wrinkle?

"I didn't see your number in my contacts. And I don't even know how to block someone," he huffs.

Of course he doesn't. He's adorable.

"Hmm. You must not have looked under Clock Tower Girl, then."

His eyes widen a fraction as he pulls his phone out of his back pocket. The blue light illuminates his gorgeous, chiseled jawline as he scrolls through his list of contacts, and I know the moment he finds me because his eyes light up and the briefest hint of a smile cuts through.

"You're something," he mutters as he stashes his phone, shaking his head.

"You don't even know the half of it. But you will."

The smirk leaves his face as he processes my reply. *Shit. Too far.*

"Look." He leans closer and rests one forearm on the bar. "What happened last weekend wasn't cool. You tricked me. You let me think you were just some random girl, when our families have a shared history, and you know it. Could you imagine if our roles were reversed? If someone took away your ability to make an informed decision like that?"

Yikes. Not only did I lose him, but he's gone into full lecture mode on me.

I try to school my expression, but it's hard to resist the urge to roll my eyes. Plus, I can't help but think that if things *had* gone the direction they were heading last Friday night, he wouldn't give a shit who I am or who I'm related to.

"Don't bother apologizing. Sorry's not enough. And something tells me you don't really feel remorse for what you did. You're just mad you got caught."

Busted.

"But it doesn't matter," he continues his lecture. "Now that I know who you are, we both know what can't happen."

"And what's that?" I ask innocently.

He glares at me with so much heat that I know without a shadow of a doubt he still wants me.

"You know what," he mutters. He turns and grabs a rag off the back bar, then wipes down the spot in front of me. "What happened last week won't ever happen again, Maddie. I'll make sure of it."

Challenge accepted.

I roll my lips to resist sassing back. Rather than argue with him, I'm going to prove to him just how wrong he is.

"Okay," I whisper. "But we can be friends, can't we?"

He stops his wax on, wax off routine, his forearm frozen in the most delicious flex while he gives me a dubious look.

"Okay, fine," I relent before he can argue. "Maybe not friends. But mutuals? Acquaintances?" I try. "I'm here all summer, and I honestly feel like I don't know anyone in this town anymore. It would be nice to have a friend... or something."

His glare tells me I'm pushing it, but I'm hoping he's too nice to completely shut me down.

"I'm not making any promises. And I definitely don't trust you, Maddie. But if I see you around town, I won't blatantly ignore you."

"How charming," I quip. When he gives me another disapproving dad glare, I reel it in. "That's fair. How late do you work tonight?"

"Jake's off, so I have to close," he explains.

I know that, of course, because I made fake plans with Jake tonight, only to ditch him at the last minute. I'm nothing if not scrappy when it comes to getting what I want.

"I don't have anywhere else to be, so maybe I'll hang out here, then I can get you your jacket before I leave. Would it be okay if I stayed awhile?"

Dempsey pushes off the bar and looks around, then puffs out his cheeks and blows out a breath.

"I won't tell you that you can't sit here," he relents. "But I'm only serving you soda. And I swear to God, Maddie, if you pull out that sparkly pink flask—"

I hold up both hands in defense. "I came in empty-handed," I declare. "Besides—where would I store a flask in this outfit?" I cock one eyebrow playfully and do a silent happy dance when his eyes scan up and down my body. I'm wearing a white spaghetti strap crop top and my fitted boyfriend jeans. I came in carrying only a wristlet. I couldn't stash a flask on me right now if I tried.

"You're something," he mutters again.

"So you keep saying... Hey. Would you save a seat for me if I went next door and ordered food? You can say no if you want. I'll just DoorDash my order like last time. I'm sure Jake loves paying those extra fees," I snicker.

"I'll save your seat. But you have to do something for me."

"What's that?"

"Order me extra tots, please."

Can do, Dempsey Haas.

Chapter 12

Dempsey

Every fiber of my being is screaming at me that this is a terrible idea. But I've already let things get this far. And I have no idea how to reel it in now.

Maddie Wheeler hung out at the bar all night, and I didn't hate it.

She's fun to be around now that I set some boundaries and we're not dancing around an attraction I refuse to pursue. She's also more extroverted than even my brother, which is saying something. She's quick. She's hilarious. And she has this way of convincing anyone to do what she says, which would be scary if I didn't see right through her sweet-as-sugar pout.

I spent the night mixing drinks, keeping an eye on her, and laughing as she made Cole and Tristan compete to see who could catch the most tots in their mouth. She even fashioned a drink napkin crown for the winner, Cole.

Now it's the end of the night—way past last call—and everyone has vacated the premises, including the rest of my staff.

I don't know what possessed me to insist they head home. I hadn't meant to be alone with her at the end of the night like this.

Yet here we fucking are.

"Ready?" I ask cautiously, watching as she lifts her lithe body off the stool and walks the length of the bar.

"Ready when you are," she declares as she stops near one end.

I freeze where I stand, hesitating and holding my breath. She's all smiles as she waits for me, her hip cocked out to one side as she runs the other hand through her hair. She's got on these loose jeans full of holes, then this ridiculously tight white shirt that only covers her boobs and the top of her stomach. What do girls call those? Crop tops? Might as well be a Cock top for the thoughts it's inspiring in my body.

Dammit.

There's nothing but sweetness behind her eyes. True to her word, she hasn't made a single inappropriate comment or innuendo all night. She's acting like she genuinely wants to be friends. And yet, something tells me she could transform that sweetness into sex appeal in the blink of an eye if I gave her the go ahead. Which I won't. Because I can't. I really fucking can't.

I blow out a long breath as I work up the courage to step out from behind the bar. When I do, she takes a step forward, coming within arm's reach. The scent of strawberries fills the air around me again, and my dick instantly twitches in remembrance.

Dammit. What was I thinking sending the other guys home?

It's too late to dismiss her now. All I can do is grab my jacket and put her in her car.

"I have to lock both doors. Let me get the back taken care of, then I'll meet you out front. Don't walk out without me," I add. I'm not about to chase after her across the green again.

"Oh, Dempsey," she sing-songs as she turns on her heel and heads toward the front of the bar. "What do you really think's going to happen to me on the streets of Hampton after dark?"

"Just wait for me," I huff, too annoyed by my reaction to deal with her sass.

I stalk through the narrow hallway that leads past the bathrooms and the liquor cage to the back. I make quick work of locking and bolting the back door, then hit the lights as I backtrack.

I can see her silhouette against the front door as I approach. I watch, transfixed, as she runs her hand through her thick blond curls. I'm standing all the way across the goddamn bar, and yet I swear I can smell her scent when she shakes out her hair.

I hit the main panel, dousing the bar in shadow. The blue-teal backlights that line the liquor shelves behind the bar are the only source of light that remains.

I can't see her anymore. But I can feel her.

Her sass. Her sweetness. That inexplicable lightness I feel when she's near.

Her eyes are on me. I don't have to see her to know that. My body's humming with want, my insides aching for an encore of what happened the last time we left this bar together.

I steel my spine and scowl as I make my way over to her. I've got to get this shit locked down. Nothing can happen tonight. Nothing can ever happen again with Maddie Wheeler.

I'm nearly to the door when she pipes up.

"Permission to exit the building, Mr. Haas?"

I itch to smack her ass or nip at her lips—anything to put her in her place. She knows it, too, based on the way she bites the corner of her lip as she eyes me from head to toe.

I refuse to play this game, though. My resolve is dialed in and locked tight, so all she gets from me is a deeper scowl as I reach past her, push open the door, and hold it open with one arm.

"After you." I nod my head. I follow her, then turn around and make quick work of locking up.

"Where are you parked?" I ask as I pull on the handle to ensure it's locked.

When she doesn't answer, I look over my shoulder to find her standing unreasonably close. She's got one eyebrow raised, and this wicked glint behind her eyes.

Fuck, this girl's trouble. All she has to do is look at me and my body is ready to betray my sensibilities. I don't care if she wants to be friends... mutuals... acquaintances. Nights like this cannot happen again. If I've learned anything in the last few hours, it's that I have no control over my reaction to her.

"What?" I press when she gives me a once-over again, ignoring my question completely.

She blinks in slow motion, her lashes resting against her cheekbones before she opens her eyes and beams up at me.

"I parked out back," she reveals, giving me a look that's anything but innocent. "But don't worry," she adds. "I know a shortcut."

Before I know what's happening, she grabs my hand and pulls me toward Clinton's with a surprising amount of strength.

"Maddie, stop," I insist, pulling my hand out of her grasp just as she turns down the narrow alley between the buildings.

Calling the walkway between Clinton's and The Oak an alley is a generous assessment—it's barely wide enough for two people to walk through side by side.

My frustration ratchets up as she struts through the space at a brisk pace. She's more than halfway into the damn alley before she turns back and calls to me.

"Come on, slowpoke! Keep up!"

"Maddie," I grit out as I stalk after her. What choice do I have? Let her trek through an alley alone after midnight? It would take me three times as long to walk around the building and meet her on the other side.

She knew what she was doing by running down this way. And yet here I am. Chasing after her. Playing her game.

I half jog, half sidestep through the narrow space, trying to keep pace with this girl.

The next time I look up, she's stopped, standing stock still, her back to me.

"Are you okay?" I ask on an exhale when I finally catch up to her. I'm breathless from the adrenaline rush of chasing her.

She doesn't answer. Not verbally, at least.

I don't know if she steps back or if I shift forward. Maybe we both move at once, but I hiss as her ass brushes against the front of my pants.

I desperately need to put distance between us. I reach out to grip her hip, intending to shift her forward so she's not right up on my dick. But thanks to the darkness of the alley and her ridiculous half shirt, my fingers find purchase against the soft flesh of her stomach.

Her abs contract against my hand, and she gasps in response to my touch. Without conscious thought, I tighten my hold, digging into her skin and pulling her back toward me.

"Dempsey." Her head lands on my chest as she cranes back to meet my gaze.

"Dammit, Maddie." I grunt as her strawberry sweetness fills my nostrils and leaves me senseless. I inexplicably bend lower, tug her closer, and nuzzle into her hair like an addict craving his next hit.

She smells *so good*. She feels even better.

She rolls her hips against me, and desire shoots through every nerve in my goddamn body. My dick's hardening behind my zipper, and my balls are practically weeping with want.

Did I experience a lobotomy when I followed her into this alley? What the fuck am I doing? There are so many reasons why this is a bad idea.

She's her.

I'm me.

And yet here we are, pressed together, hidden from view, in a private moment of our own making.

"Dempsey?" She repeats my name, her tone full of questions. She's not pushing me like before. She's not trying to manipulate me or trick me again. This time, she sounds genuinely concerned and a little unsure.

It's the way her voice quavers that does me in.

Fuck it.

I grab her shoulders, then shove her back against the bricks with a force that startles us both. My anger is still bubbling under the surface, but over the last few seconds, it's transformed into something needy and frantic. I look down at her and suck in a ragged breath.

The high-voltage thrum in the air between us—the one that nags at me any time I'm in her presence—intensifies. It's this goddamn connection I've been trying to ignore all night. Every time I look at this woman, I want her more.

"This can't happen," I exhale, grinding my knuckles into the rough bricks behind her as I cage her in.

"What can't happen?" she whispers as she pushes up onto her toes.

There's barely any room in this goddamn alley as it is, so I can't escape her closeness. I shudder when she trails a featherlight kiss along my jaw.

My breathing picks up and my brain goes haywire as memories from the night we met come flooding back to my consciousness.

Those. Lips.

I know exactly what they taste like. And just how good they feel on mine.

The heat of her breath inspires goosebumps on the left side of my body as she lingers in my personal space. I'm so focused on what her mouth is doing that I jump in surprise when she slips her hand between us and traces down the center of my stomach. I clench my abs in anticipation when she stops at the waistband of my jeans, lifts the hem of my shirt, and teases one fingernail along the muscles she exposed.

She peers up at me through her impossibly long lashes, biting down on her lower lip and giving me a look that's pure temptation.

I'm a statue before her: not willing to give her the permission she's seeking, but too damn tired and horny to turn her down.

In the end, it doesn't matter. Maddie Wheeler doesn't wait for permission.

I hiss in a sharp breath when she dips into the front of my pants. Her fingers curl into the end of my happy trail, pulling until I give up a grunt and she gets the reaction she wanted. She raises one eyebrow, bites down harder on her bottom lip, and smirks.

This. Girl.

I close my eyes in frustration, knowing what I'm about to do is an absolutely terrible idea. But I really am tired. I don't want to fight this anymore. I just want what I want for once.

And what I want is her.

I crash my mouth into hers, and her whole body responds instantly to the kiss. She grabs me by the belt loops and pulls me flush against her form. She grinds her body against me as she pushes her tongue into my mouth in what feels like a claiming.

I'm not letting her have all the fun tonight, though. I push back, greedy and desperate to get my fill. I have to quench this pent-up desire inside me and get her out of my system once and for all.

She's savage in the way she kisses: like premium gasoline being poured over fire. Every time I push, she pushes back harder. Every time I move, she matches my stance. We're devouring each other, and when she moans into my mouth, my cock literally jolts.

I'm lost. Adrift. So fucking gone. And so fucking happy.

I roll my hips into her as I bite down on her lush bottom lip, her sweetness overwhelming me as she moans again. She finally releases my belt loops, then hikes one leg up and hooks it around my thigh. Never letting up, I graze my hands down her arms, then work them behind her back, pulling her forward to separate her from the bricks.

I grunt at the loss of contact as I abandon her sweet, pillowy lips, but relief finds me again as I kiss down her neck. Every kiss is an exploration of uncharted territory. It's a reckoning of something wrong and forbidden.

This girl isn't mine to claim. And yet my body is determined to take her.

She whimpers when I find her sweet spot, halting my path of discovery so I can savor the delicate skin between her neck and her collarbone.

I lick.

She mewls.

I bite.

She hisses.

I suck, and she goes silent, instead answering my marking with the rhythmic grinding of her hips.

She careens and shifts under me as she aligns our bodies and puts me exactly where she wants me.

My dick's hard enough to punch through this damn alley wall, and I'm more than happy to oblige as her body seeks the friction we both crave.

When she finally makes contact—lining up her sweet, forbidden cunt with the pulsing bulge in my pants—she cries out. She cries for *me*. And then she moves, working her center against me and gripping my shoulders with both hands.

She sets the pace, and I gladly follow her lead, dry humping the shit out of her so I can hear her make that noise again.

She pants.

She whimpers.

She grunts.

And suddenly I worry that I'm being too rough. I slow my thrusts and work a hand between her torso and the coarse brick and mortar at her back.

"Don't," she groans as she wiggles out of my hold.

"Don't what?" I demand, halting all movement to make sure she's okay.

She's breathing so hard she can barely speak. *Fuck*. We're both so worked up I completely forgot where we are.

She cups my face, then traces my jawline, working her hand into the hair at the nape of my neck and giving it a sharp pull. "Don't try to cushion my back or treat me with kid gloves. I want you just like this. I like it rough."

She wants me like this. She likes it rough. And I'm so wrapped up in this I'm seconds away from pulling my dick out and giving it to her in an alley.

But this shouldn't happen like this.

This shouldn't happen *at all*.

I stare down at the woman panting in my arms and admire the curve of her neck, the swell of her breasts, the strength in her thigh as she keeps that damn leg hitched up, holding me to her.

I know what she wants. I know what *I* want.

I could justify this in a million ways if I just let it happen.

But then I see his face.

The sad, lonely boy who looks just like me. My brother, who isn't getting better, and who doesn't need another reason to prolong his heartache.

It doesn't matter if he never found out.

I would know. And it would kill me.

In this world where we only have each other to rely on...

I can't sully the version of myself he loves—the version of me he *needs*—to scratch an itch or satisfy an urge.

I'll choose his happiness over mine every time because there's just so little left in this world that makes him happy.

I groan my frustration, the magic of the moment dissipating into the warm night air as I force myself to pull back and put a stop to this.

"This can't happen," I lament as I drag in a breath and try to slow my breathing. I pull back from her as best I can in the tight space, then gently unhook her leg from around my thigh. I lower it to the ground in slow motion, taking a knee and bowing my head in shame for how far I let things go tonight.

She brushes a hand against my forehead and smooths her thumb over my brows, but she says nothing, and I don't dare look up. Instead, I lean forward, caress down her pant leg in the dark, and place a kiss on her thigh through one of the holes in her jeans.

I rise to my feet, regret rolling off me in waves. There's none of the anger or hostility of last week coursing between us now. It's as if she finally gets it.

This isn't rejection. It's acceptance.

"I'm sorry," I whisper as I look over her head and tuck a strand of hair behind her ear. I can't bear to look her in the eye.

She closes her eyes and huffs out a breath, the warm air tickling my neck and tempting me all over again.

"It's because of them, isn't it?"

Her question catches me off guard, but I quickly school my expression at the reminder of them—of *him*.

"I don't even know what happened, you know. No one ever told me. If it matters, I'm nothing like either of them."

She may be nothing like them. But I'm exactly like him.

"It doesn't matter what happened. All you need to know is that things went too far—and I'll be damned if I let history repeat itself," I declare as I find the small of her back and encourage her forward.

"I don't want to hurt you," she whispers, her voice soft and unsure in a way that doesn't sound like the girl I chased into this alley minutes ago.

"Then walk away right now."

I guide her until we reach the end of the alley, then I watch as she crosses the parking lot to her car.

She turns to me before unlocking her white Lexus, and we stare at each other through the darkness for what feels like forever. If she doesn't get in that damn car, I don't know if I have it in me to make her leave.

I brace my arms on either side of the alley, pushing against the bricks in frustration and desperately trying to anchor myself in place.

"Go," I whisper under my breath, urging her to get out of here so I can force myself to walk away.

Eventually, she does. She climbs into her car and starts the engine. The night is quiet enough that I hear the click of a lock before she buckles her seatbelt. Once I'm sure she's safe, I turn and start back down the alley to the front of the building where I parked.

I continue without another glance. I can't stand the thought of watching her drive away.

Chapter 13

Maddie

A drawn-out yawn escapes me as I reach over and splash water on my legs. I've got music playing through the outdoor speakers, and I made a huge batch of spiked lemonade, yet nothing feels good or right today.

I've practically become a hermit over the last three days: leaving my phone in the house all day while I lounge in the pool, going for long runs, and essentially blocking out all rational thoughts that don't involve *him*.

I'm a woman obsessed. And I don't even care.

It's been three days since Dempsey Haas almost fucked me in an alley. Three long, torturous days in which my every waking moment has been spent replaying Wednesday night in my mind.

How he felt. How he made me feel.

And then the moment that breaks me every time I recall it: how he pulled back, mentally warred with himself, and lost. He stopped what I started. Pumped the brakes when I was ready to fall over the edge, consequences be damned.

I've never, in my life, experienced anything like the chemistry between us. There was no denying what we both wanted. And yet, he pulled back.

He chose restraint over happiness, control over cravings. It was infuriating. And so damn sexy.

I couldn't help myself when I reached down and smoothed that damn wrinkle between his brows. Just like I couldn't help myself when I cried all the way home. If that was the only comfort I could offer him, then that's what I would give. I didn't walk away on Wednesday night because I wanted to go. I walked away because it was the kindest thing I could do for him.

He guided me out of the alley with soft, gentle care. But he didn't walk me to my car, and I didn't push him. It felt like he'd already surpassed his limit. And I didn't want to contribute to the self-loathing I knew he was already drowning in.

In the blink of an eye, my silly little game of cat and mouse became a quest for control and survival. And now I don't want to play anymore. Not if my actions caused the look on his face when I left him in the alley and drove away.

I'm heartbroken for him.

To yo-yo from one extreme to the next... to snap back from the moment and refuse himself of what he clearly wanted...

I can't think about what happened Wednesday night without feeling guilty. And horny. I've had to recharge my vibe twice over the last seventy-two hours, yet nothing comes close to dulling the ache he left between my thighs.

We're both responsible for what happened. I'm the one who took off down the alley. I'm the one who led us down that path. But I know he's a big boy, and he had a choice. I may have extended the invitation, but he's the one who pushed me against those bricks and kissed me first.

I texted him on Thursday to say I was sorry about what happened and to offer to bring his jacket back the next time he worked. I knew he had to be working that night since Jake was off. But I felt like I needed permission before I just waltzed back into The Oak.

When he didn't respond, I tried to call him on Friday, knowing he wouldn't answer. I don't know what I would have said if he had, but I wanted to hear his voice and know that he was okay.

Any semblance of friendship that could have existed between us went out the window on Wednesday, but I hate that he might hate me—or worse, that he hates himself because of me.

I woke up this morning in a daze. I dreamed of him. We were swinging at the park, and he kept telling me to be careful. I kept pumping... pushing, pushing, pushing... until I disappeared into the clouds. He didn't follow.

I was still half asleep when I texted him this morning. This time, offering to just drop his jacket off when he's not at The Oak so we won't have to see each other. The message seemed to go through. I believed him when he said he didn't actually know how to block someone, but he has his read receipts turned off.

I keep asking myself if I want to hear from him for my own peace of mind or for his sake.

Why do I keep trying? How did I go from wanting to get in his pants to caring deeply about whether he's okay?

I use one arm to paddle myself toward the stairs, decidedly done with laying out for today. My tan looks awesome, but I need to do something with myself before I go crazy.

That stupid party is tonight, and I've never wanted to go to anything less. But Paige is excited. And I know if I back out now, it'll hurt her chances of getting to spend time with Kyle, and I'm not that kind of friend.

I climb out of the pool and towel off, turning the sound system off with my phone, then checking my messages.

He hasn't responded to any of my attempts to reach him over the last three days. But I'm still disappointed when I don't have anything from Dempsey.

I send Paige a text asking if she wants to pregame at my house or hers beforehand, knowing she'll end up here like always. After all, I have the whole house to myself.

Chapter 14

Maddie

Paige parks her car on the side of the road behind the other twenty plus vehicles lining the street. Now that I'm here, I remember this house. Andrew Adley lives on the north side of town, near where Jake grew up. He was a grade ahead of me in school, and he was captain of the boys' lacrosse team his senior year. His family has a huge historical home, as well as this old, converted barn with a built-in bar, a makeshift stage and dance floor, and a loft filled with beanbag chairs and Jerry Garcia posters.

Groovy, baby.

"I have a feeling tonight is going to be epic," Paige proclaims as she flips down the visor mirror to reapply her lip gloss.

I try to garner up even a fraction of her excitement as I watch her primp her perfectly made-up face.

She's wearing a hot pink corset top and her favorite jeans—I spent more than an hour helping her choose this outfit earlier. Her dark hair is parted down the middle and straightened to perfection so her layers frame her face and the tips tickle the top of her chest. She looks smoking hot, and I wish she'd go into this party with an open mind. But she's only got her sights set on one guy.

One guy who just so happens to be approaching the car right now, along with his sidekick.

"Shit, here come the guys. We're doing code words tonight, right?" I ask, double-checking that my phone's not on silent in my wristlet.

"Yes, Mads," Paige huffs out with an eye roll.

It's silly to ask—we've had this system in place since high school—but I don't really want to be here, so any excuse to duck out early is a priority for me.

"Lucky Lucy if you're leaving with a guy. Rodger Dodger if we need to leave ASAP, no questions asked," I remind her.

"I hope Lucky Lucy is on both our sides tonight. Okay, let's go!" She opens the car door before I have a chance to reply.

I blow out a breath and follow, circling the car to join her where the guys are waiting. Before I've even opened my mouth to say hi, Travis throws his arm around me and pulls me into an awkward side hug.

"Hey, Maddie," he whispers against my hair as I spin out of his embrace.

"Hey," I mutter, sticking both hands on my hips to ward off any additional affection.

"Sup, ladies," Kyle says with a smirk. "You look good, Paige," he adds, crossing his arms over his Nike T-shirt as he gives my best friend this sort of smarmy perusal. The dude didn't even make eye contact with her when he spoke. Twenty-year-old boys really are just out here doing the least.

"You look hot as fuck," Travis whispers in my ear, jolting me back to the moment.

I didn't realize he'd inched closer until he was right up on me. We haven't even walked into the party, and I'm ready to Rodger Dodger everyone's ass and call it a night.

But I won't do that to Paige. I agreed to come to this party for her, so now I have to see it through. I can suck it up and fend off Travis's lame attempts at flirting if it means my best friend has a good time. Lord knows she'd do the same for me.

"Are we gonna party or just stand in the street chit chatting?" I tease, linking arms with Paige and starting the trek past the line of parked cars.

"Lead the way, ladies," Kyle announces with a flourish, his arm extended toward the house.

Paige giggles, and I don't have the heart to tell her he's not being charming or chivalrous; he's probably about to Snapchat a picture of our asses to lord knows who.

Whatever. My ass looks really fucking good in these white jeans.

Snap your heart out, Bare Minimum Boy.

I'm regretting my choice of footwear by the time we reach the long-ass driveway that leads to the main house. Four-inch wedges may look good, but they are not meant for long-distance treks. Truth be told, I only wore them because they make me a solid inch taller than Travis. I'm five foot seven on flat feet. And although I've heard Travis say he's six feet tall on more than one occasion, the guy's pushing five-ten on tiptoes.

Not that I have anything against short guys. I just don't particularly care for a little man with an overcompensating ego. If you're average, own it.

We don't bother knocking when we reach the front door. Instead, we walk into the house and are instantly hit with booming bass and the stink of weed. We pass a formal living room that's been taped off with yellow caution tape—clever, really—and head for the commotion in the kitchen.

There are two separate beer pong games going, one on the eat-in kitchen table, the other on the kitchen island. I make a beeline for the drinks lined up near the sink and pour myself a vodka lemonade before the others even make their way over.

"That's my girl!" Travis praises as I glare at him over the rim of my upturned glass. "Let's get this party started!"

I lean against the counter as I watch my friends make their own drinks. Kyle's already got an arm slung around Paige, and he's just said something that has her giggling.

Good. At least this night won't be in vain.

I glance around, surveying the crowd to see how many of these people I actually know. There are a few familiar faces from high school, but most of the people in the kitchen are strangers.

They're strangers. And yet they're all so familiar and predictable.

Any combination of these types of people in this type of setting would turn me off right now. It's not them—it's me.

I don't know when parties like this stopped being fun and started to feel like a chore. But as I glance around the crowded kitchen, the smell of weed mingling with expensive aftershave and the sticky sweetness of spiked punch, I can't fathom anywhere on planet earth I'd rather be less.

Travis perches next to me and takes a long sip from his cup before speaking. "You want to go check out what's happening in the barn?"

I already know what's happening out in the barn: girls are grinding up on each other on the dance floor, vying for attention, while other people light up in the loft. But I don't have anything else to do. And this kitchen really is crowded.

"Why not?" I shrug, resisting the urge to roll my eyes when Travis smirks and looks obnoxiously proud. Yeah. No. My willingness to check out the barn has nothing to do with him, and everything to do with my desire to be anywhere but here.

I scan the room and spot Paige and Kyle waiting for next game at one of the beer pong tables. Paige and I make eye contact, and I point toward the door so she knows where I'm headed. She gives me big eyes and an excited grin before schooling her expression and turning back to listen to whatever Kyle's droning on about. Probably crypto. Or a podcast he listened to this week, which now makes him a certifiable expert in whatever subject they covered.

Travis leads the way out the sliding glass door and onto a deck that's just as crowded as the kitchen. At least it's cooler out here. I grab a water bottle from an open cooler, then I follow him down the stairs toward the back of the property.

He reaches for my hand, but I hold up my double-fisted beverages and feign an apologetic smile.

"How do you like school?" he asks, slowing his pace to match mine as I traverse the yard in wedges.

"It's awesome," I answer honestly. "I love my school and my program. I'll definitely stay out there for law school, as long as I can get in."

"You go to University of California, right?"

"I go to UC Berkeley," I correct.

"Oh. But that's still in California, right? So the parties must be pretty cool?"

I open my mouth to tell him that I haven't attended a single college party since starting at Cal, then think better of it.

My major is in legal studies, and I'm double-minoring in gender and women's studies and political science. I've consistently taken eighteen credit hours a semester since the second half of freshman year. I have neither any interest in nor any free time to party.

I'm not a hermit. I have a group of girlfriends I met my freshman year in the dorms, and we get together for drinks on Thursday nights. But I mostly hang out with my cohort for my major.

But none of that is worth explaining to Travis. He doesn't actually care. And I don't really want to share that part of my life with him.

"Yep." I pop the *P* for emphasis and pray he doesn't realize I'm mocking him. "Awesome parties."

"Well, let's just hope this California girl still has a thing for this Ohio boy, because I've been looking forward to tonight all week."

My eyes are involuntarily rolling as a scream catches our attention. Saved by the... what? Fight club?

There's a group of guys circled up next to the far end of the barn. We're close enough to hear them yelling and cussing, but too far away to make out what's actually happening.

Travis looks at me with wide, questioning eyes. "I wonder if they're taking bets."

Typical. He would be the type to want to throw down dollar bills instead of fists.

"Let's go see," I relent.

We head toward the ruckus, and I finish off my vodka lemonade, discarding the cup in a pile of empties on a picnic table.

By the time we're close enough to see anything, the circle's closed in, making it hard to distinguish what's actually happening. I'm not about to get close enough to catch an elbow, and I doubt Travis's wallet could protect me if I got mixed up in their little game.

"Hold on," I mutter as I backtrack a few feet. I grip the edge of the picnic table to keep myself steady in these stupid shoes, then carefully step onto the bench to get a better look.

The first thing I see is a guy flying backward as he takes a punch to the face. Fuck. That had to hurt. I grit my teeth as another guy winds up and hits the same man in the side, causing him to double over on impact.

I have to hand it to the human punching bag. I'm surprised he stayed on his feet after that one-two combo.

Travis tries to join me on the bench, but his body weight makes the whole picnic table teeter. I'm not about to go down with the ship—or be in a position where he conveniently has to stand behind me—so I step up onto the table portion.

Now that I'm higher up, I have a clear view into the circle of mayhem.

My heart jumps into my throat and my stomach plummets out my butt now that I can clearly see who just took those hits.

Shit.

The man who's starred in every one of my R-rated fantasies over the last week is hunched over with both hands covering his head as some asshat beats on his back.

Dempsey.

Fuck.

Except as he stands up, I see that his hair's longer. He looks different. Sure, he's bloodied and beaten. But that's not the man I thought it was. My gut twists in realization.

That's not Dempsey.

That's Fielding Haas.

Chapter 15

Maddie

"Stop!" I wail as I tear across the yard, wedges be damned. I roll my left ankle, but the pain is nonexistent as I push to break through the wall of bodies surrounding the boy in the middle.

"Stop!" I scream again, finally busting through a sea of elbows and coming to stand in front of Fielding.

He's doubled over and panting. Someone comes at us from behind, and I see red as I spin around and insert myself between the stupid fucker and the man who's clearly in no shape to defend himself.

"I said *stop*," I hiss when a guy swings wide and barely misses decking me in the face. I don't even flinch as I feel the force of wind skim my cheek where the punch almost landed. I'm too furious to care.

"What is wrong with all of you?" I demand, keeping my back to Fielding because I sure as hell don't trust any of these goons to back off just because I said so.

"Yo. Bitch. Stand down. This guy wanted it."

I have no idea who said that. Just like I don't know what the heck to do next. I search the crowd for a familiar face but come up short. I'm surrounded by angry assholes in polos and multiple phones pointed in my direction.

"Go home, Maddie Wheeler. This doesn't concern you. Leave my boys to their games."

I whirl around and lock eyes with Andrew Adley. Fuck. This is his house. His party. And these are "his boys," apparently. I keep scanning the crowd, looking for an out or a solution that doesn't exist.

Fielding grunts behind me, and I risk turning my back to the crowd for just a second to make sure he's okay. When I glance over my shoulder, he's trying to rise up to standing.

"Field—sit down. Or better yet, lie down," I command. The last thing he should be doing right now is standing.

He nods—sort of—and his head lulls from side to side, but I'm pretty sure he heard me. When he drops to his knees, he groans.

I steel my spine and stand as tall as possible. My left ankle is throbbing with the pain I didn't feel when I rolled it, but for the first time tonight, I'm grateful to be wearing these damn wedges. I clear my throat once, and I say a silent prayer that words actually come out. If this doesn't work...

"You're all done here. This is over. Call your guys off, Adley."

There's a storm light shining on us from the upper level of the barn, so the smirk on Andrew's face is illuminated as he cocks one eyebrow in challenge.

I keep my gaze steady and try my best not to physically react as Andrew takes several steps forward into the circle. None of the other guys seem keen to join him, so even though I'm surrounded by assholes, it's a mostly fair fight.

"The prick wanted this. He showed up here tonight, snorted who knows what, then started raging about how he could take all of us at once. He wouldn't shut up until we formed a circle around him and made him."

Andrew spits toward Fielding, and my vision darkens around the edges. I suck in a slow breath and try to calm my temper. I can't physically go after him. All it would take is one meathead to lift me up or pull me away, and I'd be gone.

I'm racking my brain, desperate for a solution, when some rando calls out to me from the crowd. "Move, princess. We've got unfinished business here."

Princess. How original. He's not the first person to call me that this week.

Dempsey.

Fuck.

I can't let them hurt his brother. I won't let them touch him again.

Looking Andrew in the eye, I unzip my wristlet and pull out my phone. I raise it up, slowly and deliberately, so they can all see what I'm doing, then open up the camera app and hit record.

My body is literally shaking, but I spread my legs a little wider and dig my wedges into the soft grass of the yard for balance.

I bend my knees slightly, and I pull in a deep breath. When I speak, to my relief, my voice comes out loud and clear.

"Assault is a first-degree misdemeanor in the state of Ohio. The penalty for the offense could include a jail sentence of up to six months, a fine of up to a thousand dollars, or five years' probation."

A few guys in the crowd snicker—and I know exactly why. A grand is a drop in the bucket for most of these assholes.

"That is, if the charge is a first offense."

I pause for dramatic effect, then scan my phone around the full circle, ensuring I get every single person's face on camera.

"If a person being charged with assault already has a record, the penalties can increase."

I clear my throat and continue. "Let's say, for example, you were caught driving under the influence in high school. Or maybe there were charges filed by someone claiming you sexually assaulted them." I look at Andrew for that one. The girls in my class didn't call him "Handy Andy" for no reason.

"Suddenly, you're looking at increased jail time, more fines, and your name in the press. Everything is Google-able these days. Nothing ever stays quiet in a town like this."

The posture of a few of the guys in the crowd has deflated a bit.

"It would suck so hard for assault charges to prevent any of you from getting into medical school. Or for your name to be flagged on a background check for that social studies job you want so you can coach high school football."

I fight back a snicker at my own dig—I know my audience.

"Walk away right now, and no one gets named. Keep going, and I'm calling the police."

Andrew lurches toward me, and I can't help but flinch this time.

"You've got some fucking nerve," he jeers, looming over me, just inches away. He's so close I can feel his hot breath on my face. It's then I realize his proximity isn't accidental.

He's close. Too close. He doesn't want anyone to hear our exchange.

He's going to back down.

That realization gives me courage.

"It's your call, Adley. I can get him out of here quietly... or I can call for help."

He's glaring at me with beady eyes the color of mud. The pungent scent of his deodorant is working overtime. He leans in closer so we're standing toe to toe. We should be eye-level, but I swear he must prop up on his toes to give the illusion of being taller than me.

Four-inch wedges for the win!

"Not a word of this to anyone. And don't try to defy me. You made your choice."

I don't know what the fuck that's supposed to mean...

"Fine, Wheeler," he declares loudly.

He reaches one hand toward me, and I lean back, but the threat in his eyes makes me pause. I swallow—hard—as I let him touch the side of my face. His meaty hand skims my jaw, then trails down the side of my neck.

I shudder.

He grins.

Then he reaches out and swipes a strand of hair off my shoulder, twirling it between his fingers before he gives it a little tug.

"Maddie and I have reached a *compromise* that I think is more than fair. Fight's over, boys. Go get a drink."

I don't move a muscle as the circle shifts. Some guys wander off, others stand around and heckle Adley about our supposed agreement.

I don't dare even blink. The crowd may be gone, but the threat is far from over.

Adley leans in again, this time his words intended just for me. "Did you come here with friends tonight, Wheeler? You might want to let them know you won't need a ride home. I'll find you later."

My eyes water without my fucking permission. I'm livid that he thinks he can manipulate me. I stand stock still and bite down on the inside of my cheek. I refuse to let a single tear fall.

"I'd rather eat glass and shit out the shards than hook up with you, Adley," I hiss so only he can hear. "Remind me—was it one or two girls who accused you of assault your junior year?"

Andrew pales, and I go for the hail Mary pass.

"That's what I thought. You so much as try and touch me, and I'll drive myself down to the hospital and tell them you forced yourself on me without my fucking permission. A dozen guys just heard you stake your claim—do you think they'd all stay quiet if they were called in for questioning?"

He backs away from me, his steps slow as he moves toward the barn. "You're going to be sorry you came here tonight, Wheeler."

At least we agree on one thing.

I watch him retreat into the barn as I calm my racing heart rate and steady my breathing. Seconds pass as I mentally recover from what just happened—what I fucking did.

The mess is far from cleaned up. Fielding's still lying on the ground, and I have no idea how I'm going to move his big-ass body on my own, but we need to get out of here as quickly as possible.

I drop to my knees at his side, and mud squelches under my weight. I close my eyes in anguish, taking a moment of silence to mourn my favorite white jeans.

"Hey, Fielding."

He's on his ass, knees pulled into his chest, head hanging low. I glance around again to make sure no one's lingering. I'm relieved to see Andrew hasn't returned, and the other guys must have gone inside the barn with him. He won't leave me alone for long—I've just gotta get Fielding out of here before he comes back looking to prove a point.

"Fielding," I whisper with more urgency, shaking his knee to try and get him to come to.

He sort of grunts, but I can't tell if it's a grunt of recognition or a grunt of pain.

"Fielding, come on. Get up. We have to get out of here."

He curls up, like maybe he's going to try to stand, but then falls flat onto his back instead.

Fuckity fuck. What am I supposed to do now?

I pull out my phone and realize it's still recording. I end the video, then scroll through my recent calls until I get to Paige's number. I click it and hold my breath as the phone rings.

The call goes to voicemail on the second ring, and a text comes through before I even hit end.

Paige: OMG Mads! I'm upstairs with Kyle. Lucky Lucy for the win!!!

Ugh. What now?

The next person in my contact list is Travis.

Wait, Travis was with me on the picnic table. Where the hell did he go?

I glance down at Fielding's outstretched body; he's lying with his arm pinned behind his back. Shit. That doesn't look comfortable. Or natural. I have no idea how long those guys were beating on him before I got out here. What if he's really hurt and needs medical attention? I'm afraid to move him and hurt him further, but I need to get him out of here—fast.

Travis answers on the third ring.

"What the fuck was that, Maddie?"

Oh. So he *did* see what happened. And he decided to—what? Stay out of it and let me face off with at least ten guys by myself? Charming.

"Are you still here? I could really use some help."

He scoffs into the phone. "That was fucking reckless, Maddie. I heard what Adley said to you. I'm sorry, but I'm not getting mixed up with him."

Talk about a fair-weather fucker. I end the call without saying goodbye.

I focus on my call list again, eyes landing on the name I probably should have started with. He's going to lose his freaking mind. But at least he'll help me.

The phone rings once, then twice, then a third time. It kicks over to voicemail after the fourth ring, and it takes every ounce of willpower I possess not to chuck my phone across the yard.

I call him again, because maybe he just didn't get to his phone in time.

I wait.

Fielding groans.

Panic bubbles up inside me as the call goes to voicemail again. *Think, Maddie. Think!*

Dempsey hasn't answered any of my calls or texts over the last few days. He's ignoring me.

"Field—I'm gonna look through your pockets and find your phone, 'kay?" I experience a surge of déjà vu the moment I feel his device in his back left pocket—right where his brother keeps his.

I pull out the phone and swipe up, then scowl when the facial recognition doesn't unlock.

Shit.

"Fielding. Can you hear me? Listen, I need you to open your eyes for me."

I crawl toward his head, gently lifting his skull and laying it in my lap. "Field, come on. Open your eyes for one second..."

I position the device in front of his face and swipe up again. The phone vibrates its rejection. I try one more time. That one fails, too, because of course it does. Not only are his eyes closed, but one is completely swollen shut. I'm not sure facial recognition would work even if he could cooperate.

The phone stops trying to open with Face ID and asks me for a passcode instead.

Four numbers. Six attempts. There's no way this'll work, but I punch in Dempsey's passcode just to rule it out.

Shit. Yes! These goofballs. *Why would they have matching lock codes?*

I brush Fielding's hair out of his eyes and keep his head on my lap as I use the other hand to scroll through his contacts.

When I get to where "Dempsey" should be, there's nothing. I switch over to his recent calls instead.

Random names and numbers are listed, but about halfway down, there's one that says "Dumpy." I click it rather than waste time comparing it to what I have in my phone.

It only rings once.

"Hello?"

Tears of relief flood my eyes, but I hastily blink them away. We're not out of the woods yet.

"Dempsey, it's Maddie Wheeler. Please don't hang up on me," I rush to get out.

"Maddie? What the hell? The caller ID said my brother was calling..." He trails off, checking the display on his phone, I'm sure.

"You've got some nerve—" he starts, but I cut him off before I lose him completely.

"Dempsey, listen to me. I'm with Fielding. We're at a party. There were these guys, and they said he snorted something—" A sob rips through my chest unbidden.

If those guys come back... if Andrew finds me out here alone with no one but the unconscious dude in my lap... Fuck. I have to make Dempsey understand.

"Fielding's hurt. They hurt him. I stopped them, but I don't know—"

"Where are you?" he demands. There's rustling in the background, followed by the faint rumbling of an engine.

"Haymarket Street. The house is on Haymarket. There's a ton of cars… you can't miss it. We're out by the barn, but I need to get him out of here. If they come back…"

"I'm already in my car. GPS has fourteen minutes, though. Where are you right now?"

"I'm sitting with him in the grass. He's so out of it, I can't get him to stand."

"Are you safe?"

Are we?

"No," I whisper as my lip quivers with the confession.

If those guys come back out here looking for a fight… or if Adley decides to make good on his little stunt and prove a point… neither of us is safe. Another sob croaks out, and I curse myself for acting like such a sissy right now.

"Tickle him," Dempsey demands.

"Wh-what?"

"Tickle him. Stomach, armpits—Fielding's super ticklish. Unless he's literally unconscious, that'll at least get him moving."

"Okay…"

"I'm going to stay on the phone with you until I get there. See if you guys can get to the road or somewhere safe. I'll be there as soon as I can."

I switch the phone to speaker and stick it in my back pocket, then make sure my wristlet is secure before standing. My legs are asleep from kneeling, which is probably a good thing because my left ankle has its own pulse and is twice the size of my right.

I brush off some of the grass and dirt on my knees, then bend to where Fielding lies at my feet.

I go right for the kill shot and jam my fingers into his armpit. The man shoots straight up, then is on his feet and screaming like a banshee a second later.

"Field! Shh! Shh! You're okay! It's just me!"

His lagoon-blue eyes are wild and hazy. He's looking right at me, but it's clear he hasn't connected the dots.

"It's Maddie," I soothe, reaching out and placing a hand on his arm. "Maddie Wheeler."

"Fuck," he hisses, his right hand coming up to gingerly press on his swollen eye. "*Fuuuck*," he groans again, but with real feeling this time, as he skims his right hand over his left arm.

We lock eyes, and he blinks.

"Maddie?"

"Yes. Your brother's on his way. We have to get out of here, though. Can you walk? We have to get to the road—"

"Grab my wrist," he grunts, cocking his head toward the left arm hanging at his side.

"Field, I don't want to hurt—"

"Just do it," he commands.

I swallow down a lump in my throat. *Get it together, Maddie.* He's standing. Dempsey's on his way. We're gonna be okay.

"Like this?" I ask as I gingerly circle his wrist in my hand.

"Both hands," he growls.

I don't know if he's hurt or pissed or both.

"Hold on tight," he says before jerking away from me. I keep my feet firmly planted but still lose my balance from of the momentum. I hear it and *feel it* before I realize what's happening.

"Jesus fucking Christ," he grinds out as he doubles over in pain.

"No, no, no," I panic as he takes a knee. "Please don't sit down. We have to move, Fielding. We have to *go*."

He stays propped up on one knee, panting. When he looks up at me, he's impossibly pale.

"You just put my shoulder back in place, Little Wheeler. I'm gonna need a minute to recover unless you want me to pass out on you again."

I look from the house to the barn. A few people have passed and paid us no mind. But I can't help but feel the sense of dread that Andrew or one of his goons will be back out here to check on us soon.

"Thirty seconds," I offer. "Thirty seconds to get it together, then we're fucking out of here."

"I hear you," he groans. "And I heard what Adley said to you."

We lock eyes, and I see the gravity of the situation on his face.

He heard Adley? So he knows what I did. I gulp down my fear and silently count the seconds as we stare at each other.

As soon as I reach zero in my head, I step toward him.

"Time's up. We gotta go."

I offer a hand, which he willingly accepts. But when I try to pull him up, my ankle throbs in rejection of the extra weight.

I hiss through my teeth, and Fielding's eyes shoot to my face.

"Did they hurt you?"

I shake off his concern and bend down to undo the buckles of my shoes. There's no way I'm going anywhere fast in these things now. RIP, braided tan wedges. I'm going to have to hold a memorial for this entire outfit after tonight.

"I twisted my ankle earlier," I explain. "I just need to ice it, then I'll be fine."

"Well, aren't we a pair," he snickers as he takes a tentative step forward. He looks like shit, but he's with it enough to hold a conversation.

"Did you say my brother's on his way?" he asks with a grimace.

Dempsey. *Shit*.

I hold up a finger to Fielding and pull out his phone from my back pocket as we make our way across the yard.

"Hey, sorry," I start.

"Fuck, Maddie. I've been screaming at you for the last five minutes!"

His fury burns through the line. But my priority was getting Fielding up and moving—not giving him a play-by-play.

"Relax, Haas. We're good. Where are you?"

"I'm two minutes away. So he's okay? He's walking? Did he say you're hurt?"

I ignore his questions and go into no-nonsense mode. "I'll send you a pin so you can find the house. Pull up to the driveway so we don't have to walk any farther than necessary."

"Mad—" he starts, but I end the call.

"Here ya go."

I hand Fielding his phone, and he turns it over twice in his hand.

"Wait, is this... How the hell did you get it unlocked?" he marvels.

Uh. About that...

"I used your face to open it, dummy. I had to get a hold of your brother somehow, didn't I?"

I side-eye him as we walk, noting how his brow furrows and forms that stupid-adorable wrinkle above his nose, just like his brother.

Balancing my shoes in one hand, I pull my phone out of my wristlet and quickly send Dempsey a pin of our location before Fielding has a chance to notice that I have his brother's number.

"Who are you texting?" Fielding asks.

"My friend Paige," I reply without hesitation as I open up a new message.

Maddie: Lucky Lucy for me, too. Call me tomorrow.

I blow out a sigh of relief and stash my phone as we reach the end of the driveway. I scan the street in front of us, desperate for any sign of Dempsey.

"He drives a Range Rover," Fielding murmurs, peering past the row of cars.

Fuck. Right.

Fielding thinks I've never met his brother. Dempsey's about to pick us up, and I'm going to have to pretend that I wasn't five seconds away from riding his cock in an alley three nights ago. How the hell am I going to play this?

Chapter 16

Dempsey

I spot them near the end of the driveway. They're tucked between a huge planter and a bank of mailboxes, hiding from view well enough that I wouldn't have seen them had I not been looking.

My brother's face is jacked up, and he's standing at an awkward angle.

Maddie has mud and grass caked all over her pants, and she's got her arms wrapped around herself in a way that makes my stomach bottom out.

Goddamnit.

I leave the car running and sprint to get to them. I whip my head from side to side, unsure who to focus on first.

"Are you okay? Is he okay? What's he on?" I demand, hitting them with a flurry of questions. "You said he snorted something?" I ask Maddie, turning to Fielding to assess the damage.

I smack his cheek to get him to focus on me. I know this game. He's not going to tell me shit. I grip his chin and try to force him to look at me. Trouble is, one eye is swollen shut, and the other is frantically darting around like he's a kid who got caught with his hand in the cookie jar.

"I don't know. He seems okay now. Can you give me a ride?"

Fielding's mouth turns up in a sly smile before he speaks.

"You already know Little Wheeler, bro?"

I purse my lips and suck in a long breath.

Right. My brother has no idea that I know Maddie Wheeler. And he can never fucking know just how intimately we're acquainted.

"What did you take?" I try one more time.

He never admits when he fucks up, which is a dangerous game we've been playing for the last year. He's upright and conscious, so that's a good sign. My nerves settle a little as I palm the outline of the single-use Narcan nasal spray in the front pocket of my jeans.

"Relax, Dumpy. I only used my own stash. You know Benny Bennett doesn't play games."

Maddie snorts. "You have a drug dealer named Benny Bennett?"

"They breed 'em different in Cascade Falls, Fourth Wheel."

I study my brother for another moment and decide he's fine. Well, not fine. But he's not overdosing, and even though he looks like someone beat the shit out of him, he's not worse for wear.

Maddie, on the other hand... Fuck. Her hair is wild, and her white pants have so much dirt on them they'll never come clean.

She's shifting uncomfortably from side to side, and she keeps wrapping her arms across her chest like she's trying to hold it together.

"Get in the car," I instruct my brother, gripping him by the shoulder to guide him toward the vehicle.

"Fuck, fuck, fuck!" he screams, spinning out of my hold and practically face planting on the hood of my car.

"His shoulder," Maddie murmurs behind me.

I look from my brother back to my—to *her*, unsure who to give my attention to or how the fuck to play this.

"I think he dislocated it during the fight. I helped him put it back in place."

What. The. Fuck?

"Who was he fighting?"

"Literally everyone," she deadpans.

"Dude. Dem." Fielding lifts his head off the car, then drops it back down with a thud and a groan. "You should have seen this girl tonight. She was like Chris Pratt fending off the raptors or some shit. She was screaming and cussing, and then she threatened them all with misdemeanors and blackmail. It was epic. Wait 'til you see the video."

"What video?"

I turn back to Maddie and search her face, but she's looking at the ground. I follow her gaze, and it's then that I notice she's barefoot and purposely keeping her weight on one leg.

"Hey." I reach out tentatively, the urge to comfort her dominating all my racing thoughts. I have no idea what happened tonight. Or what she needs right now. As my fingertips graze her arm, a cackle of laughter erupts farther up the driveway. It sounds like a group of guys. They get increasingly louder as they get closer.

Maddie grips my arm and digs her nails into my skin. She looks up the driveway, then back at me, the definition of terror painted on her face.

"Shit. I can't stay here. We have to go. Dempsey... please."

The fear in her eyes and the tremble in her voice spur me into action. I can't deny this girl. Her plea echoes through my body as I instinctively move closer.

I skim one hand down her arm and take the shoes from her, then guide her toward the car. I lean down to whisper in her ear as we walk, that all-too-familiar scent of strawberry sweetness making my nostrils flare.

"You're safe now. You're coming with us."

I lead her to the passenger door and note how she grimaces when she hoists herself into the seat. She's hurt. She's a mess. And I can't help but feel like this is *his fault*. And now it's *my mess*.

I glance through the windshield to where my brother's still sprawled out on the hood of my Range Rover. If he dents the thing, I'll be even more pissed.

Maddie buckles her seat belt and lets out an exhalation that feels horribly heavy.

I brace my arms on the top frame of the open door, because if I don't do something with them, I'm liable to reach out and wrap her in a hug. "Are you sure you're okay?"

"I don't know," she admits, looking up at me with wide eyes brimming with tears.

I don't know what she's been through tonight, but I'm livid on her behalf. Whoever did this is going to fucking pay. And if my brother contributed in any significant way...

The question that's been eating at me since the second I got the call comes to mind. Again. And even though I know now's not the time, I can't help but ask.

"Did you come here with him?"

Her eyes double in size as she looks from me to my brother, then back again.

"*What*? No! What the fuck, Dempsey? Do you think I'm out here trying to bag any Haas who'll take my calls?"

I give her a pointed look. But I still feel like an ass.

"I came here with friends," she continues, peering out through the windshield to where my brother's rolling around and groaning on the hood of the car. "On a double date, in fact. Not that it's any of your business. I was walking out to the barn when I saw this group of guys doing some sort of dumbass fight club thing. Except it was all of them—at least ten of them—against one. When I saw who they were beating on, I stepped in."

"What do you mean you stepped in?" I snarl. What the fuck is my brother even doing at this party with high school and college kids? And why the fuck did Maddie Wheeler have to be his knight in shining armor?

"I intervened." She shrugs. "I got into the circle and made them stop."

I see red.

Ten against one?

And she put herself in harm's way to stop them?

Rage and gratitude wrestle for dominance in my mind. I don't even want to think about what would have happened if she hadn't stepped in. And yet knowing she fucking had to because Fielding decided tonight was as good as any to put his mortality to the test...

Without another word, I slam her door closed, then stalk to the front. I grab my brother by the collar of his shirt, hauling his ass off the car and practically dragging him around to the back seat as he stumbles to keep up.

He snarls and tries to fight me until he realizes who's dragging him. By the time we're to the car door, he wordlessly climbs in and spreads out on the bench seat with a groan.

I get behind the wheel and buckle up, turning for one more glimpse of her before the cabin light dims and casts us in darkness.

I avoid the meandering drunk people as I weave slowly down the side street. Each time we pass under a streetlight, I look over at her. She's docile, almost sweet, right now. It's disconcerting. As much as I thought I hated that bratty fire behind her eyes, now that it's gone, I miss it.

I reach over in the dark and grip her leg to make sure she knows she's not in this alone. When I pull my hand away, it's covered in mud.

"You're filthy," I mutter, lifting my hand closer to my face to inspect the grass and mud caked into the fabric of her jeans before wiping it on my pant leg.

Fielding snorts from the back seat.

"Dem thinks you're a dirty girl, Little Wheeler."

I whip my head around so fast I panic and hit the brakes. Fielding *umphs* in the back, and Maddie reaches out to brace herself on the dash. I scan the length of the girl in the passenger seat. When I meet her gaze, I swear we're wearing matching expressions.

Fielding's comment was a joke. But it hit way too fucking close to the truth.

I shake my head subtly, desperately, and she nods in understanding.

He can never know.

I reach for her hand and squeeze it once in gratitude, easing the car back up to speed as I make my way out of the development.

We drive in silence from the north end of town toward downtown Hampton. Maddie's staring out her open window, and Fielding's snoring in the back—he can literally fall asleep anywhere. I'll be up every hour all night to make sure he doesn't have a concussion. But sure, bro, take a nap while I safely get you home and save your reckless ass. Again.

I slow the car when the speed limit drops from thirty-five to twenty-five near the green. Then I startle when Maddie takes my hand in the dark. She squeezes once, but she doesn't let go like I did. I close my eyes for the briefest moment and try to garner the strength to shake her off. The resolve doesn't come.

I should pull back. I should brush her off. I should stop letting things go too far with her. But her tiny hand is a comfort I didn't know I needed tonight.

We sit quietly, each of us lost in thought, the sounds of my brother's snoring and a train horn blasting off in the distance the soundtrack to our ride home.

We sit like that, and we settle into a kind of comfort that doesn't feel like mine to claim.

We sit together, and for the first time in a long time, I don't feel so alone.

We're still holding hands when we drive past the clock tower a moment later.

Chapter 17

Dempsey

"Listen, I really need to get home. I'm supposed to be taking care of my mom tonight, so I have to get back and check on her, and if he needs medical attention—"

"That's fine," she interrupts. "I don't want to be home alone tonight anyway. I'll stay at yours."

Um. That's not what I was offering. Once again, Maddie Wheeler doesn't wait for permission. She takes and she takes and she takes.

And for some inexplicable reason, the more she takes, the more I want to give her.

I blow out a sigh of frustration and drop her hand, then casually run my fingers through my hair to brush off the dismissal.

What the hell am I supposed to do? I don't want her at mine. She doesn't want to be home alone. I can't *not* be at home tonight. And my brother clearly won't be any help. We're idling at the main intersection of downtown Hampton, which means I have a decision to make.

Straight, and I'll drive under the train bridge toward the Wheeler house, where I'll what? Force her out of the car and insist she suck it up and lock the doors once she's inside?

Right, and I'll drive out of the town center, down 303, and toward my place. I'll be forced to let her see the mess that is my life. We've got eight guest rooms, any of which I could put her up in, but being under the same roof as Maddie feels like the exact sort of trouble I don't need tonight. Or ever.

"Hey," she says quietly, pulling me out of my thoughts and forcing me to look over at her. She's got her knees tucked under her now, sitting in a way that makes me furious as I recall the panic on her face when she asked to go with us. I *hate* seeing her like this.

"You don't have to worry about me. I'm out of fight tonight."

My jaw ticks of its own volition. This girl has been nothing but spunk and sass since the moment she stepped into The Oak last weekend. Since the moment she led me to believe she was a stranger looking for a one-night stand. What the fuck happened at that party to completely steamroll her spirit?

"I'm not worried," I assure her—and myself—as I make the right-hand turn and head toward home.

"Holy shit," she murmurs as she steps in from the garage to the side hallway of our house. Fielding perks up and stands straighter beside me at the sound of her voice, like he just noticed she was still here.

"You let Little Wheeler come over?"

Believe me, brother. I'm as surprised as you.

"It was the least I could do after she saved your ass," I retort, breathing heavy as I support most of his weight and drag him into the house.

He's favoring one side and grunting with each step we take. I won't be surprised if he broke a rib. There's no point in suggesting he go to the hospital, though—he'll refuse, like he always does. And we've got plenty of painkillers to choose from. Just another rowdy weekend for my brother.

The sound of music hits us, and he stiffens under my arm.

"Fuck... it's that kinda night, huh?" We both know what sort of mood our mother's in if she's blasting Joni Mitchell.

I knew I was in for it this weekend when she came down for dinner with that glassy look in her eyes and told me how she loves me so much and that I'm such a good son. She was with it enough that I knew she hadn't totally gone off the deep end, but she was definitely on something.

"Why do you think I texted you and told you to fucking behave tonight?" I scold, loosening my grip on my brother near the kitchen island as I hustle around and gather what I need.

Water... tea... Unisom. If I can at least get her settled for the night, I'll only have to worry about one of them until morning.

"Why don't you go shower?" I suggest as I dig through the pantry in search of crackers. I doubt my mom's eaten anything all day, which is probably exacerbating the effects of whatever she took. "I'll patch you up when I'm done."

"How can I help?" Maddie asks, leaning her elbows on the quartz countertops of one of the kitchen islands.

Shit. I'm on autopilot like it's any other night. But tonight is different. I don't have two people to take care of... tonight I have three.

"I'm gonna need help getting my clothes off for that shower," Fielding leers, giving her the up and down as he shifts closer to her on one side of the island.

I'm about to scold him when Maddie speaks up.

"Nice try, fuck boy." She scoffs and pitches one eyebrow in his direction. "Now that I know your brother specifically told you to stay out of trouble tonight, you're even lower on my list."

"But I'm still on the list?" Fielding gives her a pointed look and tries to wink, only to end up cursing because his eye's so swollen.

Dumbass. Serves him right.

Maddie puts her hands on her hips and turns to me. "I'll make sure he doesn't pass out in the shower. You go take care of your mom and find me when you're done."

With that, she turns on her heel and holds out one arm, indicating Fielding should lead the way. They disappear down a long hall toward his section of the house.

Okay then.

Chapter 18

Maddie

I helped him out of his shirt, assuming he'd struggle with it, having dislocated his shoulder only an hour ago. Then I wandered around his bedroom while he got in the shower.

I found clean underwear and athletic shorts in one of his dresser drawers, then left them on the sink for him to put on himself. There's a vanity at one end of the bathroom, making it easy to stay close without getting right up in his business.

Of course, he tried to flash me his junk more than once. And I'm woman enough to admit that I was tempted to look. Mostly because I'm curious. Dempsey and Fielding are identical twins: so does that mean they're identical *everywhere*?

I decided against peeking and griped at him for indecent exposure instead. I still intend to see what the full Haas package looks like, but I want to see it on the other twin.

Now Fielding's sitting on the counter, shirtless, while I stand between his legs and clean the cuts and scrapes on his upper body. His forearms and hands are achingly familiar: I've drooled over his brother's for the last week, wanting nothing more than the arms that match these to pin me against a wall of bricks and do all sorts of delicious things to my body.

"You could be a nurse when you grow up, Little Wheeler," Fielding murmurs as I clean a gash above his eyebrow that is somehow *still* bleeding. He really could use a few stitches in this one, but no one has mentioned anything about going to the hospital.

"That's sexist," I murmur, pressing down on the gauze until he hisses in pain.

"Fine. You could be a lady doctor. Happy?"

"That's even more sexist!" Heat flares in my cheeks until I see the glint in his unswollen eye.

He's goading me.

"What *do* you want to be when you grow up?" he asks.

I look through the bandage options spread out on the countertop, deciding on a butterfly closure for his eyebrow.

"I'm going to be a lawyer."

"Oh yeah? A good guy lawyer or a bad guy lawyer?" he asks, before adding, "And I mean 'guy' as a casual expression of slang, not as gendered term, so don't come at me with your patriarchal bullshit again."

I smirk. He's quick. Just like Dempsey.

"I haven't decided. I think I would do well as a corporate lawyer or a high-profile defensive attorney. But I also have a soft spot for the underdog."

"Clearly," he jibes, wincing when I apply ointment to the cut at his temple and put one more bandage in place.

There. I've patched up every injury I can find.

"Why'd you do it, Field?"

When he doesn't answer, I push harder.

"Why would you go to a party and pick a fight when you *knew* your brother was preoccupied with your mom tonight?"

He turns his head, and I wonder if I've gone too far. At least he has the decency to look remorseful.

He sighs, then slides off the countertop, leaning back and crossing one tan, sinewy arm across his bare chest. I've been watching his movements since he got out of the shower. He's barely using his right arm. I make a mental note to mention it to Dempsey.

"I didn't set out to cause chaos tonight. Sometimes... sometimes the night just gets to me."

"That sounds like a cop-out to me," I muse. "We've known each other a long time, Field. I've never seen you like this before."

Fielding scoffs. His eyes get this glassy, faraway look, and his next words come out just above a whisper.

"You don't know me anymore, Little Wheeler. *I* barely know me anymore."

That doesn't make sense. But it sounds honest.

He clears his throat and perks up two seconds later, all the somberness of his confession dispelled like it never happened.

"Ya know, *I* was almost a doctor. We would have made a pretty awesome power couple."

I roll my eyes and pick up the trash from the bandages and gauze. "You mean you were almost a *gentleman* doctor?"

He barks out a laugh that makes me feel lighter. His laugh is louder than Dempsey's. More jovial and free. But they have the same cadence. I wonder if Dempsey ever laughs that hard.

Speaking of...

I feel his eyes on me without looking up to confirm he's there. He lights up my insides in a totally different way. All he has to do is enter a room, and it's like the 5G maxes out with five bars of service in every limb of my body.

As much as he wants to deny it, he and I just work. He feels easy. Inevitable. I know he feels it. I think he hates it. But there's no denying the energy that courses between us every time we're in the same room.

I catch Dempsey's gaze through the bathroom mirror, then smile softly to reassure him that I'm okay. That *we're* okay.

"He's all patched up," I declare as I turn around and throw away the little bits of trash. I take in a sharp breath when I put too much weight on my ankle. Thankfully, the throbbing stopped on the way home, so I know it's just a sprain. It's an inconsequential injury compared to the bruised and battered wounds all over Fielding's body.

"He *did* try to convince me he needed someone to check the bruising on his balls, so you might want to have him strip and lie down spread eagle for you before you tuck him in," I quip.

Both sets of eyes go wide: Fielding's in shocked amusement, and Dempsey's in outrage.

"Kidding," I snort.

Fielding shakes his head and grins, but Dempsey's expression stays sullen. He's got that stern brunch daddy vibe going on that would be doing naughty things to my lady bits if I didn't feel so disgusting right now.

"Um, so, I was hoping I could get a shower?" I try, looking between the boys as Fielding smirks and Dempsey still looks huffy.

Dem's expression softens. "Yes, of course. I'm sorry you had to wait so long."

He reaches out one arm and grazes the small of my back as I come to stand beside him.

"This girl's good trouble, Dumpy. We should keep her around."

I stiffen at the compliment, searching Dempsey's face to gauge how he'll react to Fielding's off-handed comment. He just keeps scowling at his twin before he spits out a warning.

"She's sleeping in my wing. Stay in your room, brother. I'll be down to check on you throughout the night."

His words are a threat intended to put Fielding in his place. I try to offer him a smile, but Dempsey ushers me out of the room before Fielding even looks my way.

Once we're in the hall, his steps overcome mine, and soon he's leading me back through the kitchen, then up a set of stairs I hadn't noticed before.

"You'll be staying in one of the guest rooms in my part of the house."

I nod mindlessly, like it isn't weird at all to live in a house so big each brother has his own wing on a separate floor. "There's a bathroom next to your room. It's fully stocked with everything you should need, and I set out clean towels for you."

As we make our way up the stairs, I have to grip the handrail tighter than normal to lessen the pressure I put on my left foot. When Dempsey reaches the landing, he stops and turns, probably looking at me for the first time since we left Fielding's bathroom.

"Shit... here." He reaches out his hand and supports me the last few steps, then wraps one of my arms around his neck as we slowly walk down a long, dark hallway.

"I've got you," he murmurs, peeling my arm off his body and opening a bedroom door, then flicking on the light so we can see inside.

The room is airy, with lavender walls and crisp, white bedding. There's a queen-size bed on one side, and a little sitting area across the way. My attention is immediately drawn to the French doors on the far end of the room that open onto a balcony. Even in the dark and from across the room, the view is spectacular.

"I'll get you some clean clothes," Dempsey says, back to business like I'm just another item on his to-do list. I'm honestly too exhausted to tease him about it.

If my head is spinning, he must be drowning in the stress of it all.

"I'll drive you home in the morning," he continues. "It'll have to be early... ideally before anyone else is up. Is that okay?"

"Mm-hmm," I murmur my assent.

"I'll leave some clothes in here for you while you shower. Lock your door when you turn in for the night."

That gets my attention. I've spent plenty of time with Fielding over the last few years. He's not harmless or innocent, but he's no threat to me.

I cock one eyebrow and open my mouth to tell Dempsey as much, but he stops me with a frustrated sigh.

"Can you just do what you're told for once?" he snaps.

He's teetering on the edge, and the thinness of his request proves it. He doesn't need to be pushed; he needs to be pulled in and wrapped in an embrace. I refuse to be the cause of any more stress for him tonight.

I nod instead of pushing back, then run my hand down the barely there stubble of his jawline. He stills under my touch, then closes his eyes and inhales what I'm sure is the deepest breath he's taken all day.

"Goodnight, Dempsey," I whisper, shifting past him to the bathroom down the hall.

Chapter 19

Maddie

Showering in the guest bathroom is like being at the spa. It's just as big as Fielding's, and it's filled with all sorts of expensive soaps, shampoos, and moisturizers. A selection of robes and clean towels was waiting for me, and if I didn't know better, I'd have sworn the tile floor was heated under my feet.

I lingered in the shower, enjoying the rainfall effect and the hot steam that washed away all traces of this horrible night. Then I took the time to blow dry my hair and work it into a loose braid. I used a few unidentified products in bottles so pretty they doubled as décor and even found a lotion that smelled like sparkling champagne and strawberries—my favorite.

I hadn't bothered asking which room was his when we came up here.

But as I sneak out of the bathroom wearing nothing but a fluffy robe, I can't help but notice the light on in the room next to mine.

I pause outside his door, staring at the thin line of light shining into the hall. He mentioned he'd be up to check on Fielding. Will he even let himself sleep tonight?

I walk into the lavender room and take it in for the second time. It's somehow even more beautiful than when he showed it to me.

There's a pile of things on the bed: perfectly folded sweatpants and an Archway Prep LAX shirt that I recognize from my brother's wardrobe. He also left me a cold bottle of water and a baggie of ice for my ankle, neither of which I thought to ask for but genuinely appreciate.

I slip into his clothes, pulling my braid out of the shirt collar as the fabric settles against my skin. Both items are comically big, but they feel right. This is the closest I've been to him since those seven minutes of heaven in the alley last week.

I lift the shirt to cover my nose and mouth, inhaling the clean scent of fabric softener with a distinctly Dempsey undertone. He's got this sweet scent that gets more complex the longer I inhale. Fresh tobacco? A hint of caramel? I've never thought about how he smelled before. But now that I've gotten a whiff, I'm craving a hit directly from the source.

I crack open the water bottle and suck down half of it, but it does nothing to sate me. I stare at the inviting bed. Then I look back at the door.

I pad into the hallway and pull my door closed behind me, unsure what I'm doing, but confident it's the right move. I creep down the hall until I reach the next door. When I try the handle, I half expect it to be locked.

The handle turns, and my desire lights up with the promise of what's next. I don't have a plan. I'm not working an angle. I haven't thought through any of this—I just want to be where he is.

His room is larger than mine, all grays and charcoals with a built-in bookshelf for a headboard against one wall. There's an enormous flat screen on the opposite side of the room, along with an executive-style desk in one corner.

I peruse his personal space, but there's no sign of the man himself. It's not until I hear a sigh out the French doors that I know where I'll find him.

He doesn't startle when I come to stand before him. He's slouched in a cushioned chair, his legs spread wide and his head resting back. He sits just a little straighter and drags his cerulean-blue eyes up and down my body, taking me in as I stand before him in his clothes.

His focus shifts to my face, and anger colors his expression before he speaks.

"You shouldn't be standing on that ankle."

"Agreed."

My voice trembles, but I swallow down my doubt and steel my spine, then take three steps forward until my knees are pressing into the cushion of his chair. When he doesn't immediately swat me away, I make my move.

I climb into his lap, then spread my legs wide, straddling him and lining us up in the process. His body tenses below me as he gives me the most threatening glare. We stare at each other, unblinking, silently warring over what's right and what's real. But then his hands slide up and grip my ass, one hand digging into each cheek as he pulls me closer and pins me in place.

"Who takes care of you?" I ask, my voice breathy as I lean in and test the waters. I run my lips against the sandpaper stubble of his neck, then trace a line from his throat to his ear with my tongue.

"Hmm?" I ask, nibbling on his earlobe and grinning in satisfaction when his hips shift beneath me. I run my hands through his hair, over and over again, caressing him until he sighs and lays his head back against the headrest, granting me more access.

"Maddie," he scolds. His protest is halfhearted, at best. He's still squeezing my ass. And he grunts when I swivel my hips, the fabric of the sweatpants he loaned me making it all too easy to feel the growing hardness of his arousal.

"Tell me to stop and I will," I whisper in his ear before placing a trail of kisses down the side of his neck. "Immediately. Without hesitation," I promise, pulling back to look him in the eye and show him my resolve.

"I just want to do this for you. Without expectation."

He tenses when I brush both hands down his torso, stopping at the button of his pants.

"I know you," I declare.

He shifts up slightly and scowls, but I keep going before he can object.

"I'm learning you," I amend, softer.

I undo the button while maintaining eye contact with him, then pull on his zipper. Down, down, down. Painstakingly slow as I slither down his body and kneel before him.

He sits up straighter, then lifts his hips and pulls down his pants and boxers, baring himself to me. I resist the urge to look—*not yet; you've almost got him*—maintaining eye contact as I make my closing argument.

"I let you pull back and send me away in the alley because I could tell that was what you needed. But tonight? Tonight, you need something else. Something I really want to give you."

His expression is filled with so much emotion I have to fight the urge to look away. He nods once—making his consent clear—and it takes all my willpower not to squeal in delight. I bow my head and bite the corner of my lip as I finally allow myself to take in the gloriousness of his dick.

It's perfect. Like I knew it would be. Ramrod straight. Veiny like his arms. Stoic like his attitude. It might be the biggest cock I've ever seen in real life. But I'm not one to back down from a challenge.

I bend low and kiss the tip, swirling my tongue to collect the bead of precum glistening there for the taking.

When I look up, his mouth is hanging open and his pupils are blown out, his eyes completely fixated on my mouth.

"You're allowed to take something for yourself, Dempsey. Especially because it's something I really want to give you."

I wrap my hand around his dick, and he thrusts into my palm almost involuntarily. I give him one last salacious smile, then throw my braid behind me and get to work.

I take my time exploring, licking up and down his length and figuring out what, exactly, draws him out of his rigid shell. Right under the rim seems to be a favorite. And he wraps his hand around my braid in the most delicious way when I turn my head and cover the base of him with my mouth.

He's so fucking big. I can't help but grunt my own pleasure as he rolls his hips and fills my mouth with his cock. I grip him at the base and develop a rhythm, jerking him as I continue to bob up and down and give him what I hope is the perfect amount of suction.

"Fuck... Maddie. That feels amazing. You're doing so good for me. You're doing so fucking good."

What the hell is this? The man barely talks to me all night, and now he's got all sorts of things to say? I've never had a guy do anything but grunt when I've given head before. Spurred on by his words and somehow turned on by all the encouragement, I double down.

But Dempsey's not just any guy—he's a man. And his words are doing more for me right now than most guys can do with their hands and their mouths and their dicks combined.

Fuckity fuck. I'm so into this guy.

I squeeze my thighs together in need, then mindlessly tweak my nipple through his T-shirt as I drive him wild.

"Take that off for me," he instructs as he slows his thrusts into my mouth.

I pop off his dick in surprise, caught off guard that he noticed what I was doing.

He smirks, then runs a thumb along my swollen bottom lip. "Take it off," he urges, gentler, nodding toward my shirt as I scurry to pull it over my head.

"Fucking perfect," he murmurs as he hauls me up on my knees and stares at my chest.

My nipples were already pebbled from the arousal coursing through my body. Now they're painfully stiff because of the night air and his sultry appraisal.

He reaches out confidently, squeezing a tit in each hand as he licks his lips. He brushes both thumbs over my aching nipples, and I can't help but whimper at his skillful touch.

"Can I fuck these?" he pants, massaging and plucking at me like he already knows exactly what I like.

Slickness runs down my thighs, and I panic as I realize I'm not wearing any underwear. I couldn't possibly drip through a pair of thick sweatpants. Could I?

"Yes," I breathe, scrambling to position myself in a way that gives him better access.

He groans in approval, then takes both my hands and places them on either side of my chest. "Hold these for me, baby." He's got the most wicked grin on his face, and I can't help but grin right back.

"It'll feel better if I'm wet," he teases, and I waste no time taking him back in my mouth, leaving a slick trail along the underside of his dick. A string of saliva stays connected as I move to pull away. He leans forward, catches it in his hand, and pushes two fingers into my mouth.

"You're a bad girl, aren't you, Maddie?"

I nod and suck on his fingers, wide-eyed, as his words slam into me like a freight train. It doesn't matter what he says. Every word out of his mouth tickles my clit and sends me higher in my own hazy state of bliss.

"You like being bad for me."

He lines up his cock, and I push on my breasts harder, creating resistance as he glides his length up and down my chest.

"Fuck," he groans, rolling his head back for a second as he picks up the pace.

I'm mesmerized, watching him slide up and down, faster and faster. Every time the crown of his cock emerges, I'm tempted to take him back into my mouth and make him lose control. But this feels so naughty and too fucking good to stop.

I hear it first, and when I feel it, I glance down and find a pool of spit glistening on my left tit. With two fingers, he rubs it in, painting my areola before he pinches it hard. I cry out, and he pulls again.

"Do you like that, princess? If I reached inside those sweatpants right now, would I find you as wet as these perfect tits?"

Fuck. Wasn't I supposed to be the one pleasuring him? Why does it feel like I'm seconds away from detonating?

"Eyes on me," he murmurs.

As soon as I look up, he spits again. I swear to God I may have just peed a little based on the amount of moisture dripping down my thighs. He massages my other breast, then tweaks my nipples in tandem with his thrusts.

"Fuck, Maddie. Fuck. You feel *so* good. You're doing so good for me. I'm so fucking close."

I don't know what comes over me. I pull back and put him in my mouth again, desperate to finish the job I started. I take him as deep as I can manage, then inhale through my nose and push down farther.

He's a mess of curses and thrusts, totally in the moment, until he gives me a courtesy tap.

All I've wanted for more than a week is to make this man come undone. He's out of his goddamn mind if he thinks I'm not about to drink down every fucking drop he gives me.

"I'm coming." He grunts softly as the first shot of cum hits the back of my throat.

I take him deeper and feel out his rhythm, swallowing down his length every time he pulses in my mouth.

"Yes, yes, fuck..." he chants as I drain him completely. Even when he's empty, I don't release him. Instead, I lick up and down his length and kiss the tip before finally going still.

My legs are half-asleep below me, so I don't dare try to stand. I rest my cheek on his thigh, blissed out and teetering on the edge of my own release.

I'm tempted to reach between my thighs and put myself out of my misery. But I know Dempsey would feel obligated to take over, and that's not what this was about.

After we spend a few peaceful, quiet minutes catching our breath—and Dempsey plays with my hair—I rise up, unashamed, as he drinks in the sight of my bare breasts with a look of total satisfaction.

"Come here," he mutters under his breath, outstretching his arms and inviting me in. I just shake my head and smile.

I bend low and kiss him once, pulling back when he tries to wrap me in an embrace. "Goodnight, Dempsey," I murmur as I pick up his shirt and slip it back over my head before exiting his room.

Chapter 20

Dempsey

I lie across my bed sideways, shame and bewilderment coursing through me. It's been more than three hours since Maddie Wheeler waltzed into my room and gave me the best head of my life. I've hated myself a little more every second since.

We're playing a dangerous game. Every time we get away with something like this, we deceive ourselves a little more, like what we're doing is okay. Like if we do this, it won't bleed into other parts of our lives. Like we can give in to our mutual attraction, and it'll never get back to him.

I've spent the last few hours trying to decide what makes me hate myself more. What I allowed and how it could affect him? Or what I accepted without reciprocating?

I let her have her way with me, and I was too mind-fucked by the whole encounter to return the favor. I basically used her mouth and tits to get off, then sent her back to bed.

I should never have let her straddle me. Or undo the button of my pants. Or wrap her mouth around my dick. The second I saw her tits, I knew it was over. There's no fucking way I won't be back for more.

She pushes me constantly. And all I want to do is take.

The alarm on my phone vibrates, so I haul myself out of bed like I have three times already tonight and quietly head downstairs.

By the time I make it to his room, I've let my frustration about Maddie bloom into anger.

If he hadn't done what he did... if he hadn't gotten mixed up with another man's wife... none of this would be a problem. He made such shitty choices. Now I have to live in the shadow of the consequences.

"Field," I call out, loud enough to startle him. When he doesn't move, I go for the kill shot, jabbing him in the armpit of his good arm until he jumps off the mattress.

"Fuck," he hisses, whether from the pain or the abrupt wake up call, I'm not sure. He comes to and shakes out his mess of blond curls before reaching over for a sip of water.

"Good. You're still alive," I mock as I turn around and head back out of the room.

"You're usually a little nicer to me when I'm possibly concussed," he mutters before taking another sip of water and sitting up straighter in bed.

"Not tonight, Fielding," I chastise. I'm tired. So fucking tired. And I have no interest in getting into it with him at four a.m.

"It's because she's here," he says in a knowing tone.

I freeze where I stand, tempted to tell him to shut up but also morbidly curious to hear what he has to say. Is my connection to her really that apparent?

"You're all twisted up with Little Wheeler sleeping in your wing."

I turn in time to see him flop back down on his bed, then let out an obnoxiously long yawn.

"I get it. She's hot," he offers nonchalantly.

"She's twenty," I counter, my tone full of vitriol fueled by my own self-loathing.

"She always did want to meet you," he muses as he rolls to his side and yawns again.

"She's twenty," I repeat. It's the only argument that feels safe. We both know the real reason Maddie Wheeler is off limits. It has little to do with her age and everything to do with who she's related to.

I wait a breath, then another, listening for the sound of his breathing as he drifts back to sleep. When I'm almost certain he's out again, I walk back into the room and bend low, kissing his forehead and brushing the curls out of his eyes.

"It would be okay, you know," he whispers without opening his eyes.

I freeze. Is he awake?

"Wouldn't bother me," he continues. "I'm fucked up enough already. You hooking up with Wheeler's little sister wouldn't do any additional damage. There's nothing left to destroy."

The truth of his pain crawls inside me and claws at my heart. He thinks he wouldn't care—but I know him too well to believe the lie he's telling us both.

"Go to sleep, Fielding."

"Stop waking me up, Dumpy," he grumbles.

I leave his room and pull his door closed, satisfied that I won't have to wake him up again. I peek in on my mom and find her fast asleep, too.

Everyone's settled. Everything's fine. Maybe now I can finally get some sleep.

The climb back to my wing feels heavy. As soon as I hit the landing, I know why.

I'm pulled toward her room by a magnetism unlike anything I've ever felt in my life. This connection between us is as strong as the one that ties me to my brother. It's a force I know I can't fight forever.

I pace outside her door, drowning in indecision. I want to see her. I want to return the favor and rock her world the way she rocked mine. And even if she's fast asleep and that's not an option, I just want to hold her tonight.

I decide to go for it, twisting the doorknob as slowly as possible. But after a slight turn of my wrist, I'm met with resistance. I check again and get the same result. The door is locked.

"Good girl," I mutter, spinning on my heel and heading back to my room where I belong.

I didn't tell her to lock her door to keep him out. I told her to lock her door to keep me away.

Chapter 21

Maddie

I wake up without an alarm as the sun peeks through the French doors of the balcony. I'm stiff and cranky but rested enough. Dempsey wants to take me home early, and I plan to be nothing but compliant after everything he went through last night.

Speaking of last night...

I smile at the memory of the fun we had on the balcony. That's exactly what it was: good trouble and big fun. It could be like that all summer if Dempsey would pull the stick out of his ass and play along. He'll be hard-pressed to look me in the eye and pretend he wasn't as into that blow job as I was. I've *never* had a man moaning for me quite like that.

I practically ran back to my room when I left him, locking the door and leaping into this bed so I could finish. I PRed in getting myself off last night, then couldn't resist rubbing out one more to the memory of him spitting on my tits and playing me like an instrument.

My body tingles in remembrance, but I shove down those thoughts and force myself to focus on why I'm up so early to begin with. I grab my phone off the nightstand to check the time, then stare, slack-jawed, when I see every social media icon on my home screen maxed out with 99+ notifications.

Fuckity fuck.

All I have to do is open up Instagram to confirm what I already know. I've been tagged in dozens of videos from the party.

I click the first one that pops up; it already has more than three thousand views. I jolt when I hear my own voice through the device. I keep scrolling and clicking. Each video was shot at a different angle or with a filter applied to cut through the graininess. Some start long before I arrived on the scene. I can barely watch as they beat on Fielding, a mob against one. But Andrew wasn't wrong: Fielding rallied them all together, then wound them up until they started wailing on him. He really did ask for it.

A lot of the videos have added reactions or stupid emojis over my face. A few of them have a filter applied to Adley, or music added in the background. These Hampton fuckers really put some effort into their content, that's for damn sure.

A knock at the door startles me. I set my phone down and look up to find Dempsey standing in the doorway.

"Hey. Good morning. Is it okay if we go soon?" He speaks softly, his tone matching my mood.

Sucking in a steadying breath, I offer him a tight smile before nodding. I figured it would be like this between us this morning—measured and reserved. But I'm okay being at neutral with him when I'm feeling so raw.

I pick up my phone but accidentally swipe the screen in the process, unpausing the video I still have cued up. Fielding's muffled voice fills the room, and Dempsey's eyes dart to mine.

"What is that?" he demands, making it over to the bed in four strides and hovering over me until I'm forced to sit back down.

"It's a video from last night," I explain. "It's... they're all over social media."

"They're?" he growls.

"There's a lot of them..."

"Show me," he demands, perching on the end of the unmade bed.

I tuck my legs under me and place my phone in his hands, then exit the video to scroll through all the options.

"These are the ones I'm tagged in. There are more from before I arrived... then others don't start until I'm at Fielding's side."

"Do I just click on it to make it play?"

I can't hold back my smile at that one. He really does act like he's forty-seven instead of twenty-seven sometimes. I lean toward him, my shoulder grazing his, and click one I've already watched so I know what to expect. Still. It doesn't make the sounds of fist against flesh any easier to stomach. Dempsey tenses beside me every time someone lands a punch, almost as if he can feel his brother's pain.

I cringe when I hear myself scream "Stop!" for the first time, my recorded voice tinny. He pulls the device closer to his face and studies it as I pick at the corner of the duvet rumpled beneath me.

"You," he whispers, forcing me to look up and meet his gaze. "You stopped them," he states matter-of-factly.

I resist rolling my eyes. Fielding and I explained what happened last night. But I guess witnessing it rather than just hearing about it secondhand garners a different reaction.

His eyes widen as he focuses on the screen, watching me take on a pack of frat boys like I'm Russell Crowe in *Gladiator*.

"Show me another one."

I want to argue that if he's seen one, he's seen them all. But something about the harrowed expression on his face tells me he needs to see it to believe it. That he needs to know everything he can about what happened last night.

I lean over and scroll through the options, clicking on a video that starts before I arrived.

After a minute, Dempsey hisses under his breath. "Fuck..."

"What?" I peer over his shoulder at the screen, then yelp as he grabs my legs and pulls them across his lap.

"Your ankle," he murmurs as he pushes up my left pant leg and massages the tender spot. "This one shows you stumbling before you even bust into the circle."

I sigh at his touch, leaning back on my elbows and sinking into the ministrations of his big, strong hands. He keeps circling and pressing into the muscle as he watches. I'm so relaxed, I let myself close my eyes and lie back completely, my legs draped over his lap. When he starts up another video without my help, I smile. He's figured it out on his own.

We lie like that for five or six more videos, the repetitive sound of my voice and the crowd's reaction easy to tune out as the scene plays out over and over again. When the room goes quiet, I exhale, relieved that we're done playing last night's trauma on a loop.

I don't need to be reminded of what it felt like to stand on trembling legs and fight like hell to make it out of that circle unharmed. I lived it.

Dempsey sets the phone down by my side. "Will the videos cause problems for you?" he asks, using both hands to massage my feet now.

I sigh in response to his touch, desperate to keep my eyes closed and live in this moment for as long as he'll let me. He's quiet for nearly a minute before he pushes.

"Maddie... answer me."

I open my eyes and curl up to sit, straightening my legs out on his lap in the process. "No. I'll be fine," I answer honestly. "Some of the stuff I threatened them with isn't entirely true, and any lawyer worth their snuff would know that. But I always assumed I'd have to delete my social media accounts once I graduate from college. More than anything, it'll just be annoying to keep getting tagged in posts until this blows over. But it's nothing I can't handle."

He nods, that adorable wrinkle between his brows deeper than I've ever seen it. Wordlessly, he continues to rub my feet and ankles, so I lean back again and let him work through it on his own.

"Adley," he says softly, freezing when I stiffen in his grasp. "What did Andrew Adley say to you before he called everyone off? I could see your reaction in some of the videos. But I couldn't hear what he said."

I pull my knees to my chest, locking my arms around them and glancing out toward the French doors. The view really is pretty, with the sun rising over the canopy of trees in the Cuyahoga Valley National Forest. I guess I hadn't realized how far east we were when Dempsey drove us home last night.

"Maddie," he reprimands, one hand tilting my chin toward him. "Answer me," he insists.

I nod but stay silent. Not because I don't remember. Or because I want to keep it from Dempsey. But I can't repeat it and trust my voice not to tremble.

I lean over his lap, pick up my phone, and open the video I took last night. I hand it to him and hit play, then curl up into his side. Without hesitation, he wraps one arm around me. I close my eyes but listen intently as the video starts with me explaining assault charges to all those douche bags.

Dempsey tenses beside me at the threat Adley made when he approached me, then he squeezes the shit out of my shoulder when Adley addresses the crowd and tells them we've reached an agreement.

"Ow, Dem..." I mutter.

He loosens his grip, but I can still feel him seething beside me.

When Adley tells me to tell my friends I won't need a ride home and that he'll find me later, Dempsey pushes to his feet.

He paces the length of the bed: an animal trapped in an invisible cage. He's holding my phone ridiculously close to his face, but I had forgotten I was still recording at that point, so there can't be much to see on the screen.

The video ends and the room goes silent. There's a heavy tension between us—that electric supercharge that's always there, intensified by his fury now that he knows every graphic detail of last night's confrontation.

Without warning, he turns and stalks toward me, throwing the phone on the bed before he takes my head in his hands.

"You stupid girl," he huffs out. The words don't match the reverence in his tone. "You stupid, wonderful girl." He closes his eyes, as if he's in pain, then presses his forehead into mine.

"Why would you do that for him, Maddie? Why?"

I close my eyes and ignore his demand. He knows why. He *has* to know.

"That's why you wanted to get out of there and come home with us, wasn't it? Because of Adley?"

When I don't answer, he holds me a little tighter, his fingers wrapping around the back of my neck as if he can will me to answer him.

"That's why you didn't want to be home alone last night," he guesses correctly.

I open my eyes and meet his gaze, awestruck by the intensity of his stare. There's anger and frustration on his face, but an admiration and appreciation that's new. Something passes between us. Without me having to explain myself, I know he knows.

Why did I do it?

Why did I put myself at risk, against impossible odds, to save his brother?

I acted on instinct.

I did it because it was the right thing to do.

I did it because of *him*.

And now we both know this is no longer a game.

I gulp past the lump in my throat and will myself to speak. "I'm not scared of Andrew Adley," I insist with a shrug. "I was just shaken up and spooked last night."

Dempsey glares at me, no doubt preparing to challenge my indifference.

"Hey," I reprimand, standing up and wrapping my arms around his neck.

He doesn't pull out of my hold, and in that moment, I know: this is no longer a game for him, either.

"I don't regret anything about last night." I give him a heated look as I cling to his neck. "I would do it all over again if I could, even knowing the outcome in advance."

I lick my lips, and he tracks the movement. But he's not done with his overprotective tirade.

"You'll tell me if he tries to contact you, or if you see him around town."

"Oh will I?" I challenge.

He shakes his head and smirks before wrapping his arms around me and hauling me into an airtight hug.

I sigh contentedly before I can hold back my reaction. I love the way I feel in his arms.

"You will," he growls into my ear. "You're not alone in this, Maddie. I'll be damned if I let anything happen to you because of my brother's dumbass choices."

I say nothing, instead savoring the feeling of his arms wrapped around me. I nuzzle against his chest, soaking in his warmth and protectiveness. I tilt my head back to meet his gaze, silently begging him to kiss me.

Instead, he loosens his arms, bends low, and places a peck on my forehead. "Come on," he urges, taking my hand and pulling me toward the door. "I have to get you home."

Chapter 22

Dempsey

We're silent for most of the drive back to her house. It's not an uncomfortable silence—it feels more like a peace offering on her part. How the hell she knows when I need to be with my own thoughts shocks the shit out of me. Even my own twin rarely picks up on that. Or if he does, he ignores it. Somehow, she just knows.

Regardless of the silence, I can't help but steal about twenty glances at her over the course of the fifteen-minute car ride. Loose strands of hair have fallen out of her braid, and she looks beautifully fresh faced, albeit tired.

She has the waistband of my sweats rolled over at least three times to keep them on her hips. The way my shirt falls over her chest—a chest I haven't stopped thinking about since she whipped off her shirt and let me play last night—does all sorts of twisted things to my brain. And my dick.

There was never any question about whether I was attracted to Maddie Wheeler. But watching those videos unlocked an all-consuming sense of duty in me. That, paired with permission to take something for myself, as she put it, has my mind finally on board with this scheme.

She's mine. Mine to have. Mine to keep safe. Mine to protect at all costs. I haven't been able to think of anything else since she clicked play on that first video.

I pull into her driveway, a sense of déjà vu slamming into me as I recall the first night we met.

That was only a week ago.

Since then, everything has changed.

The second I put the car in park, she's reaching for the door handle.

"Maddie—wait."

She freezes on command, then slowly turns to look at me. She's got this adorable smattering of freckles across the bridge of her nose that I hadn't noticed until now. I've been so determined to push her away over the last week... it's disorienting to let myself appreciate all the little things about her I've been working so hard to ignore.

"I..." I reach out and take her hand in mine, willing her to feel my sincerity. "I wanted to say thank you."

She scoffs and side-eyes me. "Don't make it weird, Dem."

Dem. I never told her she could call me that. Like it matters. We've already established that this woman does what she wants.

"I mean it," I insist, leaning in and bringing her hand to my mouth so I can kiss her knuckles. "Thank you for helping Fielding last night. And thank you for..."

For what? The best head of my life? Letting me slide my dick between her perfect, perky tits?

I blow out a breath and try to get my head on straight. "Thank you for really seeing me," I try.

She raises her eyebrows in challenge, but she doesn't call me out on the overly simplified description of what we shared last night.

"So what happens now?" she asks quietly, tracing her thumb over the veins in my hand.

"What do you mean?"

"Are we going back to our roles as grumpy bartender and pesky brat with a schoolgirl crush? Or are you done pretending this isn't real?" she fires back with that signature sass I love.

I give her a pointed look anyway.

"I never thought of you as a pesky brat, Maddie. I just... I just didn't want to drag you into my mess." I let out of heavy sigh and drop her hand. "But after last night, there's no point in trying to hide the shitshow that is my life."

"Does this mean I can hang out with you at The Oak again? Because those were undoubtedly my two favorite nights of summer so far."

I stare out the windshield as I think through her request. I'm done pushing her away. I was done fighting our attraction the second I watched the first video this morning. Or maybe I gave up the game last night, when I let her straddle me and suck me off until I saw stars.

"I'm not going to send you away if you show up at The Oak. But we still have to be careful. I have to think of my brother."

"I understand," she insists. "I can be sneaky." She gives me the most salacious smile. As if I need to be convinced that she can be sneaky.

"Maybe I'll just happen to find you in a dark alley again one night—"

"Maddie," I scold.

"I'm just saying!"

"There's no fucking reason for you to be in a dark alley without me, baby girl. Is that clear?"

She smiles sweetly before leaning over the center console. "I like it when you call me that." She bats her eyelashes and lingers in my space, but I make no move to take things further.

If we're doing this... fuck. She has to understand.

"I'm done telling you no, Maddie. But you saw the reality of what I'm dealing with last night. My brother's a mess. My mom's a mess. My *life's* a fucking mess."

"I get it," she assures me. "I'm not asking for anything more than you're able to give. And I get that no one can know about us."

I close my eyes in anguish. I want this. She wants this. And yet—she deserves so much more.

"You're too sweet to be a dirty little secret." I lean in close, hovering my lips over hers but not giving up what we both crave.

"I think you're the only person who sees me that way," she muses.

"What way?" I challenge.

"Sweet."

I can't resist any longer. I close the space between us and brush my lips against hers. She tastes like minty freshness and that strawberry flavor I love. I groan as I pull her closer and kiss her deeper.

"You're the sweetest thing I've ever tasted," I murmur against her lips. "Probably a good thing to counterbalance all the sass that comes out of this mouth." I slip my tongue into her mouth and savor the way she reacts to the intrusion, meeting me stroke for stroke. My dick starts to harden in my shorts, but I'm too wrapped up in the smell and the taste and the feel of her to care.

"So that's a yes? We're doing this?" She pulls back and smiles, giving me a thorough up and down as she bites down on her bottom lip.

I run my hand through my hair and silently scold myself for dragging out this game. I already decided I'm all in. There's no point pretending I'm still warring over my decision.

"I can't promise you anything, Maddie. You understand that, right? I don't have anything to give except the occasional night off..."

"That's *fine*," she insists. "I don't need promises. I just want you. Unless..."

She trails off, then stares out the window toward her front door, leaving me desperate to know what she's thinking.

"Unless what?" I demand.

"Never mind." She plays with the hem of my T-shirt and purposely ignores me to look down at her hands.

"Maddie, I swear to God... If we're doing this, we're done playing games. If you have something to say to me, fucking say it."

She snaps to attention, her eyes meeting mine. I get a thrill out of her reaction—she's so quick to comply when I get bossy with her. We're going to have fun together this summer, she and I.

"I was going to say unless you don't want me," she huffs out. "God, Dempsey. I don't know. You've been so hot and cold. I can't help but wonder if maybe this whole thing's in my head. I want you more than I've ever wanted anyone, and you're just... lukewarm sometimes."

"You think I'm lukewarm toward you?"

I scoff, unbuckling my seatbelt so I can lean all the way across the center console and wrap her in my arms.

"I'm on fucking fire for you, baby girl."

I smash my mouth into hers and kiss her the way I've wanted to for days. I force myself into her mouth, our tongues dancing and exploring as I show her the depth of my desire. No fucking way is she allowed to question how much I want her. Not now. Not ever again.

My phone alarm rings out through the speakers of the car, and we reluctantly break apart. I scheduled an emergency therapy session for my mom this morning, although I doubt it'll do any good. Still. I refuse to not try.

"I have to get going," I lament. "Your house has a security system, right?"

She nods, and I open my door, intent to walk her to the door this time. I move around the car and open her side, then grab the bag of dirty clothes and ruined shoes from the footwell before taking her hand and ensuring she gets inside safely.

Chapter 23

Dempsey

"I'll give you all decade to shoot that," Harold yells as Marty lines up.

He sends the ball flying, but it bounces off the backboard.

"Hit the showers, Marty," Harold hollers as he hobbles down the court. "Your game *stinks* today!"

I can't help but laugh as I watch them wrap up their ridiculous game of one-on-one. We have the court reserved for another five minutes, and although we're all dripping in sweat and out of steam, these two refuse to waste a second of our designated time.

I run a towel over my face, soaking up the sweat that pours off me after playing two games. These guys don't let me rest, insisting I'm their "lucky charm" on the court. Never mind that I'm thirty years younger than every other guy in our league.

I open up my gym bag to stash my towel and pull out my phone in the process.

I've got two texts from her waiting for me, and I feel like a fool as I rush to unlock my device and read them.

The first one is a picture of her long, gorgeous legs spread out on a pool chair, water glistening in the background.

Maddie: Wish you were here to help me cool off.

The little spitfire.

The second one doesn't have a picture, but it has me groaning all the same.

Maddie: Is it still okay if I come up to The Oak tonight?

This girl. Whenever I think she's going to zig, she zags. She doesn't ask permission. Until she does. She's a puzzle I'm eager to solve; a paradox I yearn to uncover.

I haven't seen her for three days. But tonight... tonight she'll perch her perky ass on a barstool and eye-fuck the shit out of me my entire shift. I've never been more excited to get my ass to work.

"Whoa-ho. Who's got you smiling like that?" Richard taunts next to me on the bench.

I don't bother hiding my phone or acting ashamed. He can't see anything with his safety goggles covering his glasses, anyway.

"Just a girl," I insist, giving him a light shove before rising up and offering a hand to help him to his feet.

"A girl? Did I hear someone mention a girl?" Marty asks, clasping me on the shoulder as we head to the locker room.

"I may be getting up there in years, but that wasn't a 'just a girl' smile, Dempsey. If someone's got you smiling like that, you lock her down and keep her."

I plan to do just that, all summer long.

My head shoots up every time the front door chimes and another person enters the building. I'm disappointed time and time again.

Until I'm not.

Maddie Wheeler walks into the bar for the third time in less than two weeks, and this time, I let myself succumb to her presence. I am instantly and completely enchanted.

She's got her hair pulled up in a high, bouncy ponytail, and she's wearing another one of those teeny tiny half shirts paired with cut-off denim shorts. Except that's not the only thing she's wearing tonight. She's also wearing my jacket.

She takes her time making her way over to the bar, surveying the crowd. She has to feel my eyes on her—she fucking has to. But she makes me wait. It's worth it. When she hops onto a barstool and lifts her head, I swear the lights flicker around me.

She's electric.

Her pull's magnetic.

I'm stalking over to her two seconds later.

"You look really good in that jacket," I open, leaning in close so no one else can hear our exchange.

"I look really good out of it, too," she quips, rising up a few inches to hover closer. I lock her in my gaze and hold her there for a few seconds, desperate to get my fill the best I can with her right in front of me but technically out of reach.

"Hi," I finally breathe out as I let myself blink.

"Hi." She smiles, then bites down on that bottom lip again as she assesses me.

It's going to be so much harder than I expected to focus on anything but her when she's sitting there wearing my clothes.

"You're back!"

Cole's exclamation catches me off guard. He's talking to Maddie, of course. I school my expression as I remember that I did, in fact, spend most of her last visit purposely ignoring her while she chatted up the other guys.

I push off the bar and shift back a few steps, but I don't take my eyes off her.

"I'm back," she confirms. "Turns out this is pretty much the only place worth being after six in this sleepy town. You'll probably be seeing a lot of me this summer."

Damn straight. I'll have her here every night I work if it means I get to see that smile.

Cole widens his stance and crosses his arms over his chest, stroking his chin in mock-contemplation. "Ya know, Maddie, I can't help but notice that you keep showing up when Jake's not here."

Her eyes shift from Cole to me for the briefest moment, but her smile never falters.

"Oh, Cole," she sing-songs. She leans forward and draws him in, a cobra hypnotizing its prey. When his posture stiffens, she strikes. "Don't you think it's more fun when Dempsey's in charge?"

He spins on his heel to gauge my reaction, but all I can do is laugh.

Maddie takes full advantage of his distracted state, eye-fucking me until heat crawls up my neck, then she settles back into her seat.

Cole scurries off, obviously bewitched by a girl he can't handle.

I rest my arms on the bar and lean back into her space. "What would you like to drink tonight?"

"Just a soda is fine."

"Do you want food?" I ask. I may or may not have already called over to Clinton's to see who's working. Tiff agreed to bring me a to-go order if needed.

"You know me so well."

"I'm learning you," I counter, repeating the words she whispered in my ear when she was straddling me on the balcony last weekend.

She doesn't respond, instead giving me doe eyes through her thick, black lashes and watching as I slowly back away.

I pour her drink and deliver it, then check on the other customers hanging around the bar. It's the middle of the week, and it's only eight o'clock, so things are under control. I've got two guys behind the bar, plus two more servers on the floor. I call over to Clinton's and order two baskets of tots, confirming that Tiff will bring them over when they're ready.

"Yo, Dem." Teddy waves me over and hands me a sticky note. "I need, like, four things from the cage, and one of them I needed yesterday."

I glance over his list, then nod absentmindedly as I pull the liquor cage keys out of my pocket. "I'll be right back."

I don't bother looking back up the bar for my girl. I know her eyes haven't left me since I walked away from her a few minutes ago.

As I wind through the narrow back hallway, I sense her.

I tilt my head, straining to gauge just how close she is, but she gives nothing away.

The moment I insert the key into the liquor cage, she wraps her hands around my torso. I hiss on contact, but more from excitement than surprise. I trap her arms against my body and spin her until she's pushed up against the metal cage.

"How did I know you were going to follow me, naughty girl?" I rest one arm over her head and use the other to cushion her back. Her hands find purchase under my shirt immediately, exploring the planes of my chest before she scrapes her nails down the length of my torso.

"I hate that bar," she pouts, running her nails up and down my stomach again before dipping them into the front of my pants.

I hum on contact, then pull her closer as I roll my hips forward. Her body melts into mine, our baser instincts taking over as we touch and explore in the privacy of the dimly lit hallway.

"Oh yeah? Why's that?"

"Because it's always in my goddamn way," she huffs, thrusting forward before fisting the hair at the nape of my neck and pulling me down so my mouth meets hers.

She kisses me leisurely, dragging it out as if she's got all the time in the world.

"I've wanted to taste you from the second you walked through the front door tonight." I pick up the pace and swipe my tongue along her lips, lapping at the strawberry sweetness I've come to expect. It takes everything in me not to bite down and draw out a moan.

"I know." She smirks against my mouth, then moves lower and kisses along my neck.

I groan with every bit of suction, then startle when she cups my rock-hard erection through my jeans. I push into her hand but refuse to make this a one-way game tonight. Or ever again.

I brush my fingers up her leg, grinning as she widens her stance for me without instruction. When I reach the apex of her thighs, I cup her through her shorts, eliciting a mewl that has me dropping my forehead to hers.

"Do you know how badly I've wanted to touch you here?" I strum my fingers against her core, letting my pointer finger and pinky dance at the edges of her panties. I'm going to be tempted by these impossibly short shorts all damn night.

She thrusts her hips against me, seeking the friction we're both craving.

"I dream about touching you, baby girl. I can't wait to learn what you feel like under my hands and tongue."

She moans into my mouth, then releases my cock so she can use both hands to pull me tighter against her body.

"I can't wait to find out how it feels when you clench around my cock."

She shivers, then her hands are gone. It takes a second to register that she's undoing the button of her pants, ready to make all my dreams come true right here against this damn liquor cage.

But it's too dark.

We'll be too rushed.

And after pushing her away over the last few weeks, I need to savor her.

"*Maddie*," I caution, drawing out her name so she knows it's agony for me to pump the brakes. "Not here."

I use all my energy to pull back, taking her face in my hands and giving her a slow, apologetic kiss.

"Yes here," she protests, pulling on the zipper of her shorts and grabbing for my hand.

"No," I state authoritatively. "Not. Here." I kiss her again for emphasis, then move to button her pants in the dark. She frowns against my skin and opens her mouth, probably ready to unleash some of that sass I secretly love.

Before she can utter a sound, I wrap her ponytail around my hand twice, then gently pull her head back so she's forced to look up at me. My breath hitches when she goes compliant and whimpers in my hold. God, she's pretty.

"I need to take my time with you. And I'll be damned if any other man gets to smell you on my hands... or my mouth." I give her a wicked grin, followed by a lust-filled kiss.

"Soon, baby girl. Soon. Just not here."

"Come home with me tonight," she offers, grabbing me by the belt loops and pulling me against her with so much force the liquor cage rattles behind us.

I sigh. "I can't tonight. Fielding has plans after work, so I have to go home."

She schools her expression and wipes the pout from her face. I have to hand it to her—she pulls it together quickly when I mention my priorities.

"You work tomorrow, right?"

"I do." I give her a wicked grin, knowing she'll catch on.

"Does your brother have plans then, too?"

"He does not."

"Come home with me *tomorrow*."

"Tomorrow," I agree, kissing her one more time before I carefully shift her to the side and swing open the liquor cage door to find what Teddy needs. "Now get back out there and eat your tots before the guys notice we've both been gone for way too long."

"You better be worth the wait, Dempsey Haas," she whispers in my ear before walking down the dimly lit hall.

Chapter 24

Maddie

I sit in front of my vanity and add more waves to my hair with my curl wand, smiling at how silly it is to do my hair for tonight. If everything goes according to plan, this mop will look like a lion's mane by the time Dempsey and I are done with each other.

"You're really going all out tonight," Paige chirps from my bed as she mindlessly flips through a magazine. "Who are you going out with again?"

We spent the day together, lounging in the pool while she licked her wounds from her latest Kyle encounter. She had sex with him at Andrew Adley's party—and hasn't heard from him since.

Typical.

But also convenient for me. If Kyle's on her shit list, she's far less likely to suggest we hang out with him and Travis anytime soon. I'd be thrilled if we didn't see them again this summer. Especially after the way Travis ditched me at the party.

I make eye contact with my best friend through the vanity mirror and smile. "You don't know him," I answer, because technically she doesn't.

"So it's a mystery man," she pushes.

She's got the *man* part right.

Somehow I went from playing a game of cat and mouse with Dempsey Haas to wanting to prove to him just how cooperative and compliant I can be. I like it when he calls me baby girl and princess. I fucking loved it when he called me his naughty girl last night.

I can't hide my smile as I think about having him all to myself. We haven't been in a position where we could just *be*. There won't be any sneaking around or holding back tonight. No stolen kisses, late night rendezvous, or lustful stares. I get him to myself. And I'm more than ready to have all of him.

"You are grinning like a fool!" Paige throws a pillow at my head, but I see it coming and shoot out an arm to catch it. Thanks, LAX skills.

"Maybe a little," I admit, turning back to the vanity and selecting my favorite strawberry fizz lip gloss.

"Does your mystery man know about your heroic efforts last weekend?" she teases.

I roll my eyes at the reminder. The onslaught of new photos and videos from Adley's party has slowed—I'm pretty sure I've seen everything that's been uploaded at this point. That hasn't stopped the flurry of texts, emails, and DMs from people making sure I've seen each one, though.

Idiots. Of course I've seen them. I was tagged in all the posts. I fucking lived the whole experience. The only saving grace is that neither Fielding nor Dempsey has social media, so no one's been able to connect them to the incident.

Paige knows a version of what happened last weekend. But we haven't talked about it much. I've brought Kyle up often to divert her attention. I'd prefer to drop the whole thing: the more we talk about it, the more I have to skirt around the truth.

"Probably," I hedge. "I'm going out with someone from school. He goes to Cal, too, but he lives about thirty minutes from here."

I feel bad about the blatant lie. But I really don't want her snooping around.

"It's someone from around here? That's awesome!"

Shit. Of course she's excited that I'm going out with someone local. I scramble for a response to curb her enthusiasm.

"He wants to stay out in California for grad school, too," I lie. Again.

Her smile drops, and she sighs as I turn back to spray my hair and add another layer of lip gloss. I'd rather manage her expectations now than give her false hope that I will *ever* be a permanent resident of Hampton, Ohio again.

California. Timbuktu. I want to live literally anywhere but here. I just don't have it in me to dash her dreams tonight.

I adjust my T-shirt and smooth down the front of my high-waisted jeans before pulling open the door of The Oak.

It's my fourth time walking through this door over the last few weeks, but tonight, everything feels different.

I'm on fire.

And I want nothing more than for him to squelch out every flame that's been building inside me since I pushed him against the clock tower.

As soon as I walk into the bar, our eyes meet, and he freezes where he stands. He's holding a bottle of something in one hand, and I watch, entranced, as he runs his other hand through his blond hair before giving up a subtle smirk just for me.

As I come closer, he wraps up what he's doing and backs up in front of an empty barstool. I take his cue and hoist myself up on the seat he's standing in front of, holding my breath and counting down the seconds until he turns around and faces me.

Our eyes meet, and my heart leaps into my throat.

It's the way he holds himself. The way he looks at me. I sit silently under his assessment as he appraises me.

Finally, he speaks.

"I like your shirt."

I bet he does.

I'm wearing the oversized Archway Prep lacrosse shirt he loaned me last weekend. But I've twisted it up and secured it with a hair tie in the back so it's fitted across my chest and shows off a good amount of the tanned skin of my stomach.

I glance down and feign surprise, then look back up to meet his gaze.

"Oh, this old thing?" I catch my heels on the base of the barstool, then rise up to get as close to him as possible. Whether he realizes it or not, he matches my posture, leaning in until we're just inches apart. "It'll look better on the floor of my bedroom tonight."

His pupils blow out, and he lifts his fist to his mouth and shakes his head.

"Tonight," he whispers, the one word lighting up my insides and confirming everything I've been dreaming about for weeks.

Tonight, he's mine.

Chapter 25

Dempsey

"I don't know if we'll make it to the bed if you keep touching me like that, princess."

Her hands are everywhere—caressing up my arms, scraping down my abs, encircling my neck, and brushing over my fully hard erection. I've got her pinned against the wall, letting her explore freely now that we're in the privacy of her house.

It was a mad dash to get here. To get inside. To get to her room. I have to keep reminding myself to slow the fuck down—we're in no rush now, and she deserves to be worshipped.

I'm practically vibrating with pent-up energy and sexual tension. The combination of resisting her and then holding back over the last few days has been nothing less than torture.

I pull her away from her bedroom wall and walk her backward to the bed.

Her room is bright yellow, with one charcoal gray wall that stands out from the rest. It's filled with framed pictures of friends and newspaper clippings touting her high school sports accomplishments. Her prom queen sash and crown hang off the end of a bookshelf next to an illustrated poster of Ruth Bader Ginsburg. She has an ornate white vanity at one end of the room, covered in products and all sorts of girly things, then above it is a wall decal that reads "I am a rich man."

The whole space is a paradox; a dichotomous collection that's perfectly her.

She sits down on her bed and smiles at me, crossing her bare legs and looking coy.

"Where do you keep your condoms, baby girl?"

Her pupils dilate when I call her that. I can't wait to see how she responds when we really get going.

"In this drawer." She crawls across the bed to the side table, then shakes her ass, taunting me to come closer.

I make my way to the other side of the bed and peer inside the drawer, finding a variety pack—open, but more than half-full.

"Good girl," I murmur, just to see if I can get a reaction out of her.

She turns back to me and beams.

"Is it okay if I use the ones I brought?" I ask, weaving a hand through her hair as she kneels near the side of her bed to kiss me.

She laughs. "Really, Dem?"

"Yes, really. What's so funny?"

"You are."

"What? Why?" "I don't know," she says, exasperated. "You're just... different. Most guys my age act like wearing a condom is a literal death sentence. I had three guys tell me they were allergic to latex during my freshman year of college. Three! It's like they all got together on Reddit and brainstormed ideas to get away with raw dogging a one-night stand."

Fury rises inside me at the thought of some asshole trying to take advantage of her like that.

"What did you tell them?" I demand. She raises one eyebrow before answering. "I told them to get lost, obviously."

"Good girl," I murmur again before dipping my head to kiss up and down the column of her neck.

"You seem to like saying that to me."

"Because I *know* you like hearing it," I retort, running my free hand along her inner thigh until I reach the hem of her cut-off jeans.

"Can I take these off?" I ask, my breath hitching as my fingers brush against her delicate skin.

"I thought you'd never ask." She smirks up at me, pops the button on her shorts, and shimmies out of them in one seamless motion. When she reaches for her shirt, I shoot out my hand and stop her.

"Leave that on," I growl, laying her back on the bed, then shifting to kneel between her legs. "Do you know how hot you look wearing my clothes?"

I kiss her exposed stomach, then run my tongue down, down, down until I'm dipping below her belly button.

"Dem..." She squirms beneath me, so I pin both of her legs to the mattress.

"You gonna open these gorgeous legs for me, baby girl?" I ask as I run my lips along the lace of her thong.

"Yes," she replies on a sigh.

She parts her legs, then I yank them open farther, revealing the thin strip of fabric covering her pussy. My dick twitches in excitement, but I ignore it so I can focus on the gorgeousness laid out in front of me.

I bow low and nuzzle against the crease of her thigh, then inhale deeply as I trace the line where her panties meet her skin. She smells like coconut oil and sunshine. I sniff her again, right along her sweet heat, and my eyes roll to the back of my head as the intoxicating scent of her essence floods my brain.

"Dempsey!" She squirms again, contorting her body and pressing her parted thighs against my hands.

"What's wrong?" I demand, immediately loosening my grip.

"Did you really just *smell* me? Down *there*?"

Oh-ho-ho. *That's* the supposed problem? No fucking way.

"I did. And I'm going to do it again"—I dip into the apex of her thighs for emphasis—"and again, and again, and again until I've committed your scent to memory. You smell fucking delicious, Maddie. So good, in fact, I think I need a taste."

I look up to gauge her reaction as I pull her panties off and toss them to the side. Her lips part, and her pupils are totally blown out. She holds my gaze as I lower my head.

I sniff her again and groan to prove my point, then I lick from her opening to up and over her clit. She whimpers, so I do it again.

She tastes fucking incredible. I graze up her thighs and use both hands to part her pussy lips, exposing her further. Glancing up to make sure she's still watching, I seal my mouth around her clit and suck.

She bucks slightly, but I keep her legs locked in place. I zigzag my tongue down her center, then push just the tip into her opening.

"Fuck, Dem," she mutters as she drags a hand through my hair.

That's it, baby girl. Tell me what you like.

Hooking my arms around each of her thighs, I shift back to sit on my heels. I drag her body with me so she's in a bridge position and I can really get a mouthful of her delicious cunt.

"Fuck... fuck. That feels *so* good," she praises.

"You taste *so* good," I reply, rushing to get my words out so I can get back to business. I establish a rhythm between tongue-fucking, licking, and sucking, and soon she's lifting her hips to meet my mouth.

"*Fuck...* okay, I'm good," she says out of nowhere.

Good?

Her words have barely registered when she tries to pull away.

"What the fuck?" I gawk as she attempts to get out of my hold and wiggle up the mattress.

"I want you to fuck me now," she pants, her cheeks flushed from arousal.

Seriously. *What. The. Fuck?*

"We're not having sex until I make you come."

Her eyes widen in—what? Shock? Horror?—before she sits up and scoots farther away from me. I'm so caught off guard, I prowl after her on instinct, getting right up in her face until she's leaning back against the headboard.

"What's wrong?" I demand, searching her face as she tries to steady her breathing.

"Nothing."

"Did I do something you didn't like?"

"No."

"Is there something else you want me to do?"

"No! God, Dempsey. I said I was ready to fuck. Most guys are more than happy to switch things up and get the party started." She turns her head away from me, but I see right through her bullshit.

"Most guys, huh? We've already established that I'm not like most guys, baby girl." I gently grasp her chin and turn her head back to face me. "Has no one ever made you come like that?"

Her cheeks turn a deep shade of crimson, and she fights to break out of my grasp.

"Answer me, Maddie," I grit out in frustration.

She grabs my wrist and pulls my arm away from her face before answering.

"No, okay? Are you happy now? *That* never works for me, and it's really fucking embarrassing having to say it out loud. I like it. And it feels good. But you're down there, and I'm all the way up here. I start to worry that it's taking too long, or that you're bored..."

I bark out a laugh. I'm as amused as I am outraged.

"I'm sorry," I apologize, shaking my head in frustration. "I'm not laughing at you. But I swear to God, Maddie, I was not *bored* when I was tongue-fucking your cunt just now. I was having the time of my life. But now I'm furious that you didn't let me finish."

I shift back down the bed, grip her ankles in my hands, and pull her with me.

"With your permission, princess," I look her in the eye and will her to feel my sincerity, "I'd like to resume what I was doing. And just so you know, I was purposely taking my time, but I can speed things up if it makes you feel better."

She puffs out her cheeks and blows out a long breath, which just irritates me more.

"Five minutes," she mutters before sliding back into position.

Challenge accepted.

"Take your shirt off," I demand. I've got a point to prove. "I saw you trying to play with those gorgeous tits when you sucked me off last weekend. You can put your hands on your chest, or you can put them in my hair, got it?"

She doesn't move. So I bite her inner thigh.

"Fuck! Okay, okay!" she laughs, sitting up to pull my LAX T-shirt off and unhook her bra in the process. "I'm setting a timer though," she retorts, reaching over to where her phone sits on the nightstand.

When she lies back down, her tits bounce, and I can't fucking resist.

"God, you're gorgeous," I praise, crawling up her body and taking her nipple into my mouth.

She hisses on contact, then moans on the next breath. I keep sucking as I let my fingers dip between her thighs. She clenches around my hand, and I switch sides with my mouth, lavishing her other nipple with just as much attention.

"Fuck... yes..." she pants as I continue. This girl loves her some nipple action. Noted.

"Keep playing with those," I instruct as I reluctantly abandon her perfect breasts to trail kisses down her body.

Wasting no time this round—I don't even bother getting an extra whiff—I get to fucking work. I go back to the rhythm I had going before she so rudely stopped me and slip one finger inside her for an extra assist.

Her pussy immediately tightens around me. I crook my finger up, then smile into her folds when she bucks her hips in response.

That's it, baby girl. We're gonna get you there yet.

After a few minutes of steady fingering and sucking, she's close. She's practically fucking my face when her damn phone alarm rings out. She freezes—and I see red.

"Hit snooze," I bark out, immediately resuming my rhythm. She's close. She's *so* close. I'm not letting some arbitrary timer tell me to stop.

"Dem—"

"I said *hit snooze*. You're dripping all over the sheets and pulsing around my fingers, Princess. I know this is working for you. Stop overthinking it and just fucking come for me."

I don't give her a chance to respond. I just need to be face down and knuckle deep in her cunt to get her there. Closing my mouth around her clit, I insert a second finger, stroking her G-spot over and over until her legs start to shake. I don't dare break pace. I don't even come up for air. I keep sucking, stroking, giving her everything until she finally starts to pulse around me.

She cries out. She pulls on my hair. She comes so hard she makes a pretty little wet spot on the sheets. I lap her up and force her to bare down around me as she rides out her orgasm.

Then I sit back proudly and grin. *Mission fucking accomplished.*

Chapter 26

Maddie

I think I just blacked out. Am I still breathing? Could I be dreaming? I'm lying here in what feels like a pool of sweat and cum as Dempsey kisses up the length of my body.

"You good, baby girl?"

As if that's even a question.

I open my eyes and pull him toward me, attacking his mouth with a sloppy, lust-filled kiss.

"Is that a yes?" he chuckles as he kisses my neck before lowering his head to my chest. The second he starts sucking on my nipple, I lose it.

"Fuck. I want you. Dem, please. Stop teasing me."

He grins against my skin, but he makes no move to pull away.

I already feel my pussy tingling again in response to his mouth—or is it *still* fluttering from the soul-shattering orgasm he just gave me?

"Dempsey! I'm serious. You still have all your fucking clothes on! Get naked and get inside me."

He hops off the bed, grinning in the most adorable way, then quickly removes his shirt. He undoes his pants, then shoves them down, along with his boxers, in one fluid motion. I prop up on my elbows and drink him in. His torso's impossibly long; so long he's rocking an eight pack. His waist tapers into his pants and forms these delicious hip indents.

"Fuck me," I mutter as I home in on his dick. The thing's an anaconda. I'm a greenhorn skipper about to embark on a jungle river cruise. How the hell did I manage to deep-throat that sucker last weekend?

Oh. That's right. Because I can do all things through Dempsey, who strengthens me. Especially when he calls me a good girl. Or a naughty girl. Or princess. I have a feeling he can call me just about anything, and my jaw will automatically unhinge to welcome him home.

"That's the plan," he retorts as he pulls a condom out of his discarded pants pocket and rips it open with his teeth.

I almost come again when he spits the corner of the wrapper off to the side.

After he rolls on the condom, he prowls toward me and joins me on the bed. He hovers a few inches above my body, just out of reach. My brain does the cha-cha slide when his forearms flex on either side of my head.

I knew it. *I fucking knew it*. This man could hold a plank for days.

"How do you want me?" he asks softly, brushing his lips against mine before peppering more kisses along my collarbone.

"Inside me," I quip as I lift my hips to line him up.

"Maddie," he scolds into my neck before nudging his tip at my entrance. "Tell me what you like and how you want it. I want this to be so good for you, baby girl."

He literally just gave me the most intense orgasm of my life. But sure. Let's talk more about what I want.

"I like to be on top," I whisper.

"Of course you do."

Two seconds later, we're rolling.

He lies back and adjusts his arms behind his head, giving me the most salacious smile as he watches me through those lagoon-blue eyes. I lean forward and kiss him, then lift one leg up to turn around.

"Whoa, whoa, whoa... where the hell do you think you're going?"

I freeze, then look back to justify my actions. "Haven't you ever heard of reverse cowgirl?"

He scoffs like I tried to convince him two plus two is nine. "Hard pass. If you turn around, I won't be able to see you. If I can't see you, I won't know what you like or what's working. Plus, I really think I need unfettered access to those gorgeous tits."

He tweaks both my nipples, which shoots kitty flutters straight to my core. I don't think a guy has ever been as openly obsessed with my boobs as Dempsey—I've died and gone to nipple-stimulation heaven.

"Convincing argument," I relent, shifting back to face him.

"I thought you'd see it my way." He lifts his pelvis until his condom-clad dick brushes my clit. I shudder at the sensation.

"Put me inside you, baby girl. Show me what you've got."

I rise to hover and line him up, surprisingly nervous to be facing him. But as soon as that first inch is in, I close my eyes and give in to the sensations. I work him in slowly, inch by inch, savoring the way my body stretches and molds around him. Once he's completely seated inside me, I open my eyes, startled to be met head-on by his heated, wanton gaze.

"Fuck, Maddie. Do you know how hot that was?"

I grin and start to ride him, using his abs for leverage as I lift myself up and off his dick. He places both hands on my hips, and then we're moving in tandem. When I rise up, he lifts me higher. When I sink down, he pulls me closer. Every time I bottom out, he shifts my body forward, putting more pressure on my sensitive bundle of nerves.

"See how pretty you look riding me, baby girl? You're a fucking dream."

I look down to where our bodies connect and watch as his length disappears inside me. It's surprisingly hot—and shockingly intimate.

When I lift my head again, we make eye contact, and I freeze. The energy that's run rampant between us for weeks encircles us now, the power of our connection ten times stronger than any emotion I've ever experienced. We could fuel a power grid with this electricity. And the best part of it is that I know—*I just know*—he's alongside me for the ride.

"You're perfect," he whispers, brushing aside a damp strand of hair. I'm so overcome with emotion, I move to turn my head, hoping to hide how strongly this moment is hitting me. But he catches my chin with one hand and doesn't let me pull away.

"I feel it, too," he confesses, the power of the moment growing as he continues to stare, keeping me trapped in his gaze.

After another few seconds, he shudders, shakes his head, and lifts his hips, effectively breaking the trance.

"Fuck... you feel too good, baby girl. I'm not gonna last long. Let's get you there again."

Say what now?

I don't have time to question him before he's sitting up, wrapping his arms around my low back, and bowing his head to spit on my clit.

Legit. Right. On. My. Clit.

Should I give him some sort of award for that? A round of applause? Talk about shooting your shot.

Before my brain can catch up, he's reaching a hand between us, stroking me in tight circles as he fucks me from below. I would protest and insist I'm good—but heat is rapidly rising up my neck.

"Fuck, fuck, fuck. Dem. Dempsey. I'm..."

"Yes, baby girl. Fuck, you feel *so* good. You're gonna come again for me, aren't you?"

I can barely nod as I let go of everything around me.

Every thought. Every worry. Every insecurity or witty remark.

It all pours out of my goddamn soul as my toes involuntarily tingle.

"Thatta girl," he whispers directly into my ear as he strokes and fucks me. "Clench around me, princess. Let me feel how much you love this cock."

I scream out and nearly dislodge his dick as my body convulses on command. I cry out with every wave of release, which only spurs him on. He jackhammers into me until he curses, buries his head between my tits, and moans my name.

We're a mess of breathless pants and sated whimpers as we cling to each other.

I've never experienced anything like this in my life.

I can't fucking wait to do it again.

Chapter 27

Maddie

I wake up to the sound of the doorbell. I'm disoriented enough that I have to sit up and rub the sleep out of my eyes before I can make sense of what's happening.

"Stay put, baby girl. I'll be right back."

Dempsey kisses my bare shoulder before rising from the bed, pulling on his pants, and leaving the room.

I pout at his retreating form. Where the hell does he think he's going? I check the time on my phone and see that it's already ten. I can't remember the last time I slept in this late.

After he fucked my brains out and made me question everything I know about sex, we stayed up talking for hours. Even when we were both yawning through every other sentence, neither of us wanted the night to end.

We talked about his job at The Oak, and I told him about my new apartment off campus. He told me all about his time at Harvard, and about the entrepreneurship contest he won his senior year. He talked a little about his mom, and I told him about my dream of living in a big city and making big bucks as a corporate lawyer.

It was like the perfect first date. Except we skipped the awkward small talk and just went right for the stuff that matters while lying naked in my bed.

And then, once we were too sleepy to keep our eyes open, he rolled on a fresh condom, sucked on my neck and tits, and fucked me so deeply I thought I wet the damn bed from the amount of pleasure that dripped out of me.

That's right. Dempsey Haas made me come thrice last night.

No man has ever made me come even once during sex—a fact I *didn't* share with Dempsey—and I'm mortified at the thought of what I've been settling for.

I enjoy sex, and I *do* orgasm, but I usually have to be very hands-on in my own pleasure with guys my age. Occasionally, I just fake it to get it over with, then rub one out while the guy's in the bathroom or once he leaves for the night.

What can I say? I'm an independent woman. I don't need a man to make me come.

Or I didn't think I did until now.

I'm still replaying last night in my mind when Dempsey strolls back into my bedroom. He's got two brown paper bags in one hand and a drink carrier in the other.

"Is that what I think it is?" I demand, shifting to the side of the bed to make room for him.

"Do you think it's Jersey Bagels and a large dirty chai latte?"

I squeal in delight as he sets the goods on the bed.

"Do you want to eat up here?"

"Might as well. I'm pretty sure we destroyed these sheets last night."

"That we did," he murmurs, joining me on the bed, then reaching over to rumple my crazy bedhead and kiss my forehead. "Good morning, by the way."

"Good morning." I beam, then take a sip of my drink.

Fuck. It's perfect. He asked about my coffee order last night, but I thought that was idle chatter. I didn't know he was taking notes so he could DoorDash me breakfast in bed. This man is a different breed.

We dig into our food, then immediately get into a heated debate about bagel rating criteria. I'm a staunch believer that bagels with stuff in them or on them are the superior bagel, while Dempsey doesn't stray from the classics.

"Okay wait—so if you only like plain bagels—"

"And salt bagels," he interrupts. Which are just plain bagels with extra salt, it turns out.

"Why did you order an assortment of two dozen?"

He smirks before answering. "I didn't know what you liked. I figured this way, you can have exactly what you want."

I would roll my eyes at his cheeseball line if I didn't know better. But I'm learning him. I genuinely believe this is who Dempsey is. At his core, he's a caretaker. He puts his people first. Everything he does and every choice he makes is thoughtful and intentional. What he lacks in spontaneity he makes up for in the care of his actions.

I've never been into the concept of chivalry, but being on the receiving end of his brand of thoughtfulness feels really good.

"When do you work again next?" I ask through a mouthful of blueberry bagel goodness.

"Saturday and Sunday." He goes quiet for a moment, then he turns to face me. "You know I don't have to be at work for us to hang out, right?"

"I know." I shrug, even though I was *not* aware of that fact until this very moment. "I just figured it's easier for you that way, right? If you're working, that means Fielding's probably home with your mom..." I trail off, suddenly not so sure that my assumptions are on target. Maybe I don't understand their system. Or maybe I'm grossly overestimating how much time he wants to spend with me.

I peek over at him through a curtain of hair, embarrassed by my overstepping. "Sorry. Maybe that was dumb. I shouldn't assume you want to spend your free nights with me..."

He catches my chin and tilts my head back, forcing me to look at him when he speaks. "I fucking love that you assumed." He bows down to kiss my forehead, then wraps an arm around me.

"If you want to come to the bar Saturday night and hang out, I can come home with you then. I'll tell Fielding he's got to be home all weekend so we can spend the day together on Sunday."

"So secret sleepovers are officially a thing?" I tease, resting my head on his shoulder and humming in pleasure when he massages the base of my scalp.

"Yes, baby girl. Secret sleepovers are officially a thing. But I think we learned last night that not a lot of sleeping happens when I get you alone. You better rest up for this weekend."

Chapter 28

Dempsey

It's just one of those nights.

We're slammed, but most of the customers are being patient, and the staff's in good spirits, too.

There are two bachelorette parties in the house, which used to be my specialty. But not one of the women wearing skintight black mini dresses and matching pink penis crowns is holding my attention tonight.

That honor's reserved for her.

She showed up half an hour ago wearing baggy jeans and a sheer lace tank top with my jacket layered over it. Her hair's wild tonight—sort of curly, but all voluptuous and big. It reminds me of how she looked when she was riding my cock and making my body slick with sweat and cum.

Fuck—I can't wait for this shift to be over so I can take her home.

I took the liberty of snagging her a seat at the bar as soon as one became available, and I've strategically avoided Jake's gaze ever since. I warned Maddie that he'd be working tonight, too—he almost always does on Saturday nights in the summer when we get this busy—but she said she didn't mind. We have to play it cool regardless when we're at The Oak since my brother hangs out with a lot of the guys who work here.

I'm trying to give her space—really, I am—but that damn magnetic pull she has on me keeps dragging me back into her orbit.

Maybe it's because I know what it feels like to be buried inside her, or maybe the reason can't be explained. But I can't help it. As soon as I finish pouring a drink, I look her way. The second I catch a breather, I'm compelled to walk to her side of the bar. I swear my ears are tuned to hear her above the music and general cacophony of the bar. Especially when she laughs—God, she has the best laugh.

She's made friends with the middle-aged woman sitting next to her, and she's trying to get Tristan to pay her new friend some extra attention. The lady's got to be in her midfifties. But maybe that's his type. I wouldn't put it past Maddie to pick up on that kind of vibe.

"How's everyone doing down here?" I ask, addressing the side of the bar she's sitting at as I let my eyes linger on her face.

She smiles sweetly at me—playing the game and biding her time. I instinctively look over to the clock—two hours and twenty minutes to last call. Approximately three hours until she's in my arms and I'm back in her bed.

But when I look her way again, I'm met with a totally different expression.

Her eyes are wide but unfocused. She's oddly pale, like the blood's drained from her face. She's rigid on the barstool, unmoving before me.

Something's wrong.

Something's really fucking wrong.

My blood pressure shoots up, and it takes my brain a few seconds to catch up as I try to make sense of what's happening. I look over at the people beside her, then scan the bar for any sign of trouble. It's not until I look back that I see it.

There's a hand.

A meaty hand. Resting on her shoulder.

A meaty hand that's now gliding up toward her neck, creeping under her jacket—*my* jacket—and fingering the lace strap of her tank top.

The fingers of that hand pull, and when the elastic snaps against her skin, my brain detonates in rage.

Multiple things happen at that moment. Maddie swats the hand away while I stalk over to get as close to her as possible. Our eyes meet, and I say her name so loudly everyone around us turns to look.

"Maddie."

She closes her eyes for a breath, and her chest rises and falls too quickly. If her heart's beating out of her chest, it's keeping time with mine.

"What's wrong?" I push, leaning forward and silently cursing the raw-edge bar keeping me from physically getting to her.

Before she can answer, a man wearing a baseball cap and a Hampton High football shirt shifts into the gap between her barstool and the one beside her. He's crowding her: slanting his body and hovering in her space to force himself closer. I watch in disgust as he slinks the arm attached to that meaty hand around her shoulder.

She tries to shrug him off.

But he latches on tighter.

"Maddie," I repeat, snapping her attention back to me. "Do you know him?"

"I do," she grits out through clenched teeth as she lifts her shoulder, attempting to get out of his hold again.

He moves his hand this time but lowers it and grips at her waist under her jacket.

"Hey!" I bark, slamming my fist on the bar in front of the fucker to get his attention.

He peers up at me from under the bill of his hat, his face red, and his eyes hazy.

"Get your hands off her," I demand, my voice carrying over the sounds of the bar.

The handsy asshole smirks, then looks over to Maddie before turning back to me.

When our eyes meet, he blinks several times, almost like he can't believe what he's seeing.

"Holy shit. Holy fucking shit." His expression is wild as he searches my face, his words loud and sloppy. "How're you already back on your feet, you crazy fucker? I thought you might end up dead after that beating."

I tense with realization, and my brain riots with indecision. My heart leaps into my throat as I inhale, calm my nerves, and figure out a way to get to *her*.

This must be Andrew Adley. The man—if one could call him that—who made sport of leading his friends in a ten against one assault on my brother. The *coward* who threatened my girl with the promise of unwanted attention after she stepped in and put a stop to his antics.

No fucking way.

I watch, helpless, as Adley leans in and whispers something in her ear. Maddie's face twists in disgust, and she bats his hand away again, squirming out of his hold and hopping off the barstool in one swift motion.

Her eyes find mine again from across the bar top, and I make her a silent vow that I know she understands.

You're safe. I won't let anything stand in the way of keeping you safe.

"Get out," I command.

Adley looks me up and down and laughs. "Yeah right, bar boy. You can't kick me out. My picture's on the goddamn wall hanging over your head. I'm a paying customer, just like this bitch over here." He cocks his head to the side, to where Maddie's standing, trapped in place because of the crowd.

I don't bother replying. Instead, I stalk toward the end of the bar without taking my eyes off my girl. I elbow through the crowd, laser focused on my target. When I reach her, I can't get her behind me fast enough.

"I said get out," I spit at Adley, gripping Maddie's hand as I guide her backward toward the bar.

He smirks again, assessing me lazily like he doesn't have a care in the world. "What are you? Her dad?" He looks past me then, directing his next comment at Maddie.

"Did you forget to tell Daddy we had a deal? I told you not to wander off last weekend. You still gotta pay up with that pussy."

She tightens her grip on my hand, but it does nothing to stop my reaction.

"Tristan!" I holler to get his attention, pointing to Maddie and aggressively shoving her in his direction. "Get her behind the bar. Now." I turn back to see the shock in her expression, but I have to make sure she's safe.

I turn back and stride forward two steps, then wind up with a right hook that lands squarely on Adley's temple. He stumbles back, crashing into a group of girls who have boyfriends that are apparently as protective as me.

Someone screams, "Fight!" as chaos ensues on all sides. Bodies move at once, some trying to get away from the commotion, others clamoring to be in the middle of the action. It's impossible for me to move in any direction.

I glance back and see Maddie standing next to Tristan behind the bar. I also see Jake storming over toward the chaos I just caused.

Enough stools are now vacated that I can hop the bar, just barely clearing it as Jake comes to a halt in front of me.

"What the fuck is happening?" he demands as he grabs for his bullhorn.

I meet his enraged gaze with a surly stare. There's not enough time or truth to explain anything now. Not with a fight breaking out on the floor.

Jake jumps onto the bar, knocking over drinks in the process. He sounds the horn for several seconds, and one of the other guys pauses the music. I move to stand next to Maddie, desperate to ensure she's unharmed.

"You're okay," I murmur into her mass of blond waves as I slink one arm around her stomach and pull her into my side. She melts into my touch, but her breathing is ragged as she tries to keep her composure.

"I've got you," I whisper, rubbing what I hope feels like comforting circles along her hip. We're both laser focused on the man standing on top of the bar, commanding everyone's attention.

"What the fuck do ya'll think you're doing starting a fight in *my* bar?"

Adley steps forward, unsteady on his feet, looking like he's taken a few more hits since I landed the first punch.

"Yo. Pretty boy. Maybe you want to ask your bartender that question instead." He lifts his fingers to his already-swelling eye for emphasis, then juts his chin in my direction.

Jake whips his head around to see who's to blame. His eyes double in size when they land on me. He looks back at Adley, then turns to me again, scanning up and down as he finally notices the way I'm holding Maddie Wheeler in my arms.

I squeeze her to me on instinct, unsure if it's for her comfort or mine, then step forward and offer a hand up to Jake to help him off the bar.

"That guy's name is Andrew Adley. He beat the shit out of Fielding last week, then threatened to come after Maddie when she stopped him. He was touching her and saying inappropriate things just now. He threatened her and said she needed to pay up with pussy. I need him *gone* if you expect me to work the rest of this shift."

Jake sucks in a sharp breath at my not-so-subtle ultimatum, running his hand through his hair over and over. "Fuckin' Maddie," he mutters, turning away from me and lifting his bullhorn to speak.

Tension coils in my gut as I worry about being so candid with Jake. But he knows me. He *trusts* me. I would never pull shit over on him, and I have to believe he'll take my word as truth, regardless of how he feels about Maddie.

"If your name is Andrew Adley and/or you're a sexual predator, get out of my bar right fucking now," he declares through the bullhorn. "And if your drink was just spilled, or you got spilled on, come up here and see me so I can get you taken care of." The bar erupts in cheers, and people eagerly line up where Jake's standing.

Andrew doesn't take the hint.

"Hey. Hey! Pretty boy!" He's trying his hardest to get Jake's attention. "I could fucking sue you for defamation for calling me a sexual predator!"

Maddie brushes past me before I can stop her, and I stalk after her as she makes her way toward Adley.

"He didn't call you a sexual predator." She places both hands on her hips and stands tall, facing off with Andrew from across the bar. "He said if your name's Andrew Adley *and/or* you're a sexual predator. Not his fault you happen to identify with the title." She shrugs casually as I come to stand by her side.

"Oh, and Andrew?" she adds, leaning forward in a way that makes both him and I lurch closer to hear her. "I'm sure someone's got it on video, just in case we need proof."

That's my fucking girl.

His face heats to crimson, and a few people around him jeer. "Get out of here," and "no means no!" can be heard as he turns his back and stumbles toward the front door.

I sidle up behind her and put both my hands on her hips. "Fuck, baby girl. Watching you go all sassy lawyer on him was so hot."

She scoffs quietly and places both of her hands over mine. We stand like that, in the middle of the bar, surrounded by dozens of people, reveling in what feels like the calm after the storm.

"Yo. Haas. You're still on the clock. A little help here?"

Jake's words jolt me back to reality. Then Maddie's peeling my hands off her hips, providing another wake-up call to the situation. She turns and meets my gaze, blowing out a long breath. Looks like the reality of what just happened—of what we just revealed—is sinking in for us both.

"It'll be okay," I assure her, glancing down to where Cole's watching our exchange before looking over at Teddy and Anwar, who are drinking at the other end of the bar.

My brother's closest friends just had a front-row seat to what feels like a relationship reveal party.

"It'll be okay," I mutter again, more to myself this time, as I take her hand and walk her over to a bar stool next to the ice machine along the back bar.

"*Please* stay here so I can finish out this shift."

"I will." She doesn't hesitate, squeezing my hand once before hopping up on the barstool. "Promise."

I give her one last glance—just to calm my own nerves—then step up to help Jake at the bar.

"Make me eight Sex on the Beaches, and please tell me you're not sleeping with Fourth Wheel," he deadpans.

I wordlessly line up glasses, my silence telling him all he needs to know.

"Fuckin' A, Dempsey. What happened to *'they can never know'*?"

Chapter 29

Dempsey

What *did* happen to 'they can never know'? How the hell did I go from swearing off Maddie Wheeler to essentially pronouncing her as my girlfriend to a room full of people, including some of my brother's closest friends?

The honest answer? I have no fucking clue.

Jake's words play on repeat in my mind as I go through the motions of closing out for the night. Maddie hasn't moved from the chair behind the bar, which is the only reason I can get anything done.

I keep glancing back to make sure she's still there. That she's unharmed. That she's still mine.

I'm desperate to know what the hell she's thinking after my very public claiming. But every time we lock eyes, she just smiles sweetly, like she's trying to reassure me.

We're supposed to be casual. A summer fling with a clear expiration date. We haven't talked about exclusivity. I've literally only participated in one-night stands since my ex-fiancée Brooke chose not to come back to Hampton with me when we graduated from college.

I don't know what came over me.

But something about seeing Adley's hand on my woman flipped a switch in my mind.

I've never been one to say consequences be damned—and fuck, are there about to be consequences—but for the first time in a long time, I want to let myself have what I want.

What I want is her.

I just hope to God I can have her without hurting him.

It's probably best if we pump the brakes on our plans for tonight. I need to make sure Maddie gets home safely, then I'll head back to my house to deal with this head-on. My brother's going to find out eventually. If anyone's going to tell him about Maddie and me, it should be me.

Except I have no idea what I'm going to say.

I don't know what we're doing. I don't know what I am to her. My life is messy enough without indulging in a complicated, just-for-summer relationship. But my baser instincts crave this woman, and no matter how hard I try to reason with that urge, she makes me want more.

I hate it. I crave it.

I want her.

I just have to make sure Fielding's okay with this before I can give myself permission to go all in.

Chapter 30

Maddie

"Where'd you park, princess?" he asks as he guides me out the front door of The Oak, his hand firm on my low back.

"I'm in the back lot." I run my nails down his arm, gently dislodging his protective hold and interlacing our fingers instead.

"How much trouble did I cause tonight?" I caution, sweeping my mass of blond curls over my shoulder and side-eyeing him as we turn to walk around the building.

He says nothing, instead striding along the sidewalk with a sense of purpose. I squeeze his hand once—but he doesn't squeeze back.

Fuckity fuck.

I could tell I was losing him as the night went on. He made me sit behind the bar, but we interacted less and less. By last call, he was essentially ignoring me. I ended up helping Tristan dry and restock glasses just to have something to do.

I should have taken care of Adley myself. A quick nut punch or a little dodge and weave to the ladies' room would have done the trick. But he had the advantage of surprise. By the time I realized what was happening, Dempsey had already noticed.

My stomach aches at the thought of Dempsey being upset with me. I had no idea Adley was going to show up—I didn't even post on social saying I was at The Oak tonight. But there are only so many places to be on a Saturday night in a small town.

I drop his hand and make a show of putting my hair into a messy bun. He makes no move to reclaim it once I'm done.

Okay then.

If he wants to play it this way, I can do cold and disconnected, too.

If he's going to call this off, I want to get it over with. It'll be easier to make a clean break now than play games over the next few days or weeks as things fizzle out.

"Am I correct in assuming that secret sleepovers are actually *not* a thing after all?" I go for casual, refusing to let my voice waver. But I dodge his gaze in case the truth of my hurt is written all over my face.

He sighs one of those long, cheeks-puffed-out Dempsey sighs before glancing down at me and replying. "Look, princess. There's no way my brother's not going to find out about tonight. It's just a matter of time. I need to be home when he—"

"I get it," I interrupt. "It was fun while it lasted, right?" I cock my eyebrow and give him a quick up and down, because *damn*. It was more than fun, and I really don't want to give him up.

We cross the street toward the back parking lot. I click my key fob, and when my Lexus beeps and illuminates, I freeze.

He must see it, too, because he stops beside me and reaches for my hand.

"You didn't have plans to meet up with someone else tonight, did you?"

His question is in jest, and we both know it. I sass back anyway.

"I thought you were a sure thing, Haas. I didn't have a plan B."

"That's what I thought..." he mutters as we walk through the lot, his body shielding me from the figure leaning up against my car.

Hunched over posture. Menacing vibe. It's the baseball hat covering half his face that really gives him away.

"Get lost, Adley," I call out once we're within earshot.

He straightens up and raps his hand on the hood of my car.

"I thought this was you, Wheeler. You gonna make this easy and drive me to yours, or is this a game where I have to follow you home and chase you down?"

I don't have time to react before Dempsey's charging the car, pinning Andrew to the passenger door with one hand, and wailing on his face with the other.

"What. Part. Of. *NO*. Don't. You. Under. Stand?" He punctuates every syllable with a jab.

Adley crumbles to the ground as soon as Dempsey pulls back.

"Maddie Wheeler is *my* girlfriend. You so much as say her name out loud again, and I will hunt you down and bring on a world of pain. In court. In the streets. I'll fight you with everything I have until you're fucking ruined. She. Is. Mine. Do you understand?"

I stand there, speechless, as Adley nods frantically from where he's kneeling on the pavement.

"Use your words, asshole. Maddie Wheeler is off limits. Say it," he spits out.

Andrew gasps for breath and struggles to right himself. He coughs and sputters, but eventually he pants out Dempsey's demands. "Maddie Wheeler is off limits."

"Good boy," Dempsey degrades, patting Andrew on the head as he turns back to me.

"Lock your car," he commands, taking my hand and pulling me toward the alley that separates Clinton's and The Oak. "You're coming home with me."

Chapter 31

Dempsey

He thought he could come into my bar and put his hands on her. He thought he could intimidate her into fulfilling some sick obligation he decided she owed. He thought wrong.

I thought I could put some distance between us and pump the brakes on whatever *this* is. I thought I could push down all the feelings I've been fighting since the moment I met this woman. I thought wrong, too.

We cross the street in silence, her hand wrapped protectively in mine, neither of us uttering a word as we walk to my car parked near the clock tower.

I guide her to the passenger side, open the door, practically lift her inside, then buckle her up like she can't do it herself. Her eyes bug out of her head, and I know she wants to protest, but she must see something in me that silences her objections.

I need to do this. I *have* to protect her. The only reason she's even on Adley's radar is because of what she did for my brother.

But it goes deeper than that.

Now that I've gotten to know her—now that I've been *inside her*—I can't imagine letting anyone or anything keep us apart. I spent the last few hours of my shift trying to convince myself we could cool things off and go back to how things were before we hooked up.

But seeing Adley waiting at her car changed everything.

I can't undo what's been done. I can't pretend she hasn't spent the last few weeks chipping away at the armor I've forged to protect myself and my brother. She's already in. Somehow, she's worked her way into my life and my heart. I refuse to make her leave.

I meant every word I said to Adley. She's *mine*, and I'm not sharing. I'll be damned if anyone thinks they have any sort of hold on her or over her. I won't stand to see her manipulated or manhandled.

I start the car and ease onto the main road, coasting slowly through town before turning right at the intersection. She doesn't bother objecting when I make the turn for my house instead of heading to hers.

Now that the adrenaline coursing through me has slowed, I feel the throb from my hand to my shoulder. I have decent form, so if I'm feeling it, Adley must really be suffering.

Good.

I can't even think about him without my vision going hazy around the edges. I look over to find her eyes on me, but even that connection that hums between us isn't enough to ease my nerves right now.

As soon as we pass under the train bridge, I pull off on a side road, then turn again into the storage units off Carnegie.

I throw the car in park, lock the doors, then unlatch my seatbelt in a matter of seconds.

I turn to her, desperate, my voice shaking as I make my request.

"Get over here. I need to fucking feel you."

She wastes no time scrambling to undo her seatbelt, climbing over the center console as I move the driver's seat as far back as it'll go.

As soon as she straddles me, she sinks down, and I wrap my arms around her. I hold her as tight as possible, burying my face into the scratchy lace of her top as she shucks off my jacket she's wearing.

"It's okay," she soothes, running her nails along the back of my head as I squeeze her even tighter. "I'm okay. We're okay."

A crushing sense of need slams into me then, and I have to pull her face down to mine and kiss her. I have an obligation to her—but it's so much more than that. Taking care of this woman isn't just my responsibility—it feels like my goddamn purpose. Never in my life have I wanted something for myself the way I want her now.

It's disorienting. And disconcerting. But I refuse to fight it. I claimed her in front of a hundred people tonight. I told Adley she was my girlfriend. And yet I'm still not satisfied. I'm desperate to know that we're on the same page. I'm determined to make sure she knows she's mine.

I lick along the seam of her lips, then dip my tongue into her mouth. I kiss her again and again, up and down her neck and chest, as I frantically unbutton and push down her pants. Her chest heaves against me, and I can't resist biting her breasts through the thin, see-through fabric of her shirt.

"Yes?" I question as I push aside her panties.

"Fuck yes," she confirms on her next breath, rolling her hips forward against my hand. Her center is wet and warm, welcoming me home as I plunge two fingers inside her. My thumb finds her clit, then her body sets the rhythm as her hips start to move. I make quick work of stroking her sweet spots, desperate to get her there as quickly as possible.

There'll be time to savor her later.

Right now, I need to feel her come undone.

"That's it, baby girl. Ride my hand and let me fucking feel you."

I kiss her again, desperate for more, as she moans into my mouth.

She locks her thighs around my arm and throws her head back in ecstasy.

"Maddie."

Her head snaps up on command.

I drink her in, wide-eyed and wanton as I keep fucking her with my hand.

"I know this is just for the summer, but while we're together like *this*," I press on her clit for emphasis, "You're mine."

She nods frantically, already on the edge of release.

"No one else touches you. No one else tastes you. No one gets to see you like this," I snarl as I smash my face into her tits and drive her body higher.

"Say it, princess," I demand.

"I'm... oh fuck..."

I don't break pace, but I double down on my command. "Say. It."

She cries out, and the walls of her pussy clench around my fingers. As she pulsates, she pants. "I'm yours. I'm yours. Fuck... Dempsey... I'm yours."

She whispers the words I need, over and over, again and again, until she's breathless. I ease my hand out of her, then stick both fingers in my mouth to lick them clean.

"That's my girl. You're so sweet, Maddie. You're so sweet, and you're all mine." I paint her bottom lip with my thumb before she greedily sucks it into her mouth.

"You're mine," I repeat before I groan from the sensation of her mouth around me. I rest my forehead on hers and pull her into another hug. "Just like I'm yours. For the rest of summer... it's you and me."

Chapter 32

Maddie

My eyes flutter open as memories of last night come flooding back.

Sneaking into the house.

Sinking into the sheets that smelled like fresh tobacco and caramel.

Riding his cock for hours as he showered me in words of praise.

The first half of the night was out of control. I felt terrified, vindicated, cherished, then disregarded all in the span of an hour. But when we got to my car and found Adley waiting—everything fucking changed.

Dempsey went total caveman on Andrew's ass, and the feminist in me leached right out of my body in that parking lot. I swear I got wet watching Dem smash the other man's face in. I should probably look for a little bone-shaped bow on Etsy and start calling myself Pebbles. Who knew caveman mode could be so unbelievably sexy?

Regardless of what today brings, Dempsey and I are no longer close to being over like I had thought for a whole five minutes last night.

I yawn, then roll back slightly to seek him out, wiggling under the sheets until we're spooning, his lean, strong body pressing up against my curves. I slept in his work shirt from last night, the black V-neck engulfing me. He teased me for wearing his dirty clothes, but there's something about being wrapped up in the fabric he was wearing when he went after Adley not once, but twice, that just fucking does it for me.

Yabadabadoo. I always did have a thing for Bamm-Bamm.

"Good morning," I murmur, reaching behind me to take his hand and kiss his knuckles. He lets me place his hand on the bare skin of my hip but quickly brushes up to hold my shirt-covered waist instead.

His touch is tentative, so I shake my ass into his crotch to tease him. Instead of reciprocating, he grunts and shifts back slightly, putting a sliver of space that feels like a canyon between us.

Huh.

"What time is it?" I ask through another yawn and reach for his arm again. Lifting his wrist out from under the covers, I catch sight of bare skin where his watch always rests.

I roll over and meet his lagoon-blue eyes. Instead of locking me in his gaze like usual, he avoids eye contact. Instead of seeing right into my soul, it's like he's looking past me.

An inkling transforms into a knowing. I analyze him for two more seconds, then I school my expression so I don't give myself away.

This isn't Dempsey.

What the fuck is *Fielding* doing in this bed?

I turn back to my side, scooching over until I can reach my phone on the nightstand. I glance over my shoulder to find him studying me, then quickly turn back to shield my phone from view.

Maddie: I just woke up to the wrong twin spooning me. He doesn't know I know it's not you. I'm gonna fuck with him.

I smile to myself before laying my phone face down on the nightstand again and crawling back to the middle of the bed. I grab his hand and drape my body over his in a way that makes it impossible for him to put any space between us.

"Baby, do that thing I like," I croon, moving his hand down so it's skimming my hip again.

"Uh, what thing?" he grunts, balling his hand into a fist when he touches bare skin.

So he *does* have some sort of limit. Interesting.

"You know. That thing," I whine, prying open his hand and lacing our fingers together. "Or maybe we could try that fantasy I told you about the other day."

I'm playing with fire here. But he's the one who struck the match. Now he needs to burn.

He clears his throat and shifts away from me. Any farther and he's going to fall off the damn bed...

"What was it again?" he stammers. He's clearly uncomfortable. He *has* to know I'm fucking with him at this point—doesn't he?

I turn around and face him. No way am I missing his reaction.

"You know. The one where you pretend to be your brother."

His eyes triple in size—he's like a cartoon character, his eyes practically popping out of his head—and this time he actually *does* jump off the bed. "Maddie, I—"

"Save your breath, Fielding," I snap. "I already texted him. You might want to make yourself scarce."

As if on cue, Dempsey comes flying into the room, bare chested and worked up into a rage. He scans the bed, his attention first landing on me before turning to his brother.

He charges, and before I know what's happening, they're both on the floor, grunting and exchanging blows.

I was proud of myself for knowing it was Fielding within seconds. But as they tussle on the floor, I can't figure out who's who, or who's winning.

"Uncle... Tony..." one of them grunts from where he's pinned under his brother. "Uncle Tony!" he yells louder, using both hands to shield his face.

Now that they're not moving, I know Dempsey's sitting on top, breathing hard as he keeps his brother pinned.

"Um... who's Uncle Tony?" I giggle.

They look over at me at the same time, their matching blue eyes and perfectly chiseled jawlines a freaking sight to behold. Dempsey hops to his feet, then reaches out one arm and helps Fielding stand.

"Code word to call off a fight," he explains, shoving his brother once for emphasis. "Uncle Tony means total forfeit. Uncle Andy means pause for a breather. And Uncle Buck means fuck right off."

I roll my eyes at his explanation, looking from Fielding to Dempsey, then back to Fielding again.

I'm here. *He* knows I'm here. And yet neither of them is acting like this is an earth-shattering revelation that's going to change our dynamic or ruin their relationship.

Dempsey walks over to the bed and props up on the edge, holding out one arm to me in invitation. I crawl over to him, careful to keep my ass covered now that we have an audience.

"You okay?" he murmurs into my hair and strokes my shoulder as I sink into his touch and hum my reassurance.

"Dude," Fielding starts, calling our attention to where he's bent over and panting in the middle of the room. "She did it," he declares. "She seriously did it."

Uncertainty shoots through me as I look between the brothers. Fielding's smirking. I don't know what the hell he's playing at. I didn't do shit. I wouldn't. Dem knows that.

"You're an idiot. If you didn't already have a broken rib, I'd break one for you," Dempsey quips.

Fielding grins, puts both hands on his head, and does a twirl right in the middle of his brother's bedroom.

"Bro. She *knew*!"

"I'm lost," I interject. "What did I supposedly know?"

"You knew I wasn't him," Fielding answers without missing a beat. "I don't know when it clicked—"

"The second you gripped my hip differently than he does," I retort.

Dempsey pushes off the mattress, strides across the room, and smacks his brother upside the head.

"Don't touch my girlfriend," he scolds, coming back to sit beside me as Fielding and I lock eyes.

Did he just...

"Girlfriend, huh? I see how it is," Fielding snickers. He raises his eyebrows and shakes his head. "That tells me everything I need to know. My work here is done."

He backs out of the room wearing the biggest shit-eating grin. "She can tell us apart, Dem," he whispers excitedly before slapping the top of the door frame and finally leaving the room.

Dempsey and I exhale in unison.

"*What* just happened?" I ask, half-amused, half-shocked.

"Fielding just happened." Dempsey sighs and wraps me in a hug before resting his chin on my shoulder. "I'm so sorry. Did he touch you anywhere else or make you uncomfortable?" he asks tentatively, his brows pulled together in worry.

"I'm fine," I laugh. It would take a whole lot more than Fielding copping a feel to scare me off. "What is he going on about, though?"

Dempsey sighs again before answering. "It's... it's something we used to play at when we were younger. We're identical twins."

"No shit." I roll my eyes. "But you're nothing alike. I'm sure plenty of people can tell you apart."

Dempsey side-eyes me, then shakes his head. "No one either of us has dated has *ever* been able to tell us apart."

My eyes widen at that revelation. So this is a thing? They pretend to be each other to trick one another's partners... and it works?

"Wait—what about your ex-fiancée?" I challenge.

He's mentioned Brooke a few times before, usually when he's telling me a story about college. I've never brought her up or pushed for details... but the man has called me his girlfriend twice in the last twenty-four hours. That gives me some sort of rights, doesn't it?

"No. And he tested Brooke three different times. She was *not* happy about it..." Dempsey looks off toward the balcony attached to his bedroom and shakes his head.

I try to bury my grin. "I guess I should be proud of myself. I could tell the difference just from his touch."

A disgruntled *hmph* rumbles in his chest as he pulls me back against his body.

"Are you jealous, Dem?" I raise one hand and wrap it around his neck, pulling him close so I can whisper in his ear. "Maybe you should remind me what you feel like so he can't try and trick me again."

"He won't be fucking touching you again," he growls before scooping me up and placing be back down in the middle of the bed.

"Hey, wait." I press my hands into his chest as he tries to join me. "Are you okay now that he knows? I thought this would be a bigger deal."

Obviously there's no turning back. But Fielding finding out about us and Fielding finding me half-naked in his brother's bed are two very different scenarios.

Dempsey sucks in a breath, then lowers himself next to me, propping his head on one hand. "It is what it is. I would have preferred to tell him myself, but I don't regret how everything went down. I did what I had to do to keep you safe last night."

I brush my hand along his jaw, and he closes his eyes and leans into my touch. He's always taking care of everyone—It brings me immense joy when he lets me comfort him in return.

"Thank you for what you did, Dem. I know... I know this wasn't how it was supposed to go. I'm sorry if I made things more complicated for you."

He opens his eyes and brings my hand to his lips. "Worth it," he murmurs as he kisses along my knuckles.

"On the plus side, we don't have to sneak around anymore, right?" I offer. "Unless—"

He cuts me off with a hard, demanding kiss on the mouth. "Unless nothing. What I said last night stands. It's you and me for the rest of summer, princess. You and me."

I smile against his mouth and let out a little squeal as I pull him into me.

"Now, what did you need, baby girl?" he asks, working his lips over my jaw and down my neck as his hands explore my body under his oversized T-shirt. "Something about a reminder of what I feel like?"

I nod so fast my vision blurs.

Dempsey hops off the bed, laughing. "Lay down and get comfy while I lock the door. I wouldn't put it past him to barge back in now that he knows you're here."

Chapter 33

Dempsey

She's a fucking mess under my tongue.

A panting, writhing, convulsing mess.

I've kept her locked in my room for hours. I've made her call out my name more times than I can count. She's come three times so far—once on my tongue, twice on my cock.

She told me she needed to be reminded of what I felt like.

Baby girl, I'm going to make sure you never forget the feel of me.

"Dem," she pants, her thighs clenching around my ears as she tries to push me away. "Fuck. Dem. It feels so good, but I can't. I can't do it."

I refocus my efforts, beckoning slowly against her G-spot, concentrating all the pressure right where she needs it. I lap softly at her clit, teasing just the tip of my tongue over her overly sensitive bundle of nerves.

"I can't," she pants again.

But I know her tells now. Her breathing is getting heavier, and her tight, swollen channel is pulsing around my fingers.

"You can, and you will," I tell her, peeking up just long enough to take in her gorgeous, naked body splayed out on my bed.

"Come on, baby girl. Give me one more," I encourage. I suck her clit into my mouth, not coming up for air until she screams and claws at the sheets.

I break away but keep massaging her G-spot, cheering my girl on as her body trembles with release. "Come, come, come, come," I murmur in time with my strokes.

She arches up in pleasure, her legs tensing as she climaxes. I press into her G-spot as she bares down, and she cries out again, then she squirts so hard she soaks halfway down my forearm.

"Thatta fucking girl," I praise, gently pulling out of her as she pants on my now very wet sheets. "Fuck, Maddie. You look so gorgeous when you soak me."

She throws her arm over her eyes and shakes her head, but I pull that arm away and kiss her. Hard. I fucking love the way her body responds to me.

"I've never done that before," she confesses, pulling me down until I'm crushing her into the mattress. We almost always lie like this after sex, naked and sated, chest to chest. I tease her about being her living, breathing weighted blanket. But I crave the intimacy as much as she does.

"You did so good, princess. You did so good for me. But now that you've told me that, I'm gonna have to make you squirt more often."

"Dempsey!" She hits me playfully, and I catch her mouth in another kiss. She knows I'm teasing. Although I would love nothing more than to spend each day trying to break my orgasm record with this woman.

"I think I need a nap," she yawns. "And I definitely need a shower."

"Sleep now," I encourage. "I have to leave for work in a few hours. I'll wake you up so you have enough time to shower and change before we head back to The Oak."

She nods sleepily, and I stroke her hair as she drifts off. Once I know she's out for sure, I get up and take my own shower, then dress so I can take care of the one thing I've been dreading all day.

Fielding's been on mom duty all weekend, like we'd originally planned. He texted me this morning before he realized I was here to say she was okay but hadn't eaten much.

I make my way into the kitchen, intent on whipping up some eggs and toast. If she's in the middle of a spell, it's not likely she'll eat. But sometimes just leaving food on her nightstand does the trick, so it's worth a try.

"Sup, bro?" he calls out, walking barefoot and bare chested from the patio, through the living room, and into the kitchen. He's wearing board shorts and dripping wet, which he knows pisses me off.

I grab a tea towel from the drawer by the sink and chuck it in his direction.

"Two extra minutes, and you'd dry off enough *not* to trek water all over the house," I scold.

He smirks and sips from his bendy straw. He won a Coke Freestyle machine at a charity auction a few years ago, then customized the thing so it dispenses more than 120 soda options, plus rum instead of water.

Clever. But dangerous.

I side-eye him as he takes another sip, the unasked question lingering between us.

"It's Dr. Pepper," he finally relents with an eye roll. "And it's not my fault I had to run in here without drying off to your specifications. I wanted to catch you while you're on break from making that girl scream your name."

"*That girl* has a name," I retort. "I figured I had to make it up to her since she got manhandled by your sorry ass this morning."

"Oh, believe me, brother. I know that girl's name. I'm less concerned with her name and more concerned with what you called her this morning. What was that word you used? *Girlfriend*?"

I say nothing, overwhelmed by shame at having him find out about Maddie by discovering her in my bed. I was going to tell him today—I knew I had to after what went down at The Oak last night—he just beat me to the revelation. I spray a misting of oil in the pan, then move toward the fridge to get out the rest of what I need.

"Is that for Mom?" he asks, jutting his chin toward the pan heating up on the stove.

"Yeah. I figured I'd try eggs and toast."

He nods, then shuffles around me before opening a cupboard and pulling down the blender. "I'll make her a smoothie."

Silence settles between us as we prepare food and he waits me out.

"How'd you know she was in my room?" I finally ask, because I've honestly been dying to know.

"I got a text last night."

"From who?" I demand.

He chuckles to himself as he chops an apple, shaking his head like he almost doesn't believe what he's about to say. "Jake."

"Jake?" I deadpan, my anger spiking as I crack an egg against the countertop.

"Believe me, brother. I was as surprised as you."

Why the hell would Jake, of all people, feel compelled to text my brother? Out of all the guys, he was the last one I expected to spill the beans. He and I are close, and he and Fielding are... not. They used to be. But things changed. I didn't even know they talked anymore.

"I don't think he did it to be malicious," Fielding defends, throwing the apple pieces into the blender before dropping a handful of spinach in a colander to rinse. "He wanted to know the whole story with Adley and to make sure I was okay. He hadn't seen any of the videos from the party."

I add another egg to the pan, then sprinkle them with salt and pepper. I watch as the edges transform from clear to opaque, my frustration at my boss and supposed friend mounting as the eggs pop and sizzle in the pan.

"He said he wanted to make sure I didn't hear pieces of the story from someone else," Fielding offers, adding the last few ingredients to the blender, then plugging it in. "He said a lot of the guys were there last night, and that the place was packed. I honestly think he was trying to do the right thing by giving me a heads-up."

He starts the blender, and the whirl of the motor cuts off my ability to speak. I shift the eggs around in the pan, spooning a little oil onto them as they get closer to being done.

I'm pissed that Jake would take it upon himself to break the news to my brother like that. Especially after he and I had a conversation about keeping this from both Rhett and Fielding.

But I guess it was naïve to expect nothing to change after what happened at the bar last night. And out of all the guys who could have texted Fielding about what went down, Jake knew the most about the context of the situation.

As the blender dies down, I realize it doesn't matter who told Fielding first. He shouldn't have had to hear it from anyone but me.

"Look," I start as he reaches for a glass. "I'm sorry you had to find out about Maddie and me like this. And I'm sorry that I kept her a secret. It wasn't supposed to be anything with her. I never expected—"

"Dumpy." He levels me with a look that forces me to stop what I'm doing. "I meant what I said to you the night she saved my ass. Whatever happens between you and her... I'm good."

"You shouldn't have to be, though. Out of all the girls in this damn town for me to—"

"Bro. Seriously. Stop." He pours the smoothie into a glass and gets out a tray, then reaches past me to pop bread into the toaster. I move the eggs off the burner and turn back to face him.

"None of what I feel for Tori makes sense. I know that. I'm still reeling from what happened... but I also realize how messed up it was. I made a lot of shitty choices. And even if I hadn't, I doubt it would have gone my way. I don't hate her. Or Rhett, for that matter."

He crosses his arms and leans back against the kitchen island, seemingly lost in thought. When he speaks again, his voice is softer, with a tremble to its tenor. "I saw your face when you ran into the room this morning. You called her your fucking girlfriend, bro. And the fact that she can actually tell us apart... fuck."

He shakes his head and smiles.

"If you want Little Wheeler, have her. Have her and hold on to her for as long as you can. Just stop using me as an excuse. You do it with everything—but you don't need to do it with her."

I don't bother replying—some of what he says makes sense. But it still feels like a betrayal to let myself be happy when he's so fucking miserable.

"I'm serious, Dumpy. You know I wouldn't say it if I didn't mean it."

That's true.

He reaches past me again, retrieving the toast that just popped up and plating it along with the eggs. Then he adds silverware and a glass of water to the tray and plucks an iris out of the arrangement on the island as a finishing touch.

It doesn't feel right to be happy without him. But being miserable right alongside him hasn't seemed to make a difference, either.

"I got this," he says, lifting the tray and balancing it on one hand as he picks up his Dr. Pepper with the other. "Love you, bro. Have a good night at work," he calls over his shoulder as he makes his way down the hall. "And hey. Look at the bright side. If you and Little Wheeler get married someday, maybe Tori will save me a dance at the wedding."

Chapter 34

Maddie

Four Weeks Later

Days turn into weeks. Weeks roll into a month. Before I know it, I'm lounging in Dempsey's arms, watching the annual Hampton Fourth of July Fireworks from my front lawn.

We spent all day sunbathing and playing in the pool. Dempsey bought fancy steak burgers from the butcher shop downtown, and I whipped up a fruit salad and a double batch of my mom's homemade mac and cheese so he can take leftovers home to Fielding. It was a low-key day, and I loved every damn minute of it.

Rhett tried to convince me to come up to the cabin for the weekend, but listening to him and Tori fuck each other's brains out while trying to hold my temper around Jake didn't sound like my idea of a good time.

Dem told me it was Jake who outed us to Fielding. Something about that really grinds my gears. Yes, Fielding would have found out eventually... but what the fuck? Wasn't that Dempsey's news to tell?

The only decent thing Jake's done lately is close Clinton's and The Oak for the weekend. Last year, they were dead on the Fourth of July weekend because so many people go on vacation around this time. That means I've had Dem to myself for the last two days.

I sit up a little straighter, craning my neck to watch some of the lower displays as they explode in the sky. Even when we were younger, we could only see about half the fireworks they shot off at the park near our neighborhood. Now that the trees have had another decade to grow, I would put visibility around 30 percent at best.

It doesn't matter. We aren't paying attention to the fireworks anyway.

His hands are everywhere. His mouth keeps finding new spots to kiss and lick. I can barely lean back against him without wanting to straddle him right here on my front lawn and put on a different kind of show for the neighbors. The way this man has learned my body over the last month out-blasts every firework in the goddamn sky.

"I wanted to ask you something," Dempsey whispers in my ear as he traces along the outline of my tank top. I look back, and he smiles down at me, his fingers dipping in and out of my shirt, mindlessly caressing my cleavage.

I'm always amped up and ready to go when we're together, but there's also a familiarity and comfort between us now. It's this deep, delicious sense of ease that I've never felt around anyone but my family. Being with him has become second nature. I feel most like the version of myself I want to be when I'm in Dempsey's arms.

"Would you like to go to New York City with me?"

I sit up so fast I make myself dizzy.

"Are you serious?"

He smiles and sticks his tongue in his cheek, peering over at me with this carefree, amused expression.

"Of course I'm serious."

"When?" I demand, already visualizing my calendar in my head. I don't have a work schedule to consider or much of anything else going on, but it's already July fourth. And I'm heading back to California on July thirty-first.

"Next weekend?" he asks, as if it's up to me.

"Yes. Hell yes. Oh my gosh, Dem. I'm so excited! But wait, why New York City?"

"I have to sign some papers from my mom's lawyer since I have power of attorney for her estate. He offered to fly out to Hampton like he normally does, but I thought maybe you'd like to go on a trip and spend a few days in the city."

He pulls me back into him, encouraging me to lean back again. But I'm way too restless to sit back and relax now.

New York. New York freakin' City. The Big Apple. Concrete jungle where dreams are made, or something like that. I'm almost positive my mom's DVD of *When Harry Met Sally* is down in the basement somewhere. I'll find it and watch it this week. Maybe I'll have time to rewatch all six seasons of *Sex and the City*, too.

"Have you been to New York before?" he asks as he strokes the skin behind my ear.

I shiver under his touch—which just encourages him to use his other hand to caress the same spot on the other side.

"Once," I reply, reaching back to run my fingers along his forearm as he plays with my hair. "My grandparents took Rhett and me on a sight-seeing trip when we were kids. We stayed at the Plaza hotel and ate our body weight in Babybel cheese from the mini fridge."

He twirls a strand of my hair in his fingers before giving it a little tug. "Wait—are you sure you're not recalling the plot from *Home Alone 2*?"

I swat his hand away and laugh. "No! I swear I've been there! We went to Top of the Rock and took a carriage ride through the park. We saw *Beauty and the Beast* on Broadway. My grandma and I spent a whole day shopping at Macy's and Bloomingdales. On our last day, we took the ferry out to Ellis Island and did the listening tour. None of that happened in any of the *Home Alones*."

"Hmm," he hums mockingly. "I'll have to ask Fielding to be sure. Those are his favorite movies—he'll tell me the truth," he teases before he continues.

"I can't promise there'll be cheese... but I booked us two nights at the Williamsburg Hotel, in the Skyline Suite. It'll take me less than an hour to get the paperwork done, so we'll have plenty of time to explore the city and do anything you want to do."

"It sounds perfect," I gush before a less-exciting thought enters my mind. "Will Fielding be okay on his own again next weekend?"

Dempsey sighs before responding. "He says he will. He's been decent all week, actually. And he's doing Dry July, which he's done before. He always sees it through when he does a dry month or a detox. I think he likes to prove to himself he's in control, regardless of whether there's any truth behind that. He was the one who encouraged us to go... so I'm trying not to overthink it..."

He trails off, and I don't push, instead focusing on the feeling of his hands in my hair. Over the last few weeks, I've started to worry about Fielding more. Maybe it's because I'm around them both so often or because Dempsey's caretaker tendencies are contagious, but either way, it's like my empathy has tripled. I feel for Dempsey, and I feel for Fielding. I care about them both in different but equally deep ways.

Spending so much time with them has unlocked a hard truth that's impossible to ignore. Fielding is no longer the jovial, cocky fuckboy I once knew. He has this darkness about him now: an underlying sadness that's always there, paired with a defensive dry humor he wears like armor. Some days, there are peeks of the happy-go-lucky man I used to know. But then other days, Dempsey says he doesn't move off the couch.

Seeing how Fielding affects Dempsey is hard for me to wrap my head around sometimes. But when we're together, Dem seems to cling to his concern less tightly. I just do my best to give him space when he needs it and to be there for him when he needs a distraction.

"Two days in the city," I sigh, already thinking about what types of outfits I'll need for a weekend in New York.

"Two days. Two nights," he confirms, moving his phenomenal hands to my shoulders. "No responsibilities. No worries. Just you and me, baby girl."

"It sounds perfect," I squeal, rising to my feet as the fireworks finale shoots off in the distance.

"Wait—where are you going?" Dempsey calls after me as I run toward the house. He can grab the blanket and citronella candles—I'm a woman on a mission.

"Dem—you just said we're going to New York City this weekend. That's only six days from now. I have to start packing!"

Chapter 35

Dempsey

We arrived in the city early after a quick, *mostly* uneventful flight. My little spitfire of a girlfriend tried more than once to tempt me into getting cozy under a blanket in first class. But sitting toward the front of the plane meant the flight attendants were right there, and I wasn't about to get us banned from the airline for indecent behavior.

We dropped our bags at the hotel, then I took Maddie to Juniors and insisted she have a piece of cheesecake for breakfast. We walked down to Bridge Park and along Pebble Beach. Then she practically dragged me to the carousel when she spotted it across the way. We watched the thing spin three times before she set her sights on what she declared to be the prettiest horse. But once it was our turn, she realized her dream pony didn't actually move up and down. She made me switch mid-ride, which resulted in a scolding from the ride operator and me ultimately riding the prettiest, albeit stationary, horse on Jane's Carousel.

Only for her.

We took the subway to Manhattan after that and spent the rest of the afternoon in Central Park. We made it just in time for the final penguin feeding session at the Central Park Zoo, then we grabbed gyros from a food cart and settled in for a picnic near Strawberry Fields.

Strawberry Fields with my sweet, strawberry-scented girl. Being in the city with her is fucking heaven. I shouldn't be surprised. She's proved to me time and time again—everything is easy when we're together.

I took care of the paperwork I needed to sign while we were in Manhattan, then we took a cab back across the bridge to get ready for the night. Now we're all dressed up, sitting in the back of one of my father's Escalades, being driven into the city by Glenn, one of my favorite drivers from when we were younger.

"Have you had a good day so far?" I ask, draping an arm around her shoulders and pulling her into my side. We barely had enough time to get into our room, washed up, and changed. We've been together all day, but my body still craves her, even when we're close.

"The best day," she sighs as she leans into me and runs her nails up and down my thigh.

I catch her hand to stop her exploration—she knows what she fucking does to me. My body's craving her too much right now to deal with her teasing. We've only got an hour until showtime, and I'll be damned if we miss the show and she gets anything less than the perfect New York City weekend.

I interlace our fingers and peer out the window to distract myself.

"We're almost to the Brooklyn Bridge," I murmur, directing her attention to the window.

She shifts into my lap so she can see, then rolls down the window for a better view.

She sticks her head out the window and screams as the wind sweeps her hair all over her face. I tighten my hold on her waist on instinct, gripping her against my body until she's fully back inside the vehicle.

"That's incredible," she exclaims, her eyes bright as she wiggles in my lap. "How well do you know this driver?" she purrs, running a hand through my hair in a way I know is intended to pull me under her spell.

The move is unnecessary. I'm completely enchanted by this girl.

"I've known Glenn my whole life. He drove us home from the hospital when we were born, in fact." I can't resist kissing up and down her throat as she melts into me.

"So we trust him?" she asks, tilting her head back and giving me better access as her fingertips trace along my neck. The vehicle slows, and I look out again to see we've just barely made it onto the bridge. Hopefully, there isn't too much traffic between here and Times Square.

"I trust Glenn completely," I proclaim, instantly missing her touch when she slides off my lap and makes her way toward the middle of the cab.

The Escalade has come to a full stop, so I don't think much of Maddie not being buckled. That is, until she shifts to stand, hits the sunroof button, and straddles the two captain's seats so half her body sticks up out of the vehicle.

"Dammit, Maddie," I grunt, but my scolding lacks fire as I unbuckle and move forward to brace her. I wrap one arm around her bare legs, then reach over with the other hand to hit the intercom as she giggles and twists in my grasp.

"What seems to be the holdup, Glenn?" I grit out as I try not to react to her silky smooth legs just inches from my face. I have half a mind to yank her back into the car and smack her ass for this stunt.

"I love you, New York!!" she screams, prompting our driver to chuckle before he replies.

"Accident half a mile ahead on the bridge, Mr. Haas. GPS says we'll be stuck here for a bit longer, but we should make it to the theatre with time to spare."

I run a hand up the back of one of her legs, teasing along the hem of her little black dress as she continues to holler out the sunroof.

"Do *not* move this car without warning me first," I command through the intercom before raising the privacy screen.

"Yes, sir." Glenn chuckles again before the intercom goes silent.

I release my hold on her and make sure her feet are balanced on the seats before running my other hand up her leg. She freezes at my movement—then she peers down at me. Predictably, the look in her eye tells me she's up for whatever version of trouble I'm willing to give her.

"Brace yourself, baby girl. We're about to give NYC a different kind of show."

I shuck off my jacket, then roll up my dress shirt sleeves before hiking up the skirt of her dress to expose her to me. She's not wearing any underwear, and the sight of her perfect cunt has me straining in my pants.

I kneel between the seats she's standing on, wrapping both arms around her body and digging my hands into the back of her thighs. When I bring my mouth to her pussy, she quivers; it's the most satisfying feeling to know I affect her just as much as she affects me.

Her whimper from outside the sunroof is barely audible when I blow against her center, and her pleasure surges down my face when I pierce her with my tongue. But it's the subtle little roll of her hips—her silent demand for *more*—that has me digging my fingers into the flesh of her ass and sucking her clit into my mouth with such intensity she grinds against me.

I loosen my grip on her legs and plunge two fingers into her heat, then grunt in satisfaction when I feel her desire gush around my hand. Her legs are shaking, but we're on a time limit. I stroke her G-spot in rhythm with the way I suck her clit. We're a perfect orchestra of motion as she fucks my face and claims what's hers.

When I feel the first flutters of her release, I rise up higher on my knees, determined to fucking get her there by any means necessary. When I peek up to check on her, she's massaging her tits through her dress—in full view of literally anyone walking or biking along the bridge—her head thrown back in ecstasy as she races toward the finish line.

I nip at her clit, then she shatters, crying out, pounding on the roof of the car, and pulsating around my hand harder than I've ever felt her come.

"Open your eyes, baby girl," I demand when I finally move my mouth away from her pussy. I stroke her G-spot through her orgasm, just how she likes, watching up through the sunroof in reverence as she takes in the view of the Manhattan skyline with the sun setting in the distance.

Even when she comes down, she doesn't get back in the car, instead gazing down at me with that wicked grin that lights me up inside. That look is everything. I'll do everything I can over these last few weeks together to make her smile like that again and again.

She reaches down to run her palm along my chin and mouth, wiping the evidence of her pleasure off my face before I snatch her hand and lick it clean. She doesn't move away immediately—instead caressing me with tender care. I lean into her touch, and she strokes my face, her fingers tracing my jaw and cupping my cheek in a way that feels intimate and sincere.

What this girl has done to me this summer is indescribable. The mark she's left on my spirit—on my *heart*—has been so unexpected.

I silently adjust her dress and try to clear my head of the heavy feelings that hit every time we share a moment like this. I know our end is inevitable—but I want to feel alive with her for every second until then.

She'll be gone in less than a month.

But I have her in my arms for now.

"We're about to move, Mr. Haas," Glenn announces through the intercom.

I tug on Maddie's dress to encourage her back into the car, but she peers down at me and pouts.

"I want to stay up here," she insists, her eyes alight with wonder.

I puff out my cheeks and consider arguing, but to hell with reason and safety when she's flushed with satisfaction and looking down at me like I'm her whole damn world.

"Brace yourself with both hands and hold on, you hear me?"

She nods and does a little dance that has me half-tempted to hitch up her dress again and have my way with her.

"Slow and steady, Glenn," I direct through the intercom as I grip Maddie's waist and hold her tight.

"Yes sir," he replies, his smile apparent in his voice as the Escalade picks up speed.

Chapter 36

Maddie

The beams overhead pass in rapid succession.

The sky is ethereal: light pink and orange. Dusty rose and soft coral.

I've never felt more secure than I do in this moment, standing out of a panoramic sunroof, nothing holding me to this earth but his grip on my thighs.

I'm flying.

I'm free.

The cables and cords of the bridge blur together as emotion overwhelms me.

This is it. This is the happiest I've ever been. If this is the happiest I'll ever get to be, then I'll die a satisfied woman.

There is a magic to being in a relationship with this man. From the way he draws pleasure from my body to the way he embraces who I am, I have never felt so seen.

He doesn't want to change me. He doesn't want to use me. He lifts me up. He lets me be.

There is beauty in being seen; in knowing that this man knows the shape of my soul, and that even if given a chance, he wouldn't change a damn thing.

I'll never forget this moment.

I'll never forget this trip.

I'll never forget this summer or what it was like to be adored by Dempsey Haas.

Chapter 37

Dempsey

I wake up after the most restful night of sleep with her by my side. We spend almost all our nights together nowadays, but there's something about being in the city with her that just feels different. She's asleep on her stomach, her head turned toward me, her pouty pink lips parted and her thick eyelashes fluttering while she dreams.

She's an angel.

A gift I never expected.

This bright, effervescent force that came barreling into my life at the most inopportune time.

Nothing about us makes sense. And yet—we've made this work.

Watching her wistfully as she sleeps, I brush a strand of blond hair from her face. I caress another tendril resting on her bare back.

I look out at the perfect view as the sun starts to rise and shine its reflection on the Manhattan skyline.

My attention drifts back to her gorgeous sleeping form. Is this what it would be like? If this was an option, is this how it would feel?

For one single minute, I let myself envision that this could be my life.

We'd live in a big city: New York or Los Angeles, Chicago or San Francisco. I'd wake up early, like I always do, and get in a workout in our home gym. I'd shower, then prep the coffee. She'd never need to set an alarm clock—I'd wake her up eating her pussy each and every morning, then I'd bring her breakfast in bed.

We'd get ready together, dancing around each other in our penthouse suite or restored loft with an epic view. I'd head into the office; she'd go down to the courthouse. She'd look so fucking hot dressed up for court. She'd smoke all their asses, I'm sure, then we'd meet up in the city for lunch. And maybe a quickie.

Our nights would be spent at fundraisers and sitting on the same side of a booth in dimly lit restaurants. Our weekends would be filled with lazy mornings, runs across the Brooklyn Bridge, and trips to Trader Joe's. Maybe we'd get a dog. I've always wanted a dog.

We'd build a life together. No matter how busy we got, we'd make time for each other. No matter where life took us, we'd be each other's priority. I would never have to worry about her reciprocating my love. If the last several weeks have taught me anything, it's that I can trust her completely. In the privacy of our apartment, in the sanctuary of our bedroom—we'd always come back to the home we made in each other.

I sigh as the dream thins in my mind and all the reasons my life can't be that way bubble up and stain my fantasy.

She rolls over and cuddles closer. "What are you thinking about over there?" she asks through a yawn.

I smile warmly, even though her eyes are still closed. Leaning in, I place the softest kiss on her lips. "I just had a really good dream. The best dream, actually."

She nestles into my chest, and my heart pitter-patters in response. "You deserve to have good dreams, Dem."

I wrap her in my arms and sigh again before we both drift back to sleep.

Chapter 38

Maddie

"Pick out whatever you want," he declares as we push through the rotating doors. I beam back at him over my shoulder, striding into Tiffany & Co. like I own the damn place.

The space is smaller than I expected, but it's still sparkly and amazing—and there are multiple floors. I inhale deeply, my eyes flitting from display case to display case as I soak it all in.

I'm in Tiffany.

I'm in Tiffany on Fifth Avenue in New York City.

I'm in Tiffany on Fifth Avenue with my boyfriend, and he wants me to pick out whatever I want.

I would pinch myself if I was sure he wouldn't notice.

"Anything?" I challenge as I turn to face him and walk backward into the store. He's giving me *that* look, but I know he secretly loves it when I test him.

"Anything, princess. Although keep in mind that it'll be hard to pack fine china for the flight home if you pick tableware or dinnerware."

I stick out my tongue and turn on my heel before skipping toward the first display.

Running my fingers along the seam of the case, I peer through the crystal-clear glass with wide eyes. Everything is so gorgeous—I can hardly decide where to look first.

A case of diamond tennis bracelets catches my eye. They're so bright, I feel compelled to pull out my sunglasses to protect my retinas from the way they glisten under the display lights. A bracelet seems too matronly, though. It's a present a man would buy his sister or his mom, not something he'd buy his temporary summer girlfriend.

I scoff at my own bad joke. Humor always has been one of my favorite defense mechanisms.

We've still got more than three weeks until I leave for California, but since we arrived in the city, it feels like time is moving at warp speed. When I woke up this morning, Dempsey had this far-off, dreamy look on his face. I couldn't help but think about what it would be like to wake up to him every day, even after our summer together is through.

But those kinds of thoughts are pointless. There's no version of our future where I don't go to California to finish school and he doesn't stay in Hampton to care for his mom and brother. My reason for leaving and his reason for staying are equally valid and more than a little similar. We're both stubborn, yes, but we both have rock-solid convictions at the core of who we are as individuals.

I've always dreamed of this big, bold life for myself, regardless of what I have to sacrifice to make it happen. He's determined to care for the people he loves, regardless of what he can't hold on to in the process.

I would never ask him to leave his family. I would resent the hell out of him if he dared to ask me to stay. Our fates are cemented in stone: two separate paths that crossed for one summer but will never merge again.

I clear my throat and focus on the here and now, which garners the attention of the salesperson behind the counter. She asks if there's anything I'd like to see, so I mindlessly point to a pair of earrings to distract myself from my morose thoughts.

When she presents me with the earrings and tells me the price, I almost laugh out loud. There's no way in hell I'm letting Dempsey spend twelve thousand dollars on earrings. I know he's loaded, but that's not the point. It's way too much, especially compared with just how little I can give him in return.

Every minute we're together feels more supercharged than anything I've ever experienced. I refuse to put a price on what our time together has meant to me.

If he wants to buy me something, it needs to be small. Something delicate and unexpected. Something that encapsulates how brilliantly we burned together this summer, for just a blip in time.

I'm shaking my head and saying no thanks to the earrings as Dempsey smooths one hand along my hip. He sidles up behind me before whispering in my ear.

"The money doesn't matter. Pick out what you want and let me buy it for you."

I reach back and take his hand, and we study the pieces behind the glass together as I seek out what feels right. If this gift is the only thing I get to keep when we say our goodbyes, I want it to be something I'll wear every day. Something that reminds me that what we had was real and true.

I circle back to the middle of the store and ask to see a necklace I noticed earlier. I tentatively accept the little blue cardboard backing from the salesperson, then trace one finger along the length of the impossibly thin chain. I look up to find Dempsey's focus on me.

There's a small diamond no bigger than a quilting needle head encased in platinum suspended on the chain. It's unassumingly elegant.

"This one. This is what I want."

He takes the necklace from my hand and balks at the price—only four hundred dollars.

"You're sure?" he challenges, eyeing me skeptically to make sure I'm not just trying to pick something cheap.

I can't explain my reasoning to him. I won't. This is what I want because this is how I want to remember us. Years from now, when I think about this summer, I want to remember how it felt to be with this man.

"I'm sure. It's perfect."

He puts it on for me rather than having them bag it up, and I savor the way his fingers brush my hair aside and caress my skin as he secures the necklace in place. He pays and insists on purchasing the lifetime warranty plan, which makes tears prick behind my eyes without my permission. Damn him for caring about what happens when we're done.

Even after we're ancient history, I'll still have a lifetime guarantee that I'll never forget this summer.

I blink back tears as he takes my hand again and leads me toward the circular doors.

"It's beautiful," he praises before bending down to kiss me on the forehead. "Come on. We've got tickets to the four o'clock showing at The Paris. It's close enough that we can walk."

He guides me out of the store and onto the streets of New York, completely unaware that I'm mentally unraveling about the end of us.

Chapter 39

Maddie

We're pressed together in the same side of a booth at a rotating bar on the forty-eighth floor of a hotel in the middle of Times Square. The fringe of my blush pink cocktail dress tickles my thigh every time Dempsey brushes against my leg. Which is often. So often.

We're drinking Cosmos at my insistence. He's been such a good sport this weekend, indulging all my tourist-y wishes and being the perfect guide. I take another sip of my drink and listen intently as he tells me about the time he helped his brother break into the headmaster's office when they were thirteen so Fielding could steal back the weed that had been confiscated earlier that day.

"Glenn was in on the whole thing. He's the one who drove us back to school that night for the recon mission." He smirks before taking another gulp of his vibrantly pink drink. It's only the second or third time I've seen him drink all summer. I like that he feels free enough here to do things he doesn't let himself do at home.

"When our parents showed up for the meeting the next day, Field and I could barely keep it together. The poor headmaster's face when he went to pull the weed out of the drawer and couldn't find it." Dempsey throws his head back in a fit of laughter, and I can't help but join in. I seriously love seeing him like this.

"Our mom was so pissed that she'd canceled her luncheon for nothing. I'm pretty sure our father suspected there was more to the story, but he never pushed, and we never told. Glenn didn't either, obviously. Fielding and I are legends in the hallowed halls of Fletcher Rigby Academy for Boys."

Our server stops by, and Dem orders us another round, then pulls me closer beside him.

"You look so fucking good tonight, baby girl," he whispers in my ear as he plays with the fringe along the hem of my dress. "I can't wait to get you back to the hotel so I can fuck you with this on and feel this fringe tickling my dick."

I squirm along the booth bench at the idea. "Do we really need another round?" I tease, biting down on my lower lip as I work my hand dangerously high up his pant leg.

"We do," he retorts as he lifts my hand from his thigh and laces our fingers together. "It's our last night in the city. I want to make every minute count."

A figure steps in front of our table, blocking out the glow of Times Square from the floor-to-ceiling windows. I look up to thank our server, only to see a woman standing before us instead.

"Dempsey?"

I watch, perplexed, as Dempsey rises and greets the woman with enthusiastic familiarity. They hug and gush, each one insisting they can't believe the other is here. I cross my legs and recross them again as the seconds tick by, growing increasingly aware of how comfortable they are with each other as they interact.

When they finally remember they're not the only two people in the room, Dempsey turns to me and grins.

"Maddie—this is my friend Brooke. Brooke, this is Maddie."

Brooke. *The* Brooke? Holy shit. This is Brooke.

I rise to stand and offer her my hand as we not-so-subtly assess each other. She's gorgeous—dressed in this striking silky pant suit with her dark brown hair twisted into an intricate crown on her head.

Her eyes aren't unkind, but they aren't welcoming either. We exchange "nice to meet yous" and she immediately turns back to Dempsey, only regarding me again when she catches him brushing his hand with mine.

I get the innate sense that she wants nothing more than for me to skedaddle, and I'm so out of my element that I'm more than happy to oblige.

"I'm going to go to the bathroom," I whisper in Dem's ear. Not because I actually have to go. But because giving them a few minutes of privacy feels like the right thing to do.

He squeezes my hand once and pecks me on the cheek in a move I know she notices. His hand slides down my back as I angle to move out of the booth, and he fans his hand along the fringe that's just barely covering my ass as I walk away.

If there was any question about what we are to each other, he just made it perfectly clear.

Or did he?

He introduced me as Maddie, which is fine. But he's called me his girlfriend on more than one occasion over the last few weeks. He just didn't say it to her.

I glance back at the two of them, careful to watch my balance as I walk in high heels through the rotating, circular bar. They're sitting in our booth now, and she's got a hand resting on his arm. They look like long-lost friends, eager to catch up. That, or former lovers, sprinkling fuel onto embers of the past.

I huff out a sigh of frustration as I push into the ladies' room. It's actually harder to pee in this dress than to just hold it—the sacrifices we make for fashion—so I busy myself with fluffing my hair and washing my hands. As I study myself in the mirror over the sink, my new necklace catches my attention, and a wave of insecurity slams into me.

What the hell does it mean that we ran into his ex-fiancée in a city with more than eight million people? What are the chances that they're both here, on the same night, in the same bar?

I toy with my necklace and try to get my head on straight. We were only ever going to be temporary. I *know* that. So why do I keep thinking about the moment he rose to his feet without hesitation and wrapped her in a hug?

They look good together, I'll give them that. I don't know what I expected Brooke to look like, but she's gorgeous; the epitome of grace and class. Probably the type of woman who dreams of supporting her husband and raising a family. She would be the perfect partner for him now and into the future.

They make sense together.

We never did.

Maybe the kindest thing I can do for him is give him this night. Maybe there's a reason we ended up at this bar. Maybe this is why he was supposed to be in the city this weekend. I just happened to be along for the ride.

By the time I make my way back to the table, my mind is made up.

Dempsey moves over so I can sit beside him, but I give him a subtle headshake and reach past him for my wristlet.

"I'm actually not feeling well, so I'm gonna catch a cab back to the hotel."

He wraps a hand around my wrist, freezing me in place. "Did you get sick? Are you okay?"

I resist rolling my eyes as his caregiver instincts take over. I should have come up with a better excuse. "I'm fine. Or I will be. I just want to go to bed."

He starts to rise as he speaks. "We'll head back together. Brooke, it was so good to—"

"No," I insist, pushing against his shoulder and willing him to sit back down. "Stay. Catch up. I don't need you to come with me."

"Maddie."

"Dempsey," I mimic his stern brunch daddy voice.

"It was nice to meet you," I offer, turning to Brooke and mustering up what I hope is a cordial smile.

I look back to Dem and school my expression. "Don't rush. I'm fine. I'll see you back at the hotel," I insist with finality as I stride toward the exit.

I make it as far as the lobby.

I don't know what he said to Brooke or how he took care of the bill that fast. But before I can push out the doors, his arm is ensnaring my waist.

"What the hell do you think you're doing?" he hisses in my ear. The heat and stink of the city hits me at the same time I feel his solidness at my back. "I'm not letting you walk around New York City alone at night."

I don't stop, but he doesn't loosen his hold. Instead, he guides me to the corner of the bank of doors, tucked away behind a giant potted plant.

He looms over me as the marble tiles of the building façade cool my back.

"Go back to your friend, Dem. I'm fine on my own."

His mouth falls agape before he catches my chin in his hand. "What is wrong with you?" he demands, scanning my body like maybe the answer is hidden beneath the fringe of this damn dress.

"What's wrong with me? What's wrong with *you*?" I spit back, swatting his hand away from my face. "You're so stubborn. You know that? That girl—that *woman* up there is clearly still in love with you, Dempsey! Do you think it's random happenstance that she was here tonight? Maybe you were supposed to run into her here! What the hell are you doing wasting time chasing after me?"

The words tumble out of my mouth. I don't even know why I'm saying any of this. I don't *want* him to go running back to her. But we were only ever a summer fling. If there's a reason the Universe brought them together tonight after all this time...

"She's not who I came with," he growls. "And she's not who I'm leaving with tonight."

I shove my hands against his shoulders, desperate to dislodge him and send him back to her. "It's fine, Dempsey. You're being ridiculous. Just go back in there and have a good time. You deserve to put yourself first for once in your fucking life."

He smirks, then peels my hands off his body, one after another. "Nice try, princess."

"I'm serious!" I insist.

"No, Maddie. *I'm* serious." He pins me against the marble with his body, then slowly brushes one hand down the length of my torso. My legs part involuntarily as he travels farther south, my cunt a traitorous bitch under the spell of his touch. When he cups my pussy, I whimper.

"You listen, and you listen good."

I open my mouth to cut him off. He pushes my panties aside and circles my clit to silence me.

"Keep that bratty mouth closed for one goddamn minute, princess, or I swear—"

I'm already slick enough to coat his hand. He pushes two fingers into me with almost no resistance.

"*You*." He bows low and blocks me in, shielding us from view of the chaos and traffic of Times Square. Even if someone was watching, I wouldn't notice. The way he's commanding my attention in this moment—my only focus is him.

"You're my number one, Maddie. *You*. This is me putting myself first for the first time in a long time. Choosing you is choosing me. And it's fucking terrifying." He moves his fingers in and out of me slowly, creating enough friction to make me tremble, but not enough to build me up.

"I walk around every day thinking it could be our last. That you'll come to your senses. Because why would you want me? My life's a mess. My time's not my own. I've got more baggage than I know what to do with."

He's deeper now, and my body takes charge, baring down on his hand. I can do nothing but breathe through the pleasure and soak in his words as he continues working me over.

"That first night you walked into The Oak, I felt it. We both did. I did everything in my power to lock you out once I found out who you were. But you pushed." He beckons against my G-spot, and I swear my legs would give out beneath me if he didn't have me pinned to this wall.

"You pushed and you pushed and you pushed." Every word is another stroke as he drives me higher and higher.

"Even after I gave in, I assumed you'd tire of me. That we'd fizzle without the chase." He kisses me hard, then pulls back an inch before speaking his truth against my lips.

"But you didn't leave. We haven't fizzled. You're here. *You. Stayed*."

He puts firm pressure on my pulsing channel and rubs my clit so hard I'm afraid it's going to fall off. I close my eyes and shudder in pleasure as I freefall off the deep end—his ministrations and the truth of his words equally responsible.

He kisses me again, and it feels so good I want to cry. "Look at me, Maddie," he coaxes as he eases out from between my legs and smooths down my dress.

When we lock eyes, I know what he's about to say will change everything.

"That woman up there? She and I have a history. I thought she was the love of my life. I thought she'd be the mother of my children."

I turn my head as he speaks, overwhelmed by the thought of him building a life with her. He's not mine to keep. But I *hate* the idea of him being with anyone else. He turns my chin back to him, just like he's done so many times before, and forces me to meet his gaze.

"But she left, Maddie. She made her choice. She chose not to stay." He whispers the next words into the crook of my neck. "She's not you."

I shudder again as I'm overcome with emotion. All this talk about staying… and yet we're weeks away from saying goodbye. I can't think of it. I can't possibly imagine what it'll feel like to go back to a version of my life where he isn't by my side.

He barely let me get out of the goddamn building tonight. How will he let me go for good at the end of the month?

He cups my face in his hands and plants a kiss on my forehead. "You're mine. And I'm yours."

"Until the end of summer," I remind him, searching his face for any sign of uncertainty.

He doesn't give me what I'm looking for. There's no resolve or acceptance in his eyes. He looks pained—his expression matching the truth of how I feel.

Seconds tick by, and then a whole minute passes in which neither of us says anything. I hate this. And yet here we are already. Three weeks to go. It won't be enough. Part of me wants to put us both out of our misery and end it now.

Finally, his jaw ticks, and he glares at me like he's glowering into my soul before he grips my head tighter in his hands and presses his forehead into mine.

"Until the end of summer," he finally relents.

Chapter 40

Dempsey

We're both sleepy and sated on the drive from Brooklyn to JFK. Neither of us slept much, instead choosing to spend the night fucking each other senseless.

There was a desperation between us after the run-in with Brooke. We didn't speak of it; we just acted on instinct. It was a fire in my belly that I couldn't douse, no matter how many times I made her orgasm or how long I stayed buried inside her.

For her to challenge me like that... and for me to respond the way I did...

I had no intention of staking my claim, pouring my heart out, and finger fucking her in the middle of Times Square to prove a point.

But apparently that's what we both needed.

It was wild running into Brooke, in a city she and I used to dream about living in together. It was also a wake-up call.

What Maddie doesn't know is that Brooke *did*, at one time, have a hold on me. There was a time in the not-so-faraway-past where I would have run into her, with or without someone else by my side, and the night would have gone a very different direction. Things with Brooke were good and easy when we were together, but that's because my life was good and easy back then.

There was nothing good, easy, or pleasant about the end of us.

Brooke and I didn't break up as much as she just didn't show up. She chose not to follow through on her promise, and I couldn't even be mad about her choice.

Toward the end of our senior year at Harvard, Fielding declared he wouldn't be going to medical school as planned. Instead, he decided he'd move back to Hampton to take care of our mom. It was an idea I had considered time and time again. He just came to the decision first.

If it was cancer or Parkinson's or Alzheimer's or any other disease, we would have made the same choice.

He chose to pause his life, and I felt compelled to do the same. Sometimes I think he resents me for following him home, but in my heart of hearts, I know it was the right thing to do.

Brooke and I were already engaged by then. I had won an entrepreneurship grant, and she was eager to get her master's degree in art history from NYU. When I told her about my plans to take care of my mom, she was all in.

She originally agreed to pause our wedding plans and take a gap year before getting her master's. She was adamant that she would move to Hampton, and I moved into a separate wing of the house so we'd have our own space.

Plans were set. Her flight was booked. All her things were packed up and shipped to Ohio, and I'd started unpacking some of her stuff the week she was set to arrive.

But the day before her flight, she called and said she couldn't do it.

She loved me, but she couldn't wait around for an indefinite amount of time.

She wanted to be with me, but only if I could put her first.

She wasn't willing to share the podium with my mom and my brother.

The logical part of me understood. And looking back, I know she made the right call. Fielding and I have existed in purgatory for the last four years. We've put our lives on hold with no timeline or frame of reference for when we'll be able to move forward.

I don't resent Brooke. But it was heartbreaking to realize the person I considered my ride or die wasn't even willing to ride.

I pined after her for a long time. I wondered if someday, maybe—when my life was less messy. When I wasn't responsible for anyone but me—maybe we'd find our way back to each other, and we could move forward with all the plans we had made in college.

Brooke *used* to have what I thought was an unshakable hold on me. But I've learned what it means to have true, unconditional support. And I learned it all from the girl who came into The Oak and, honest to God, turned my world upside down.

Maddie showed me what it's like to be unafraid. She taught me how to trust that someone could stand by my side, even when things are tough. She gave me space when I needed space. She was flexible when plans had to change.

How the hell Maddie Wheeler taught me more about life and love in the last few months than I've learned in the previous twenty-seven years of existence is beyond me.

I kiss her hair and pull her closer in the back of the SUV. She's wearing one of my shirts, like she loves to do, under an oversized zip up hoodie she bought from a street vendor. It's navy blue, with the word "Brooklyn" embroidered on the front in gray.

Holding her tight, I breathe in her strawberry sweetness. I've learned over the last several weeks that it's not one product or perfume that gives her that summertime scent I love. It's everything. She uses strawberry-scented hair products and strawberry champagne lip gloss. She sprays her sheets with a strawberry-lavender calming mist, and she even has a little strawberry-shaped air freshener in her car.

I'll never smell, eat, or see a strawberry again and not think of her.

We sit in silence, and I savor the way she fits. In the crook of my arm. In the bleakness of my life. She forced her way in and made herself at home.

I play with her hair and watch the cityscape disappear in the distance, pretending that this summer—this moment in time, this feeling of warmth and joy, love and belonging—that it could last a lifetime.

Except a lifetime isn't an option. We have three weeks, she and I. Three weeks until she goes back to California. Three weeks until I make the choice I've always made, putting my mom and my brother first.

"We're here, Mr. Haas," Glenn announces from the front seat.

And just like that, our trip is over. Our summer is coming to an end. Our time together is vanishing like sand through my fingers. I'm not ready for this to be over. But I have to let her go.

Chapter 41

Maddie

Dempsey dropped me off at home yesterday afternoon, and we stayed at our own houses last night. Thankfully, I made it back in time for the Wheeler family Zoom call since I hadn't actually told anyone I was out of town. My parents would have asked twenty questions about who I was with and what we saw and ate in the city. Then Rhett would have pushed for the details I'm not willing to share.

As soon as our Zoom call ended, I locked up the house, showered, and put myself to bed. I hadn't slept at all on Saturday night, and I'd only napped on and off on the plane.

Now it's Monday, late afternoon, and I've done a fantastic job ignoring everyone and everything all day long.

I've spent most of the day in the pool to keep myself from being glued to my phone. This way, I haven't been tempted to text or call him, or to look through the few hundred pictures saved on my camera roll from this weekend.

I've put myself on a Dempsey Detox.

Untangling my life from his now that we've only got a few weeks left feels harsh, but it's necessary.

I saw his life in a new light this weekend. Seeing him with his ex-fiancée, even after everything he said to me about her, opened my mind to so many possibilities for how his life could have been. I believe him—she left, and he would never go back to her because of the way she abandoned him—but maybe that's the direction his life was supposed to go. Maybe they were meant to be together.

And I'm just… in the way.

We were only ever supposed to be a summer fling. Did we let things go too far? We're so much more than hot sex now. I care for him deeply. I know he cares about me. But there's a time limit to this—to us—and there always has been. There are so many forces outside our control reinforcing the idea that we are not meant to be.

We're on different life paths that just happened to spark together this summer, but our paths won't ever cross again. We were a once-in-a-lifetime cosmic collision. A spontaneous supernova that exploded and shined so damn bright when things were good. But now we're careening toward the inevitability of the end.

Maybe NYC was always supposed to be it for us—our final hoorah. I'll be heading back to California in less than three weeks anyway.

Maybe it's better if we let that trip be the capstone of our summer fling. The next few weeks might not feel so damn heavy if I end things now. We could go our separate ways. We'd think of each other fondly. This summer is already positioned to live rent-free in my mind for the rest of my life. Maybe there's something to calling it off while we're at our peak.

My phone rings in the house for the third or fourth time, so I paddle my float to the edge of the pool and call it a day. The sun's low enough now that it's probably dinnertime anyway. I might as well shower and order food, then put myself to bed early again.

I make my way through the sunroom and into the house, locking up and setting the alarm system as I go. Andrew Adley hasn't tried to pull anything since Dempsey beat him in the back parking lot over a month ago, but it still makes me feel better to have the alarms in place.

I yawn at least three times as I make my way through the lower level of the house. I'm not really hungry, but I know I need to eat. I decide Mediterranean sounds good, and will reheat well tomorrow, too, so I find my phone on the kitchen island and pick it up to place my order.

As soon as I see the screen, my heart drops.

Three missed calls from Dempsey.

Two from Jake.

One from Fielding, since I unblocked his number weeks ago.

Then one single text message.

Dempsey: Call me when you get this. It's about my mom. She died in her sleep last night.

I drop my phone on the counter, and my heart shatters into a million tiny pieces for the man I've been mentally pushing away all day.

Chapter 42

Dempsey

We've always planned for the worst. An overdose. Liver failure. A major fall. A car accident she caused.

I never expected her to go quietly in her sleep.

The official cause of death is sudden cardiac arrest. But when Fielding tried to bring her breakfast this morning, she looked like she was sleeping, her expression placid and peaceful.

It's a gift I never expected: an extended sigh of relief after all this time.

We called our family doctor, and we had some time to say goodbye to her together before they took her body away.

I checked in on her after dropping Maddie off at home last night, and we talked for a few minutes, but I wish I'd spent more time with her. I wasn't all there. Instead, I was preoccupied with a girl I have no business worrying about.

I did kiss my mom goodnight. I told her I loved her. She squeezed my hand, and she said what she's said to us our entire lives.

"I love you. Both of you."

Even if we weren't both in the room, that was always her thing. Recognizing that my life is intertwined with my brother's in a way so few people will ever truly understand. She saw us both. She loved us both. And now she's gone.

She wasn't naïve to the reality of her situation. A planner by nature, she had everything mapped out and ready. All I had to do was make a few calls and pick a date to set her plans in motion.

Calling hours and the funeral won't be until the middle of next week. That will give people time to make arrangements and come to town.

I have a task list to keep me busy over the next several days, but it feels like I'm facing this empty expanse of time. What the hell am I supposed to do now that she's gone?

I keep catching myself in the middle of a task that sparks a fresh wave of grief when I remember she's no longer here. I've absentmindedly walked to her wing of the house at least ten times over the last twenty-four hours. I've picked up my phone to text her twice, only to remember she won't respond. She'll never text me again.

I keep gravitating back to the kitchen to have something to do with my hands. I made way too much food for dinner because I don't know what else to do.

With a quick knock, I enter my brother's bedroom with two plates balanced in one hand. "I made dinner," I announce, hoping he's in the mood to tolerate my overbearing tendencies.

I don't know how to play it with Fielding. He's already so damn low—will this be what finally sends him over the edge? And if he topples, will I follow?

He's not acting any differently. I guess I'm not, either. I just worry that this is the beginning of the end and that I won't know how to handle it if he unravels further. Keeping him in line and getting through these next few weeks are all that matters.

He sits up in bed and shifts over to make room for me.

"Do you really think you can feed me into submission?" he teases through a yawn.

"I know how much you love BLTs, so maybe?"

I'm half kidding. Half not. There's an undercurrent to every conversation we've had over the last twenty-four hours. I keep expecting him to fly off the rails, and he mocks me for waiting for the other shoe to drop.

He accepts his plate and takes a massive bite as I join him on the bed. I pick at a bit of lettuce hanging over the edge of the crust. I'm not hungry. I haven't been since we found her. But he'll notice if I don't eat, so I pick up my sandwich and go through the motions. Chew and swallow. Rinse and repeat.

"I feel like I need to put you out of your misery," he declares through a mouthful of food. "I'm okay, bro. I mean, I'm not, but I am, ya know? I'm sad. I'm sure I'll have regrets and low days. But if you're waiting for me to lose it, you're going to be waiting a long time. Right now, I'm fine."

He finishes chewing, then shoves a handful of chips into his mouth. "I figured I'd just lie low between now and the services next week. Is that your plan, too? To chill here at the house?"

Relief washes over me. Relief and agitation. Lying low and being home with him should be my priority right now. But I can't help but think about the blond-haired, brown-eyed girl across town who's leaving for good in less than three weeks.

"Earth to Dumpy," he teases, shoving me in the side when I don't reply. "What the hell is wrong with you, man? I thought you were just worried about me flying off the handle, but I just promised to keep my shit together, and you're still acting like your mom just died."

"Not funny," I mutter with an eye roll.

"Kinda funny," he insists. "Seriously, though. Something's got you all twisted up, and for once I don't think I'm to blame."

He shifts over on the bed until we're sitting shoulder to shoulder. He sighs and rests his head against mine, his mass of blond curls immediately tickling my face.

"You need a haircut before next week," I huff as I readjust my head against his.

"Dumpy..."

I say nothing. But he's not done pushing.

"Is it Little Wheeler?" he asks, which we both know is pointless. He already knows the answer.

"Just leave it, Field."

"You can talk to me, bro! We *always* used to talk about girls."

We did. Until he fell in love with a married woman. And I fell in love with her much younger sister-in-law.

"She's not just a girl," I reply on a sigh.

"She's only twenty, so technically she *is* just a girl," he teases as he rubs his stupid thick head into mine.

I swat at him and shove away from the wall, giving myself space and a second to breathe. I turn around and face him head-on before replying.

"When Maddie and I were in the city this weekend, we ran into Brooke."

His eyes triple in size. "Brooke-Brooke?"

"What other Brooke do we know?" I smack the side of his head to try and knock some sense into him.

"And how did that make you feel?" he asks in a deep, mocking tone.

"You know I don't give a shit about Brooke. She didn't even try and make it work." We've had this conversation a dozen times. I've never felt more rooted in my resolve when it comes to my ex.

"But Maddie saw us together and tried to run. Like, literally tried to run out of the bar and back to the hotel without me. She pulled back, and even though we were only ever supposed to be a summer fling, I fucking hate the way this feels."

His face softens a touch, but he says nothing.

"So now, even though I'm supposed to be drowning in grief and mourning our mom, all I can think about is how I only have a few more weeks with Maddie and how I wish it didn't have to end. I was on the phone earlier confirming floral arrangements and I spaced out three times because I was thinking about her. I'm panicking. I'm not ready to say goodbye."

I huff out a long breath, but there's still a tightly wound knot straining in my chest. Saying it out loud doesn't alleviate the tension I feel when I think about time running out with my girl. If anything, it makes it all feel more real.

"Dude," Fielding whispers.

"I know."

I knew he wouldn't judge me for how I feel. But I can't help but judge myself for not keeping my head on straight or my priorities in order.

My brother kicks his leg out and knocks his knee against mine. "Mom's gone now, Dem. We're free. You could go to New York. Chicago. *California*. You could follow Maddie out there, and you could make a real go of things if she's what you want."

I smile sadly to myself. He's always been a hopeless romantic.

"Yeah. Maybe. We'll see," I murmur, mostly to redirect the conversation before it encroaches on territory I refuse to get into with him right now.

What I can't tell him is that my shackles didn't break open the moment our mom passed away. She's not the only one I watch over, take care of, protect.

Even if I tried to leave... even if I made plans, convinced her to give a real relationship a go, and followed her out to California, I'd never truly be free.

I can't live thousands of miles away from my brother, knowing he's struggling and despondent, with no sense of direction and no one by his side.

Our mom may be gone, but I'm not free. She's not what tethers me to this place. That honor goes to him.

Chapter 43

Dempsey

When I head back to my room, I shower and collapse on my bed. I reach for my phone and am relieved to finally see a missed call from Maddie.

I couldn't get a hold of her earlier, so I texted her the news. It may have been a cop-out, but it felt easier than the pressure of having to wait to say the words out loud.

I hit her name without hesitation, desperate to hear her voice. She answers on the second ring.

"Oh Dem, I'm so sorry. I'm so, so sorry," she gushes as soon as the line connects.

"Thanks for calling," I mutter as I clear the emotion from my chest.

"Are you okay? How's Fielding?"

I can't help but smile—her concern for me barely trumps her worry about my brother. Her heart is so good.

"We're okay," I reply, shifting up on my bed to lean against the headboard. "Part of me is still in shock, but she went peacefully in her sleep, so there's not much more I could have asked for."

"That doesn't mean you can't be sad, Dem. God, I wish I could come over there and hug you right now."

My heart catches in my throat with her admission. I would give anything to be in her arms tonight. But I'm where I need to be. And I need to stay put and stay focused.

"Can we switch to FaceTime?" I ask, my voice guttural and filled with emotion I can't hide.

She initiates the call without responding. As soon as I accept, her gorgeous, freckle-faced smile fills the screen, and something settles inside me.

"Hi."

"Hi," she giggles.

"You look gorgeous," I praise as she scrunches her nose at me. "Although a little sunburned," I observe.

"I was in the pool most of the day. That's why—that's why I didn't see any of your calls. I'm so sorry I didn't answer, Dem. I just…"

She trails off, then glances away from the phone, frustration written all over her face.

"Hey," I reprimand. "You're here now. And honestly, I wouldn't have had time to talk earlier anyway."

"I just feel bad. You've been through hell today, and I've just been sitting at home, worrying about the stupidest things…"

She trails off again, and this time a telling sniffle comes through the line.

"What's wrong, baby girl? Talk to me," I softly pry.

She looks like she's about to burst into tears, and I get the distinct impression it has nothing to do with my mom. She doesn't answer, instead drawing in a shaky breath and forcing a smile that I know isn't real.

"I feel bad I wasn't there for you today," she admits, wiping her eyes on the sleeve of her Brooklyn sweatshirt. It's hard to believe we were together in New York just one day ago. It seems like a lifetime has passed since then.

"You're here now. Seeing your face at the end of the day is all I need to be okay."

She nods and wipes at her eyes again. I'm frustrated by her reservedness, but I know better than to push when emotions are already so high. I'd do anything to hold her right now.

"What can I do for you? How can I make this easier?" she asks.

Now it's my turn to smile sadly. What I want and what I need are on two opposite ends of the spectrum. I blow out a long breath before steeling the courage to reply.

"I would give anything to hold you right now, princess, but I think it's best if I lie low and stick around at home with Fielding until the calling hours and funeral."

"Okay, I understand," she whispers. "Can I still call you?"

The uncertainty in her voice has me grinding my molars. I don't want to stay away from her—especially knowing that we're running up against the clock and she'll be leaving for California by the end of the month—but I don't have the luxury of getting what I want right now.

"You can and you will. We're going to talk every single night, Maddie. I want you to text me all day long, every damn day. I hate that we can't be together right now... but I need to be here for Fielding until we get through this. Calling hours will be next Tuesday, then the funeral is Wednesday. Just let me get him through the next ten days."

"Do what you have to do to get through this. But promise me you'll tell me if there's anything I can do to help," she asserts.

"Talking to you every day and knowing you'll be back in my arms when this is over is all I need. Just hang tight and be patient... I promise I'll make this up to you."

We hang up a few minutes later, but my mind is no less settled after our call. Part of me feels like this won't be enough. That I've grown dependent on her presence. That I need to see her and feel her beside me to be okay.

But then I think of him, and the trepidation settles. I have an obligation to my mom's memory; I have a responsibility to Fielding's stability.

We can get through this. I'll do whatever it takes to make sure my brother is okay and that we both make it through the next ten days.

Even if I hate the thought of wasting one single minute of the rest of the summer without Maddie by my side.

We made it to the weekend.

The days ticked by dreadfully slow, my daily to do lists and the need to keep Fielding on the straight and narrow the only things keeping me going. I slog through every day, taking care of everything I can think of. Then at night, I let myself unwind when I talk to her.

We exchange texts throughout the day, but it's the nightly calls that keep me going. Even if they start as regular phone calls, they always end up being FaceTimes. There's just something about seeing her smile that soothes me.

With calling hours and the funeral just a few days away, I'm expecting the first out-of-towners to arrive tomorrow. Soon, Field and I will have to suit up and turn on the charm, having the same conversations over and over again. I'm already exhausted.

Fielding has taken most of the calls from our dad, which I'm equally surprised by and grateful for. George won't come into town until Tuesday, and he booked a hotel in Cleveland, so we don't have to worry about seeing him at the house.

Just a few more days, then we'll be able to move forward. Just a few more days until everything hard and complicated is forgotten, our saddest and lowest memories buried alongside her.

I cut through the living room and head to the kitchen to make lunch, only to stumble upon my brother lounging across one of the couches.

He's staring at his phone, earbuds in place, cackling.

I pluck one AirPod out of his ear, and he reacts instantly, swatting at me and pulling me down onto the couch beside him.

"Why are you laughing like a hyena?" I demand, shoving him in the side for pulling me off my feet.

"Just one of your girlfriend's daily videos," he mutters under his breath before hitting play, turning up the volume, and handing me the phone. "Did she send you this one yet?" He hits restart, and a toddler with a beer bottle fills the screen, babbling about overdue rent.

I stare at the device, perplexed, when Will Ferrell opens the door.

"You said this was one of her *daily* videos?" I confirm.

"Yeah, bro. She's been sending them to me all week." He cackles in my ear when the toddler starts screaming about money, so I hand him back his phone and rise to my feet.

I can't fight back the grin that's taken over my whole damn face.

Maddie has sent me plenty of texts, mostly sweet, with the occasional flirtatious message thrown in the mix. She's also sent me a number of selfies, each one immediately saved to my camera roll. All I have to do is tell her I miss her, and she sends a picture and says she misses me, too. But she hasn't sent me any funny videos; that's not our thing. That's not what cheers me up. That's not what comforts me or distracts me in times like these.

Immature humor is *his* thing. I'm once again stunned but delighted that she never forgets about him—she sees him, she knows him, and she cares for him, too.

Fielding and I are going to be okay. We're both going to get through these next few days. I'll make sure of it. And apparently, she will, too.

Chapter 44

Maddie

I've never been more grateful to see Jake in my life. I get out of the car in the church parking lot at the same time he emerges from a black Tesla.

Huh. So much for being a Jeeper for life.

"Hey," he greets me softly as he walks over. "How's he doing?" he asks, which just puts our distance over the last ten days into context.

Sure, I've talked to Dempsey every day since his mom died. Fielding, too. But I haven't seen him in person, and I don't feel like I really know how he's doing or what he needs right now.

"I think they're both doing the best they can, given the circumstances," I answer as he wraps his arms around me for a hug. "Is Cory coming, too?" I ask as we break apart and he places one hand on the small of my back to guide me into the church.

Cory is Jake's husband, and unless one of them is working, it's rare to see one without the other.

Jake shakes his head solemnly. "He offered to hold things down at The Oak this afternoon so all the guys could be here."

We walk into the church and join the line of people angling to get to the front. I haven't been to many funerals, and none by myself, but I assume we're waiting to greet the family and offer our condolences.

I shift from foot to foot as we wait, a ball of nerves over the prospect of seeing Dempsey in person for the first time since we've been back from New York. I can see the tops of the boys' blond heads over the twenty or so people in front of us, but I can't really *see* either of them.

What I do see? The impossibly tall, elegant brunette who strides in from a side aisle and joins the gathering at the front of the church as if she belongs there.

I don't know if I make a sound of disgust or just stiffen beside him, but within seconds, Jake is scanning the room until he identifies the source of my discomfort.

"Who is that?" he murmurs as he slings an arm around my shoulders.

"That would be Brooke," I huff under my breath.

Jake looks at me wearing a puzzled expression.

"Dempsey's ex-fiancée." I raise both my eyebrows, and his eyes widen in surprise. For once he doesn't call me out for my attitude—*way to read the room, Jakey*.

"I think I'll just find a seat and meet up with him afterward," I relent, turning to step out of line and head to an empty row at the back of the church.

"Are you meeting up with the guys from The Oak? Or will you sit with me?" I ask as Jake follows my lead.

He scoffs under his breath before replying. "Of course I'll sit with you. But you're sure you don't want to go up there? Or sit closer to the front?"

I shake my head adamantly as I slide into one of the last rows in the back of the church. I busy myself arranging my dress and making sure Jake has enough room before looking up to the front of the church again.

I don't know what I was hoping to see. But Brooke in the second row, directly behind the reserved seating for immediate family, was not it.

I feel like a birthday candle compared to the blinding light that surrounds her. Multiple people move on to speak to her after speaking to the boys. They were *engaged*, after all. They were going to be married. It makes sense she's here. And that she feels entitled to sit front and center.

I double check that my phone is on silent before glancing over to find Jake's attention on me.

"You okay, Fourth Wheel?" he asks, genuine concern in his expression.

I bite down on the inside of my cheek to hold back the tears I have no intention of shedding as I nod.

"Do Rhett and Tori know?" I whisper, desperate to change the subject. I don't need anyone—least of all Jake—knowing just how affected I am by Brooke's presence or just how much Dempsey means to me.

Jake doesn't answer right away. He leans forward and rests his elbows on his knees, then he turns to me. "What are you really asking me right now?" he counters. "Do you want to know whether your brother knows that their mom died... or whether he knows about your not-so-secret summer fling?"

I roll my eyes at his non-response. "I assumed he knew about Dempsey and me, considering you made it your personal mission to out us this summer," I snap back in defense.

"*You* need an attitude check," Jake admonishes as he wraps one arm around me and pulls me into a side hug.

I shove him in the ribs but let him hug me.

"I don't think your brother knows about your summer of love. If he does, he didn't hear it from me. And for the record, I only told Fielding about you two because he needed to hear it from a neutral source. Regardless of what happened in the past or how I feel about what he did, Field's not a bad guy. He deserved to hear the full truth after that night at the bar with Adley, not some small-town gossip from an unreliable source."

I don't love his explanation. But we can't go back and change it now.

"And to answer your question, yeah. Rhett and Tori know."

My eyes widen as that little realization sinks in.

"But they won't be here," he continues. "They *were* coming. They had already booked their flights. But Dempsey called and asked them to stay away. Fielding's not... he's just not in a good place. Hasn't been for a while. Add in Gloria's death and the fact that he was the one who found her—"

My heart lurches with that confession—I didn't know Fielding was the one who found her.

"—and he's fucked in the head right now. Being around Tori would have been a gamble with his sanity, and Dempsey decided it wasn't worth the risk. It was his call to make. Rhett respected his wishes."

I nod somberly, then sit up straighter when organ music begins to play. Jake releases his grip on my shoulder and settles in beside me while my mind drifts to who's actually here, who's not, and why.

Chapter 45

Dempsey

The service ends, and we're escorted to a family waiting area as people file out of the church. That's fine by me—for the last twenty-four hours, Fielding and I have gone through all the motions of smiling and nodding and thanking people for coming.

I'm ready to be done. I'm ready to get to her.

Dempsey: Are you still here?

I spotted her before the ceremony, sitting toward the back and being comforted by Jake. I had secretly hoped she would sit next to me during the service. But I might not have been able to focus with her back in my orbit.

Fielding claps me on the shoulder as I pace. "You good, bro?" he questions, side-eyeing me because he knows damn well I'm anything but.

I've spent the last ten days stuck at home, focusing on him. I fulfilled all our mother's wishes, just like she wanted. Now, it's over. There's nothing left to do. I want so badly to focus on the one person I've missed like crazy this whole damn time.

"Dad wants to take us out to dinner tonight, and he mentioned inviting Brooke. I'm assuming that's *not* your priority right now?"

I blow out a long, frustrated breath. We both know damn well our dad has little interest in spending time with us. He's just doing what he thinks he's supposed to do. I respect the effort, but it's about ten years too late in my mind.

He wasn't here. Just like she didn't stick around. My dad and Brooke are the last two people on earth I want to spend time with.

"Tell ya what, bro. I'll handle dad and Brookie Cookie tonight."

I smirk at his dig—she hates that nickname, and he knows it.

"It'll be fun. I won't even mention it's me since we both know she can't tell the difference." He chuckles at his own joke. "Let me take care of this just like you've taken care of everything all week. You did good, Dem. Mom would be proud."

He pulls me into a hug before I have a chance to respond. "Go find her," he whispers before shoving me away and messing up my hair.

By the time I check my phone, her reply is waiting for me.

Maddie: Yes, I'm in the parking lot. I'm sorry I didn't say hi earlier. I just didn't want to overstep.

Overstep my ass.

Dempsey: Stay there. I'll be right out.

I glance around and find an emergency exit, then pray it's not attached to an alarm. I push through the door and am greeted by the sweet sound of silence. Even better: the side door dumps right into the parking lot.

I spot her immediately, leaning against the side of her Lexus and scowling down at her phone.

A few people call out to me, but I'm taking Fielding's advice to heart. I'm done. Off the clock. Out of platitudes and bored with niceties.

I just need to get to her.

She must feel me before she sees me, because she lifts her head and studies me as I stride across the parking lot.

When I reach her, we don't speak. Neither of us makes a sound. I just pull her away from the car, wrap her in my arms, and hold her like she's as vital as the oxygen in my lungs.

She returns my embrace, and for the first time in ten days, I feel at ease. The longer we hug, the more I unwind. Her arms around me feel like the sustenance I've been craving since the second I dropped her off at home after our trip.

"Fuck, I missed you, princess. These last ten days... they've been torture, Maddie. The hardest part of all of this was being away from you," I murmur into her hair before pulling back to look her in the eyes.

Every part of me feels calm and whole as I take her in.

"God, you're pretty. I missed you so much." I tuck a loose curl behind her ear and cup her face in both my hands. "Come home with me tonight?"

She gives me a pained smile, her expression a mix of pity and confliction. "Dem, I don't know if that's such a good idea..."

"Well, I do. I've spent the last ten days missing you. I'm not going another night without you in my bed."

"I'm leaving next Sunday," she reminds me.

As if I could possibly forget.

"We still have over a week," I counter.

"Yeah, okay," she relents, running her hands down her dress and looking around the parking lot before reaching out and wrapping me in another hug. "I missed you so much," she whispers. And in that moment, I feel better than I have in days.

Chapter 46

Maddie

I'm so out of my element here. And yet there's no place else I'd rather be.

I'm sitting out on Dempsey's balcony, listening to the frogs and crickets, while fireflies dance in the canopies of the trees. It's unbearably humid tonight—but that's Ohio in July. There's a familiarity to the heat and the moisture clinging to the air. It reminds me of summer nights with Rhett, Tori, and Jake. Freeze tag and skinned knees and the ice cream truck rolling through the neighborhood.

He walks onto the balcony wearing athletic shorts and a ribbed tank—a total departure from the sharp suit he had on for most of the day. When we got back to the house, he explained that Fielding was keeping their dad busy tonight. I guess it was Fielding who encouraged him to take it easy and spend the night with me.

I'm grateful for it. My own selfish reasons aside, Dempsey looks like he could use a break. His eyes aren't as bright as usual, and the wrinkle between his brows has barely left his face. I feel terrible about the passing of his mother, but I can't help but hope that now that the funeral's over and most of her affairs are in order, he can regroup and some of the burdens he carries will ease.

"Hi," I offer when he spots me in my favorite chair. It's identical to the other loungers out here, but this is the chair he was sitting in the first night we hooked up.

"Hi, you," he murmurs, grabbing for my hand as he sits down beside me.

I immediately rise to my feet. Sitting side by side doesn't feel close enough after all that time apart.

Earlier, when he found me in the parking lot and held me, something clicked back into place. The countdown is on for the rest of our time together, but if he's all in until the end, then so am I.

I straddle his lap and join him on his chair, my body melting into his solid, muscled frame as he pulls me closer. We sit like that, neither of us speaking, both wrapped up in the other, listening to the frogs and crickets in the distance.

"What can I do for you?" I ask eventually, shifting back so I can brush his hair out of his face. God, I missed touching him.

He rests his head back on the chair and closes his eyes, humming in pleasure as I play with his hair. "Just being here is enough. Everything about the last week and a half was hard. But being away from you was the worst of it. I missed you so damn much."

I feel his sorrow in my bones. Grief for his mother. Worry about his brother. I can't help but feel like I'm responsible for some of his pain as well. All I can do is be with him now and do everything in my power to lessen his heartache.

"I'm here now," I reassure him, pressing my lips to his in the gentlest kiss. "I'm here now, and there's nowhere else I'd rather be."

We sit together as the minutes tick by, then an idea comes to mind.

"Do you want to take a bath together?" I ask.

"Hell yeah, I do," he replies, rising to stand with me in his arms. "Go get all that strawberry stuff you like from the guest bathroom. I'll fill the tub." He places me on my feet and swats at my ass as I scurry out of his room and down the hall.

By the time I make it back to his bathroom, the tub is half-filled and he's already removed his shirt.

Goddamn. I really did miss this man.

I wrap my arms around his lean, muscled torso, then squeeze him so tight he lets out an involuntary *umph*.

"Arms up," he murmurs when we finally break apart, lifting my shirt for me and discarding it with his on the floor. He bites his bottom lip as he assesses me, and I preen under his gaze.

I shimmy out of my shorts, then unhook my bra and let it fall off my shoulders. I give him a cheeky grin before turning around and dumping strawberry shower gel into the tub.

He swats at my backside, then sidles up behind me, completely naked now, his erection lined up perfectly with my ass. "You better get in there before I change my mind and carry you over to the bed instead," he murmurs against my neck.

I peel down my panties, taking longer than necessary to step out of them, then climb into the tub and gingerly scoot toward the front. The thing is massive—it's honestly the size of a hot tub, so we'll have no problem fitting together. I admire the view while he climbs in and hisses slightly as he gets used to the hot water.

Once he's seated, I move back, lining up my legs with his and draping my body over him.

"Right there, baby girl," he encourages as I melt into his arms. He encircles my waist and positions me so I'm sitting on his lap, my back flush against his chest with his very erect cock lined up along my center.

It would be all too easy to slip him inside me—and goodness gracious if I don't want to *feel him* inside me again, preferably as soon as possible—but that's not what this is about.

Right now, I just want to be here with him. To let him feel me. To reacquaint our bodies and our hearts after that treacherous time apart.

He laces our fingers together, then glides our joined hands up and down my body. Everywhere he grazes feels good and solid and warm—in seconds, I'm on fire for his touch.

"You're everything I never knew I wanted," he whispers, inspiring goosebumps to erupt along my neck and down my spine. He brings our hands to rest on the inside of my thighs.

Although I'd usually be wiggling and thrusting to get him where I want him, tonight, I'm more than happy to lie here with him and just let him hold me.

He draws little circles on my skin.

I caress up and down his arms and his thighs.

Our touches are constant, our need to reconnect intoxicating. Every point of contact sparks a sense of familiarity in me. Every caress feels like the comfort of coming home.

"You got me through the last ten days, Maddie," he confesses against my skin as he trails kisses along my shoulder. "Your texts. Our phone calls. The videos you sent to my brother. Every time things felt too heavy or stressful or hard, I reminded myself there was a light at the end of the tunnel. That light was you.

"You're my hope. You're my courage. You're my sunshine, ever-present and driving me forward, even on the darkest of days."

A lump forms in my throat as I tremble at his words. Not because I don't want to hear them, but because they mirror my own truth.

Rather than replying, I turn my head and catch his mouth in a kiss, pouring every emotion and confession I'm too chicken to give voice to into my kiss.

I kiss him until we're both breathless. And even then, it's not enough. I kiss him as I collect myself, painfully reminding my heart that this is almost over. I kiss him, and I swear I feel his soul fuse to mine.

I just pray it's not welded too tightly. Because in less than ten days, I'm gone. And I can't stand the idea of causing him any more pain.

Chapter 47

Dempsey

I reach for her, but she's not there. I brush my arm down her side of the bed but come up empty. Panicked, I check the bathroom, then the balcony. Finally, I grab for my phone and send her a text. She wouldn't leave while I was sleeping, would she?

It's already nine. I slept deeper and longer last night than I have in almost two weeks. She has that effect on me. Everything is easier when she's here.

I jog down the stairs and scowl at my phone, willing her to respond so I know she's okay. But about halfway down, my ears pick up on something. I slow my pace and strain to make out what they're saying, smiling to myself as their voices carry down the hall.

They're blasting some pop song I don't know. Fielding belts out the chorus as Maddie heckles him. I can hear dishes being discarded in the sink and the rattle of the silverware drawer opening and closing.

"Okay, but if I remember dancing to this in middle school, you were probably in college when it first came out. I stand by my claim: it's embarrassing you know the words to this song."

"How dare you judge me, Little Wheeler? Miley Cyrus is an American institution. Her godmother is Dolly Parton. They're both national treasures!"

They haven't noticed me yet. They're too busy bickering while Maddie fries what smells like bacon on the stove and my brother mans the waffle iron.

I clear my throat when I reach the island. "Good morning."

Her eyes light up and she skips over to me the second she sees me, and damn, if that doesn't make me feel good.

"Good morning," she croons as she rises up on tiptoes and wraps her arms around my neck. Her hair's piled on top of her head in a messy bun, and she's fresh faced so I can see the freckles sprinkled across the bridge of her nose. "Did you sleep okay?"

"I did. I always sleep well when you're next to me." I kiss the tip of her nose and close my eyes, determined to commit this moment to memory.

She's here. I'm happy. And right now, our only concern is what toppings we want on our waffles. I *need* more of these moments with her. I can't stop the words that tumble out of my mouth without thought.

"Will you stay?" I whisper in her ear, my voice thin and more desperate than I intended. I can't imagine spending a single second away from her between now and when she goes back to California.

Her eyes are wide and questioning when I meet her gaze, and it takes a few seconds of awkward silence to realize she needs context for my question.

"Until you have to go back to California," I clarify. "Will you stay here at the house with us?"

Her expression softens, and she nods. "I'll stay," she vows, rising back up on her tiptoes to reach my lips and kiss me again.

"Thank you," I breathe out. "I can take you by your house later today and help you pack if you want. We can bring your car back here so you're ready to go."

She nods again, and my heart feels like it's been hit with a defibrillator. We don't have forever. But the time we do have left will be spent together.

"Okay, lovebirds," Fielding quips as Maddie yelps and jumps out of my arms.

Now that she's not so close, the world around us comes back into focus, and I notice my brother's got a towel twisted up and Maddie's rubbing her butt where he must have snapped her.

"We're going to be eating burned bacon if you don't let my sous chef get back to work."

In seconds, Maddie's grabbing a towel of her own from the drawer next to the sink, spinning it into a twist, and taking off after my brother. "I'm going to get you for that!" she yells as she tears around the island and Fielding skids out of her reach.

"Hey, hey, hey!" I scold them both. "No running around the stove!"

It's officially the weekend, but putting names to the days doesn't matter anymore. Jake's keeping me off the schedule at The Oak until I tell him otherwise, and Fielding quit his valet job. It's one of the hottest days of summer yet, but we've made our own version of paradise in our backyard.

I've been assigned the role of timekeeper, so I'm in charge of the stopwatch for the water slide competition. Every time Maddie goes down, I clock it perfectly, calling out her time with pride. When it's my brother's turn, I don't bother starting the timer, instead adding a few tenths of a second to Maddie's score so he just barely loses again and again.

He's catching on to me. But I think he likes letting her win, too.

She's filling up her cup at the Coke Freestyle machine now, and I can't help but watch her pert little ass in her red one-piece. She looks like a freaking Baywatch model, and I get hard every time she gets out of the water.

We learned yesterday that Fielding is a literal child and can't resist untying her bathing suit strings underwater, which resulted in her getting pissed off and him getting a beating, hence the reason she's not wearing a bikini like she usually does. That one-piece may have been chosen to discourage salacious behavior, but it's inspiring all sorts of dirty thoughts in my mind.

When her drink is topped off, she shakes her hips and peeks at me over her shoulder, smirking when she catches me watching, then she crosses the pool deck and heads my way.

I get her for eight more days.

I've got seven more nights with her in my bed.

It feels like I've pushed pause on life and stolen this time with both of them. Soon, I'll have to regroup and get back to the business of adulting. There'll be lawyers to deal with and the reading of the will and papers to sign. Fielding said our dad was on his case about what we're doing with our lives, hounding him about why either of us would stay in Hampton now that Mom's gone.

I don't have a good answer for that. I don't know what comes next. Eventually, I'll have to figure it out. But none of that has to happen right now.

Fielding loads up a noodle blaster and hits Maddie in the ass just as she's about to reach me. Her eyes flare with mock anger. A second later, she's getting a running start toward the pool and landing a cannonball inches from where he's treading.

I watch as they wrestle and she eventually declares herself the winner before mounting his shoulders and steering him around the pool by his hair.

They're ridiculous. And yet I would give anything to freeze this moment. He's laughing, she's smiling, and I'm unburdened and surprisingly free.

Fielding eventually dunks her and swims away, freeing her up to come back to me. She's a literal wet dream as she walks out of the beach entry of the pool. I'm tempted to jump up and meet her halfway to ensure she makes it this time.

She slinks over to me, dripping wet with that wanton look in her eye, then straddles my lap and soaks me.

"You're trouble," I murmur as I cup her ass and curl up to bite one nipple through the thin fabric of her suit.

"Am I?" she teases, grinding down on my erection and arching her back to offer me her other tit.

I can't fucking resist her like this, and she knows it. I take her into my mouth, then bite down harder when she mewls. I'm so tempted to peel this whole damn one-piece off her body and devour her right here on this pool chair. But I know better, and she does, too.

"Baby girl. We can't. He's not decent enough to give us privacy or pretend not to watch."

Fucking Fielding.

"I know," she relents with a sigh. "I just needed to feel you." She grinds against me again.

My dick aches from her proximity, and I press my hips up into the apex of her thighs in response.

"Tonight," I promise with a growl before gripping her by the arms and lifting her off my body.

"Tonight," she repeats with a wink before rising to her feet and extending one hand.

"Stop being a grump and come play," she urges.

What she doesn't realize is that I'm completely content to lie back and watch her.

"I'm good here. *You* go play," I encourage with a slap on the ass.

Eight more days.

Seven more nights.

I don't know how I'm going to let her go.

Chapter 48

Maddie

My week with the Haas brothers whizzed by in a blur. We did nothing remarkable, yet we made a thousand memories. We spent all day together, the three of us, every day. Then Dempsey and I got lost in each other every night.

We enjoyed "Valley Cruise" drives through the Cuyahoga Valley National Park with no real destination in mind. We made daily ice cream runs to Valley Cream at Fielding's request.

One night, Dempsey even convinced us to go see the orchestra perform at Blossom. It was shaping up to be a very mature, respectable evening until Fielding busted out the weed he snuck past security and rolled two joints.

He and I got high while Dempsey sat in his lawn chair and scowled. When we went home that night, Dem made love to me so good I swear I heard the symphony in my head when I came.

Now it's the weekend. Our last hurrah. Our final goodbye.

I don't know how either of us will survive it.

We went out to dinner, then Fielding took off to hang out with some friends. It's the boys' first night apart since their mom died, and part of me ached for them. But Dempsey asked him to give us tonight, and Fielding was more than happy to oblige.

I cornered Fielding this afternoon and made him swear he'd come back to the house before his brother wakes up in the morning. I couldn't stand the idea of Dempsey being here in this big house alone.

I come out of the bathroom to find him shirtless in bed, wearing the pants he wore to dinner, staring idly at his phone. I stripped down to my tank top and thong when I took off my makeup and brushed my teeth.

He sets the phone down the second he sees me, then beckons for me to join him on the bed.

"I'll never get tired of seeing you walk out of my bathroom looking edible as fuck."

I give him a smile, though I don't feel the joy that should accompany it.

We've been playing this game all week. Neither of us acknowledging that I'm about to leave. Neither of us willing to admit that this ends tomorrow.

But now we're here. One last night. With an alarm set for five a.m., because I was so fucking desperate to get out of Ohio that I *had* to have the first available flight on July 31 when I booked my plane ticket months ago.

He doesn't know it, but I'm not waking him up in the morning. There is no tomorrow. At least not for him and me.

I already insisted on driving myself, so the boys helped me pack up my Lexus this afternoon. My parents will drive it home from the airport's long-term parking lot when they come back to town in a few weeks.

All we have is tonight.

Whatever words need to be said… whatever this final night needs to be… this is it.

I climb onto the bed and drape myself over him as an ache that can't be quelled settles inside me. Tears pool in my eyes and fall freely without permission, landing on his chest and painting his abs with sorrow.

"Hey," he tries to comfort. "Stop that. Don't cry, princess. We still have tonight."

I nod against him and sniff before speaking my truth. "You have to let me go."

He shudders under me before replying. "I know."

But he doesn't. Or maybe he does and he's that much better at hiding his emotions than I am. I don't want to cause him more pain. But I have to make sure he understands. "This is it, Dem. After tonight—"

He interrupts me with a growl that reverberates through my chest. "I *know*," he says again. This time, his anguish is clear, pain coating those two words. He gets it.

We lie still together, accepting what we can't change while resisting the pull of what could have been.

He breaks the silence first.

"Every day we've spent together has been better than any version of my life before you."

I sniffle, the tightness in my chest threatening to pull me under as I try and hold back my tears.

He strokes both hands down my back, and I swear he trembles beneath me. When he speaks again, there's no doubt in my mind that he's fighting back tears, too.

"In another life—where you could stay, or I could go—in another life, I think I could love you forever."

A sob escapes me this time, because his feelings aren't just his own.

I love this man. I think I could love him forever, too.

But it was never supposed to be Dempsey and me. Part of me wishes we had never met—that I had never walked into The Oak that first night. Not knowing what his love feels like would be a fair tradeoff for not having to leave him and feel like this now.

There is no long-distance arrangement. We haven't bothered to talk about what'll happen when I'm back in town. It's pointless. Now that I have my own place in Cali, I'll be in Hampton less and less. I'm more likely to end up in Norfolk or at my brother's cabin for the holidays. I wouldn't be surprised if my parents put our house on the market sometime this year.

I won't stay. He can't leave. We both know that this is the end of what could have been.

All we'll have left after tonight are memories and this mutual ache I fear we'll carry with us for a lifetime.

I brush my fingertips over his lips, then trace the definition of his throat. I will my head to stop spinning and the tears to stop falling as I desperately try to memorize every detail of this man.

I resist the urge to even blink and lose a millisecond of the time we have left.

He raises his mouth to mine in the most agonizingly slow kiss, sealing a fate we both know is inevitable. He's kissing me goodbye, and the kiss is filled with so much sorrow, I think I might combust.

I can taste his sadness. There's so much regret and longing behind the way his mouth moves against my lips, my neck, my chest, my stomach as he crawls down my body and positions me where he wants me.

"You're still mine tonight," he murmurs against my inner thigh.

I say nothing. I can't. But then he hovers over my body and tilts my chin up, urging me to look him in the eye.

"Stay with me, baby girl. It won't hurt less if you pull away before time's up. Stay with me—right here, right now—and live in this moment. Let me try to show you what a lifetime of us could have been."

I choke back another sob and nod. If all I have to give him is this one last night, I don't want to cry. I want to be right here, totally in it.

He peels down my thong and savors the skin around my center, kissing, sucking, and even biting me with slow, tantric care. He licks up my folds and sucks on my clit just how I like, but he doesn't build me up high enough to fall.

He rolls on a condom and nudges in, giving me just an inch at a time, forcing me to feel every roll of his hips and tilt of his pelvis. When he's finally seated inside me, he uses those damn arms I love to hold himself above me, locking me in his gaze and stroking my hair as we revel in this connection one last time.

He thrusts gently, and we moan in unison. I'm so full of him. Our connection has never been stronger. Nothing's ever felt more like home.

I close my eyes and shudder at the intensity of it all. But he doesn't even let me get away with that.

He kisses along my neck before taking my lips in a deep, passionate kiss. "Come back to me, Maddie. Stay with me until the end."

I open my eyes and meet his devastatingly blue irises. As he stares down at me and thrusts again, I feel a surge of vulnerability. Dempsey sees me in a way no one has *ever* seen me.

To him, I'm not just something to be conquered or claimed.

He sees me for who I am. And in this moment, I realize that's my definition of love.

"Baby girl," he pants, his voice shaky with emotion. "You're everything. Right here. Inside you. This is the happiest I've ever been in my life. It may be the happiest I'll ever be."

I moan, his words fanning the flames inside me as he pulls out slowly before gliding back in.

"Let me feel you, princess," he encourages.

I clench around his dick, then whimper when he pulses inside me.

"Do you feel it?" he demands.

I know he's not just talking about our physical connection.

He's talking about the way his soul mirrors mine.

I feel it. I always have. It's this high-frequency thrumming that's dominated my world for the last two months. It's the passion he stokes in me. It's the way we breathe life into each other when we're together.

"I feel it," I pant, clenching around his cock again and making him moan. "I love it," I add without overthinking my words.

"I love it, too," he replies before burying his head in my neck and shuddering against me as he ruts in earnest.

I let myself get lost in the sensations of him, clenching every time he slides all the way in. We both know what we're not saying. We both know why we can't utter the words. It's not because we don't want to or because it's not true.

But an "I love you" from this man in this moment would be enough to keep me from getting on that plane tomorrow. And I know without a shadow of a doubt that he loves me too much to ever hold me back.

Chapter 49

Dempsey

She's gone.

I knew she was going to sneak out. Field gave me the heads-up yesterday when she insisted he come back to the house by six. She didn't want me to have to navigate the first hours of "what now?" without her.

That's why I spent the entire night awake, holding her in my arms and watching her sleep. When her alarm vibrated, I forced my eyes closed, but I didn't try to hide the tears that fell. She knew I was awake—and she left anyway.

She kissed me goodbye. She brushed the tears from my cheeks. She pressed her lips to mine one final time, and then she was gone.

I'm so proud of her. She's getting on a plane, moving into a brand-new apartment, and gearing up to take eighteen credit hours this semester. I love the way she jumps into things, charging forward as if there's no other speed. For Maddie, there isn't. She either plays full out, or she doesn't play at all.

It's been two months since she forced herself into my life and made a home inside me. Two months that have brought about so many emotions, but the gratitude I feel trumps them all.

I worried all summer that I would regret letting her in or resent how deeply I care for her.

But there was never any uncertainty about what we shared. In a way, knowing we had a time limit allowed me to feel it all. I never tried to hold back or shelter my heart with her. Our inevitable ending allowed me to be happy—truly happy—for the short time we had together.

I'm still lying in bed recalling every detail of last night when there's a rustling outside my door.

Maybe she forgot something. Or maybe…

I pick my phone up off the bedside table and check the time: 5:58 a.m.

My brother opens the door without knocking. He looks at my sorry state, crying in bed, surrounded by tissues. But instead of heckling me, he offers a sympathetic smile.

"I brought ice cream. Is it too early for ice cream?"

Today's my first day back at The Oak. Fielding teased me about getting back to work so I could support his lifestyle, but I need normalcy to distract me from missing her.

That, and being here reminds me of her.

Fielding's sitting at the bar, playing on his laptop, drinking a soda, and eating tots, which Jake now offers on a limited menu. It turns out it actually *isn't* that hard to call Clinton's and place an order for customers over here, then have one of the servers walk it over. Not that Jake would ever admit that to Maddie.

I'm glad my brother's here, honestly. Jake's been more tolerant of Fielding since our mom died. It gives me hope they might be friends again someday. Plus, I think Jake knows it helps me keep my head on straight if my brother's close by.

Keeping an eye on Fielding is a full-time job. He's been great since our mom died, but I get the nagging suspicion he's keeping something from me. I don't know if it's hard drugs or too much booze, but there's a familiarity to the way he's been dodging my questions today.

The fall is inevitable. There's a beauty and a simplicity to someone falling off the wagon. At least then they're meeting your expectations. But this is the part I hate—being stuck in limbo, waiting for the other shoe to drop.

It's a cycle I know well because it's the cycle we lived in with her. Things will be good, great even, for a while. Then it'll all come crashing down.

The bar isn't busy yet—just a few regulars sipping their usual white wine and whiskey sours. I'm looking over the schedules for the next month and making sure we'll be covered when a few of our guys head back to school in two weeks.

"Done," my brother announces with a flourish as he hits a key on his keyboard harder than necessary.

"Done?" I question.

"Done." He smirks and bobbles his head with excitement, like he's bursting to tell me something and can't wait to see my reaction. He's got that mischievous twinkle in his eye.

I sigh, knowing I'm walking straight into one of his games. "What did you do?" I ask, already exasperated.

"I registered to take the MCAT in the spring."

My brain short-circuits. What he just said does not compute. "Come again?"

"I'm going to take the MCAT again. I figure I need some time to study since we've been out of school for half a decade, but I'll take a few prep courses online and order the same workbooks I used in college. If I do as well as I did the first time, I'll have my pick of schools to choose from."

If he does as well as he did last time, I'm probably going to have to talk him out of getting his score tattooed on himself. *Again*. Who in their right mind wants "518" on their body forever?

"I'm—I mean—I think that's a great idea, bro," I stammer. But I'm reeling from the revelation that he has any plans whatsoever beyond bumming around this town for the next few decades.

Here I am, working at a local watering hole, planning my whole damn life around the fact that my brother needs me.

And yet, he's reclaiming his dreams and talking like he's ready to move forward with his life.

I'm flabbergasted. After being stuck in this town for so long, repeating the same cycle, I assumed this was our forever.

I turn away from him and wipe down the bar, the motions familiar. I thought this job and this place were my fate.

This wasn't my dream. But I was willing to stick it out for him. How the hell did he just flip the script?

If Fielding's not planning to stick around town, then what the hell am I doing here?

Chapter 50

Maddie

I take my seat on the plane and pull my hat down lower, desperate for privacy as I continue to cry.

The tears haven't stopped flowing since I closed his bedroom door.

Everything about leaving Dempsey was harder than I expected. I can't explain my compulsion to sob, even as I run through all the logical factors of the situation in my mind.

He can't leave. I can't stay.

Any compromise would end with one of us miserable.

Any compromise would ultimately be our demise.

I thought I was in control when I kissed him goodbye this morning. I thought I'd feel empowered when I walked away from my summer fling and stepped forward into the future I've always dreamed of.

But I can still taste the tears that silently tracked down his cheeks when I leaned in to give him one final kiss. And every part of my body is in a state of cranked-up awareness, adrenaline blasting through me and urging me to go back.

It hurts because he was my first. Not my *actual* first, but he was my first *real* anything.

My stupid heart keeps coming up with questions I can't answer. What if Dempsey was my first real love, and he's also supposed to be my last? What if we were meant for more than just one summer? What if he was it?

I have to believe we made the most reasonable choices for our futures.

I have to believe that even though this hurts like hell, a different ending would have hurt worse. Giving up my dreams isn't an option. Neither is breaking his bond with his brother.

We gave each other everything we could offer when it was ours to give. And now it's time to move on.

I wipe my nose on the cuff of my sweatshirt as I try to gain some form of composure. People are going to start whispering about the weird crying emo girl in seat 3A if I don't. I can't even force a smile or pretend I'm fine—my only hope is that this feeling will start to fade the moment we touch down in California.

Chapter 51

Dempsey

I walk across the pool deck, intent on filling a cup with Coke with lime and rum. It's been two weeks since she left, and I haven't heard a word from her since. I miss her so much. But I know she's out there doing her thing. I hope to God she doesn't feel as crummy as I do.

My brother is spread out on one of the pool chairs, lying on his side. I sneak up behind him, ready to throw my cup of ice on him.

But when I peer over his shoulder, I realize he's not snoozing or watching stupid videos on his phone like usual.

He's got his ear buds firmly in place, and he's scratching notes in the margins of a workbook.

I'm shocked as shit to see him studying. It's a sight I haven't seen for years, and something I doubted I'd ever see again.

My shadow gives me away. He pulls out an ear bud and turns to face me, squinting up and shielding his eyes from the sun.

"What's up, bro?" he asks with a jut of his chin.

"What are you doing?" My brain is having trouble catching up with the reality of this situation. I need to hear him say it.

"I'm studying," he replies without a hint of sarcasm. He pops his ear bud back in place and turns back to his book.

Just like that. Like he hasn't spent the last five years bumming around this house without any sense of direction, or like he hasn't suggested on more than one occasion that he's just going to be a rich prick fuck boy and live off his trust fund for the rest of his life.

I make my way over to the Freestyle machine, but skip the rum as planned. If I'm going to have it out with him, I want to be of sound mind.

I make my selections and fill my cup, warring internally over how to approach this. Fielding is wicked smart. He was in the top 3 percent of our graduating class. He earned exceptional scores on the MCAT. He could have had his pick of med schools.

I stalk back over to where he's lounging and throw myself onto the chair holding his workbook.

"So you were really serious about going back to school?" I demand, watching for signs of uncertainly.

He pulls out both earbuds this time, then scoffs at me like I'm dense. "Of course I'm serious. What the fuck, Dem? Did you expect me to sit around Northeast Ohio for the rest of my life, hoping you'd come visit me from Cali or wherever you end up?"

Now it's my turn to scoff. I've never mentioned leaving this town, let alone the state. We're so not on the same page here.

"I wasn't planning on leaving," I declare.

He looks me up and down and smirks. "I wasn't planning on letting you stay."

He lets his words sink in for a breath before he continues.

"I told you, Dumpy—you're free now. *We're* free, and I'll be damned if either of us wastes this new lease on life. Mom's gone, and it's sad, but you have to start living again. You put so much into taking care of her—we both did our best. Now it's time for your next adventure."

The day after our mom died, he told me we were free. I had never even considered that his life had been on pause because of her, too.

"Why did you bring up California?" I demand.

He cocks one eyebrow suggestively, but I just glare at him in return.

"Please don't tell me you're really this dense." He chuckles. "I watched you all summer. I had a front-row seat to the MadDem show over the last two months—"

"Don't ever call us that again," I interject.

"Whatever you say, *Mr. Maddie Wheeler*."

I roll my eyes, but he schools his expression and continues.

"Being with Little Wheeler made you happier than I've seen you in years, bro. More than happy—fucking jovial. Why *wouldn't* you go to California to be with her?" he challenges.

Because of you.

I think it, but I don't dare say it.

He never asked me to stay. The shackles between us are of my own making.

"You can't hold back because of me," he responds to the words I didn't dare speak out loud. "If you want her, go be with her."

I say nothing, instead huffing out a sigh of frustration. Why does it sound so easy when he says it?

Fielding rises to his feet and snatches up his workbook. "I love you, bro. But I refuse to be your excuse anymore. Either go be with your girl or stay here by yourself. The choice is yours."

He dog-ears the page of his book before snapping it shut and walking away.

Is this real? Will he really follow through with his intentions? Is this med school plan going to stick?

But who am I to question his desire to move forward? Maybe my happiness can't be dependent on his stability. I don't trust him enough to get his shit together. But I also don't trust myself enough not to go down in flames in solidarity.

If Fielding's going to take the MCAT and go to med school, then I need to do something with my life, too. I have to live. I have to *let* myself live. I have to unshackle my life from his and move forward, regardless of what happens next in his story.

Chapter 52

Maddie

Five Weeks Later

Each slap of a bean bag against the board reverberates through my chest and prickles the pit of my stomach.

I shouldn't have come here this weekend.

Spending Labor Day at my brother's lake cabin in Michigan is something I look forward to at the end of every summer. It's my last hurrah before I buckle down and get serious about the fall semester. But I've been living in a state of disconnected purgatory for the last five weeks. And being here—surrounded by family but not with the one person who means the most to me—feels like more than I can bear.

"Really, bro?" Jake gripes as he flips up his Ray-Bans and glares at my brother. "We were up by six and you just fucking handed them the win!"

Tori does a happy dance and kisses Rhett on the cheek while Jake's husband Cory sinks two bean bags in a row.

"Winner, winner," Cory declares, wrapping his arms around Jake from behind as Jake sulks and pretends to be salty.

He spins in his husband's arms and mutters, "I'll show you a winner tonight," before kissing him senseless.

I turn my head and fight back tears, only to see Rhett and Tori *also* making out behind their cornhole board.

Gag. Me. Now.

The constant PDA is a lot on a normal day. But add in that I'm secretly heartbroken and still reeling from having to leave Dempsey, and it's more than I can take.

Wrapping my arms around myself, I walk back toward the cabin. I knew it would be tricky to come here and not think of him, mostly because I've done nothing but think of him over the last five weeks. But being so close to him in a place that feels like home burns in a totally unexpected way.

I wave to Judy in the kitchen as she stirs what looks like lemonade. I don't bother stopping to chat—what happens next is inevitable, and I just need to be alone.

I make my way up the stairs to the loft and free fall face-first into the mattress of my queen-size bed. The tears fall silently, and I'm just thankful I've had weeks to nail down the ability to cry without making a sound.

Only a few minutes pass before I hear someone on the stairs.

"Maddie girl, I wanted to talk to you about our holiday schedules," my brother says before he even comes into view.

He flips through the calendar on his phone without looking over at me and perches on the end of the bed, but I turn my head to the side so he can't see my tears.

"We'll probably do Thanksgiving in Hampton again since Jake and Cory can't get away that weekend, but we'll plan on Christmas at the cabin, like usual. Did you want me to book your..."

He trails off, and I know I'm busted.

"Hey," he nudges me with a shake of my leg. "Are you awake?"

"I'm awake," I mutter into my pillow.

He chuckles in his good-natured way before pulling the pillow out from under my face. "Will you at least sit up and acknowledge me then?" he teases, hitting me in the back with the pillow he just stole.

I know I'm not going to get away with this now.

I sit up and sniffle, but I don't bother trying to dry my eyes.

"Are you crying?" he demands, sounding equal parts shocked and concerned.

I roll my eyes. "No, I was just moisturizing my cheekbones."

"Maddie girl," he soothes, genuinely sympathetic this time as he pulls me into a hug. "What's wrong? Why are you crying?"

I lean into his side and sigh. It was stupid to come here. I *knew* I wouldn't get through this weekend without breaking down.

"Oh, just having one of my daily cries," I admit with a shrug.

"*One* of them? What the hell's wrong with you?"

I sigh again—something I picked up from Dempsey, apparently—before pulling back and studying my brother. "If I tell you, do you promise not to judge me?"

He agrees, so I tell him everything.

About the first night, when I realized Dempsey didn't know who I was. About the clock tower and his reaction when he drove me home. The nights that followed at The Oak, and about helping Fielding at the party.

Rhett cuts me off there and makes me show him the video on my phone—he stays silent while he watches, but his jaw does that agitated tick thing it does by the end.

I explain what happened when Adley came to the bar, and I take great pleasure in ratting out Jake for telling Fielding about our secret relationship. I go on about my summer with Dempsey. I show him pictures of New York. And then I recount the harrowing time we spent apart after their mom died, followed by what I now realize was the most meaningful, profound week of my life.

I tell my brother how I left, and that Dempsey didn't ask me to stay. I sob as I confess that I've cried over him every single day for the last five weeks.

Rhett holds me and pets my hair. He soothes me and assures me it'll be okay. At some point, Judy magically appears in the loft with a box of tissues, two glasses of lemonade, and a plate of fresh-baked cookies. I would roll my eyes at her overbearing antics if I wasn't so comforted by the gesture.

"When's the last time you talked to him?" Rhett asks through a mouthful of warm chocolate chip goodness. Judy really does make the best cookies.

"The night before I left Hampton. Five weeks ago."

"Jesus, Maddie," he hisses. "You've been this upset for over a month and you didn't think to call him or reach out?"

Damn. Not exactly the brotherly love I was hoping for.

"I figured that would just make it harder! How was I supposed to know I'd become you and fall in love so easily?" I retort.

Rhett laughs and shoves my shoulder before pulling me into a side hug. "Come here," he mutters as he holds me tighter and kisses the crown of my head. "Do you really think you're in love?"

My reply is instant. "I think life doesn't feel worth living without him."

Damn. I'm a sucker. I really did inherit the Wheeler family curse. When we fall, we fall hard. I feel stupid that I didn't admit this to myself sooner.

"You have to talk to him, Maddie."

I *knew* he was going to say that.

"What's the point?" I counter. "Nothing has changed. I love school. I would never leave Cal. I want to have an amazing career in NYC or LA. I don't want to live in Hampton and be a housewife! I might be in love, but I still love myself more."

"I'm sure Dempsey's aware that you're not housewife material," he teases. "Why do you think that's what he'd want for you anyway?"

I pause before treading into uncomfortable territory.

"I don't think that's what he'd want. I think that's what I'd have to settle for. He's... he's stuck there, Rhett. Because of *him*. And I refuse to ask him to choose."

My brother's jaw ticks, but he nods in understanding.

Dempsey and Fielding's relationship is complicated and co-dependent. But they've been through hell together, and all they have left in this world is each other. I don't begrudge him for needing to be there for his brother. But I also can't imagine feeling anything but stuck if I had to live in Hampton my whole life.

"It sounds like Dempsey has some decisions to make. But you *do* have to talk to him. You can't expect him to choose you if he doesn't know you're an option."

That... makes sense. But I cower at the thought of putting myself out there and not being chosen.

"I don't know what to do," I moan, defeated.

"Maddie. We're at the cabin. You're literally less than two hours from Hampton. If you don't know what to do, then I'm not sure we're related."

"You think I should go to Hampton?" I challenge, one eyebrow raised.

He raises both of his in reply, so I know he means business.

"Okay, yeah..."

I start to formulate a plan in my head. Rhett's right. I'm so close. This is my shot. If I go back to Hampton tonight...

"One problem," I groan. "Jake picked you up at the airport, too, right? That means he's the only one with a car here."

Rhett's eyes grow wide as the realization sinks in.

"Will you ask him for me?" I beg, my hands held together in prayer with my lower lip turned out in a pout.

He shakes his head and laughs, but I know I've got him. "Only because I love you." He ruffles my hair. "And I really do want you to be happy."

Chapter 53

Maddie

The only thing more nerve-racking than asking Jake if I can borrow his car is driving the thing on the Ohio turnpike in the pouring rain. At least the self-driving technology is there to keep me company. Especially since Jake only listens to emo music from the 90s and early 2000s and I'm too scared to mess with his presets.

I ease into their driveway unannounced, entering the security code and hoping it still works.

It does, and the gates swing open as I pull up close to the garage. All the garage bay doors are closed, so I make a split-second decision to run to the front and knock.

He must have seen me coming on the security cameras, because within five seconds, the door swings open, and there he is.

I scan up and down his body and have to hold back a squeal as all my favorite features register in my brain. Six foot two.

Gorgeous blond hair and crystal-clear blue eyes I want to get lost in forever. Lean, tanned forearms. Veins for fucking days.

I'm about to make a running leap for him, Dirty Dancing-style, but then he smiles, and baby's right back in her corner. It's a megawatt smile that transforms his whole face. At that exact moment, I know.

Even at his happiest, Dempsey never smiles quite that big.

"Is he here?" I pant, the adrenaline and the rain blending together and making me feel frantic. I'm standing on the covered porch, but I'm already drenched from running to the front door.

Fielding gives me a knowing look, then smirks before responding. "He's not here."

"When do you expect him home?" I ask as I pull out my phone to check how much time is left until last call at The Oak.

"I don't. He's not in Hampton. He went on a trip."

I almost drop my phone on the stone patio as that revelation sinks in.

He's not here. He's not in Hampton at all. He's out of town—on a trip.

Did he go to New York? Did he go back to her?

I mutter something that sounds like thanks, then turn on my heel so fast I almost slip on the wet pavement. My power walk quickly transforms into a jog. My stomach churns and my lungs riot as I push harder to get back to the car. But running is futile. Getting in the car is pointless. Jake would never forgive me if I barfed in his Tesla.

I drop to my knees near a bank of bushes and let loose. I sob as my stomach convulses. I expel every pent-up emotion, and even then, my heart still tries to escape with the purge.

"Fuck, Little Wheeler," Fielding bemoans as he drops to his knees beside me. "Please don't tell me you're pregnant."

I shoot up like a shot, then shove him as hard as I can.

"No, you asshole. Girls can puke and not be pregnant! I'm literally on my period right now!"

"Well that explains your charming demeanor," he quips. "I wasn't trying to offend you. I was just checking. The last thing we need right now is a little Fielding or Dempsey running around."

He may be an asshole, but he has the decency to hold back my hair as another surge of vomit releases from my body.

"He's gonna be so pissed he missed you," he mutters as he rubs my back.

Eventually, I calm my stomach and catch my breath, then Fielding helps me to my feet. The rain has slowed to a drizzle. Slow, sad tears from the sky that match my mood.

"Where is he?" I dare ask as Fielding ushers me back to the porch. He guides me over to a set of rocking chairs on one end, then settles into his before answering.

"He's in California," he finally declares.

"He's *where*?" I practically scream. He could have led with that, and he knows it.

"He's visiting some buddies from college who live in the Bay Area and following up on a few leads at some start-ups he might want to invest in. I guess he's out there looking for his next move. But between you and me"—he leans in close, searing me with his lagoon-blue eyes that make me miss Dempsey even more—"I think he went out there for you."

For the first time in five weeks, hope blossoms inside me.

I hear the familiar tune of a FaceTime call before I realize Fielding's even got his phone in his hand. I quickly try to smooth down my hair and wipe the mascara out from under my eyes, but what's the point? I'll be crying again in a minute, regardless of which way this call goes.

"Look what just showed up at the house," Fielding sing-songs into the phone before pointing the camera at me.

I choke out a sob when I see him. It's still daytime in Cali, and he's outside. Tears of joy stream down my face before either of us can utter a word. I don't know what any of this means.

But if he's *there*—and I'm *here*—we both want more, and we're willing to try.

I take the phone out of Fielding's hand, then barely manage to choke out a "Hi."

Dempsey's face screws up with emotion. He looks away from the camera before looking back to me.

"I'm a mess," I lament as I sniffle and try in vain to do something about my soaking wet hair. There's a smattering of vomit on the corner of my shirt—so gross.

"You've never looked more beautiful to me," he replies without missing a beat.

"*Ugh*," Fielding groans beside me as he stands to his feet. "I'm going inside to give you two some privacy. Bring me my phone when you're done, Little Wheeler. You're gonna need a shower to get some of that puke smell off you before you get back in Jake's car."

Heat flares in my cheeks from the callout, but I guess I better get used to Fielding being, well, Fielding, if Dempsey and I are really doing this.

Dempsey clears his throat and calls my attention back to the screen. He's wearing a button-down shirt without a tie, and his hair's slicked back and styled. He's the epitome of California cool. Seeing him there, looking that good, increases my confidence that this could work.

"You're in Hampton?" he asks. "For me?"

I nod my truth as the tears keep coming.

"You're in California?" I ask, even though I already know the answer.

"I came out here to scope out some businesses I'm considering backing. I have a few meetings planned this week, and depending how those go, I planned to call you," he explains, his voice low and gruff. "I just didn't want to give you false hope without having things figured out. If we're doing this, I need to do it right."

"This?" I question.

"Us, baby girl. Me, here in California. Permanently. I know we haven't talked about any of this... and we'd have so much to figure out... but I want to be where you are. Nothing has felt right since you left. I couldn't ask you to stay. Not because I didn't want to, but because I didn't want to trap you. But I want to be with you, Maddie. Wherever you are—in whatever way makes sense—I want to be with you."

"I've missed you so much," I admit. I hate that we're doing this over FaceTime. I smile through another onslaught of tears, this time evoked by his willingness to pursue a relationship, to come out to California, to leave his brother—all for me.

"I know. I feel it, too. I came out here to make sure—to be sure that I could promise you more and hold up my end of the bargain. But just seeing you now is all the assurance I need. When do you come home?"

"I'll be back tomorrow night."

He pauses, then and glances off past the camera, his face fraught with indecision.

"Is this okay, Maddie? Is it okay that I'm here? If this isn't what you want, or if this is too much—"

I cut him off before he can make any sort of argument against what we both know is right and true. "There's no such thing as too much when it comes to you."

"Oh my *God*!" Fielding moans from inside the house. So much for giving us privacy.

"Now when it comes to your brother…" I holler to make sure Fielding hears me.

Dempsey chuckles to himself and shakes his head. "He's the one who encouraged me to come out here," he confesses, his words soft and just for me. "I don't think I could have done this without his prodding. He's going to take the MCAT and apply to medical school again. At least, that's his plan. I've decided to believe him and to let go of the idea that I have to make sure he's okay before I do anything for myself. If there was ever a time to take a risk… it's now. It's for you, Maddie."

I blush at his confession, but quickly shiver as the night air reminds me that I'm soaking wet and coming down from an adrenaline spike.

"I was up at my brother's cabin in Michigan," I whisper, because that's a particular detail I don't need to rub in Fielding's face. "Jake let me borrow his car, but I think I'll sleep here if that's okay with you."

"Absolutely. There's no way I want you driving back tonight."

I would roll my eyes at his overbearing protectiveness if I hadn't missed it so damn much.

"I didn't bring anything with me. I didn't even know what I was going to say when I got here. I guess I'll just have to steal your clothes and sleep in your bed tonight," I tease.

"You're gonna FaceTime me later from my bed."

"Oh, am I?"

"You're gonna use your own phone for that, Little Wheeler!" Fielding hollers from the house.

My eyes widen in rage, but Dempsey sees me and immediately quells the situation. "I'll text him and tell him to behave. You go inside and get cleaned up. Call me when you're in bed, okay?"

"Okay," I mumble before yawning from sheer exhaustion.

"We're going to make this work, Maddie. If you're all in, then I'm all in, too."

I tilt my head to the side and consider his words. As much as I ache to touch him and hold him right now, there's something so special about having him waiting for me in California.

For the first time in five weeks, I feel like I can finally exhale.

"I've always been all in with you."

Chapter 54

Dempsey

She got home later than expected last night, then she had an eight o'clock class this morning. I had already scheduled a lunch meeting with an old friend from school, and I didn't want to cancel on what sounded like a promising lead.

Now I'm sitting in a coffee shop near campus, next to a park called Strawberry Creek Park. Ironic, but serendipitous in a way.

I don't know why the hell we agreed to meet up in public. We've been talking nonstop since she FaceTimed me from my brother's phone two days ago. There's no question about how this will go, but I still have the distinct urge to throw up as I wring my hands and wait for her to arrive.

She wants this. She knows I want this, too. I have exactly zero reasons to be as worked up as I am about seeing her right now.

But still.

I send my brother a text to pass the time. He replies with a picture of himself sitting in the living room, his workbook splayed open on his bare chest. I smirk at his ridiculous commitment to those workbooks. But before I can type out a smart-ass response, I sense her.

My head snaps up. Our eyes lock. And I swear to God, in that moment, I feel everything around me slot into place.

She's glowing.

She's ethereal.

Holy hell, does California look good on my girl.

This is where she's supposed to be. It just took me a while to realize I'm supposed to be here, too.

She rushes to me as I rise up from the booth I've claimed and meet her halfway.

"I can't believe you're here," she gushes as she throws her arms around my neck and pulls me tight against her.

I let myself savor this moment. The smell of her. The truth to how right she feels in my arms. How the fuck did I ever think I could live without her? Just hugging her centers my mind and helps me feel more like who I'm supposed to be.

"I can't believe you went to Hampton," I murmur as I smooth a hand down her hair. I let my other hand skim along her low back, the urge to touch her everywhere drowning out all reasonable thoughts.

"Let's sit down," she insists as she reluctantly peels herself out of my arms. She must sense that I would have spent all night awkwardly standing in the middle of this coffee shop holding her if I could. I miss her touch the moment we part.

We take our seats, and I slide over the dirty chai I ordered when we arrived. She smirks at me as she takes a sip, then gives up a little moan when the piping-hot liquid hits her lips.

"This place is my favorite," she confesses. "My apartment's two blocks from here."

She takes another sip of her drink, then gets quiet, eyeing me like she has a million questions but doesn't know where to start. I reach across the table and take her hand, then wait for her to take the lead.

"What are we doing, Dem?" she asks, her voice soft and timid.

I inhale and sit up straighter, preparing to deliver the speech I've rehearsed in my head for the last two weeks.

"I don't know. For the first time in a long time, I don't have a plan. I'm so out of my depth here, princess. But I need a fresh start. And I'd like to make it out here, with you. Or, at least in close proximity to you, if you're really willing to go all in."

She raises an eyebrow and opens her mouth, but I don't give her a chance to sass back.

"I should never have let you leave the way you did. I should have realized when you were still mine just how good we had it. But I let my concern for my brother cloud my judgment. I let my love for him suffocate every other emotion I dared to feel."

I run my thumb over her knuckles in a way that I hope comes off as reassuring. I've never been more sure of anything in my life.

"Fielding's the reason I'm here. He's the one who told me to come. I'm so sorry I had to wait for him, of all people, to knock some sense into me... but you're where I'm supposed to be. What I said to you a few days ago is true—I'm committed to making this work. I'm all in with you."

She grins at me from across the table and squeezes my hand, inspiring a confidence in me that we're on the same page and that this is going to work.

"I want to be with you, but we can take things slow. I know school is your priority right now, and I'm looking into a number of opportunities with various start-ups in the Valley. I haven't decided if I want to work or if I just want to invest, but I'll keep myself busy and out of your hair. I'll get my own place—"

She holds up a hand and glares, effectively silencing me with one look.

"You'll do no such thing," she quips.

"Wait. What are you objecting to? Me getting a job, or—"

"You getting your own place!" she exclaims. "That won't work, Dem. My schedule is packed as it is, and if you're planning to work in the Valley, we'll never see each other!"

She lowers her voice and continues.

"If we're going to do this, then I'm all in, too. You'll move in with me. We'll spend every minute of free time together. If you're gonna be here, *be here*. Be with me," she appeals, squeezing my hand again for emphasis.

My heart practically leaps out of my chest.

"Get the fuck over here right now," I demand, pulling her arm gently until she's rising up and joining me on my side of the booth.

I can't hold out any longer—I have to kiss her. The moment our bodies connect, sparks fly, and the connection that was forged up against a clock tower and hidden in an alleyway erupts into so much more. I kiss her like there's no tomorrow. Then I slow my pace and kiss her like we have all the time in the world. When I finally pull away, I keep her face cupped in my hands.

"Do you know that I love you?" I ask as I catch my breath.

She bites down on that pouty lower lip that I've fantasized about for weeks before replying. "I do now."

"You didn't know before?"

She smiles sweetly and kisses me again, wrapping me in her arms before whispering in my ear.

"I knew it," she confesses. "I just wasn't willing to admit it to myself if we couldn't have forever. I love you, too, Dempsey Haas."

My insides light up at her declaration, and I'm tempted to pull her onto my lap right here in the middle of this damn coffee shop until I remember she said her place is just two blocks away.

"We can have forever now," I vow. "It's you and me, baby girl. We were always meant to be more than just one summer."

Dempsey

Epilogue: Two Years Later

I beam with pride as she walks across the stage. Although walk isn't the right word, because my girl never does anything by halves. She struts past her peers like a woman on a mission, head held high, blond hair perfectly styled under her graduation cap. When she accepts her diploma, she does a little twirl.

Anne Wheeler squeezes my arm as I end the recording and lower my phone.

"I can't believe she's graduating with honors and a perfect 4.0."

I chuckle before I reply. "I can. I've never seen anyone work as hard as Maddie."

"I don't think *you* even graduated with a 4.0 for undergrad, did you, Ev?" Tori teases from farther down the row.

Rhett scowls at her before cracking a smile and shaking his head. "No," he admits. "Maddie girl got me there. I only managed to swing a 3.89 in undergrad."

The ceremony wraps up a few minutes later—one of the few benefits to having to wait for the majority of the alphabet to go by before they got to Wheeler. Once the dean makes her final remarks, the graduates throw their caps, and their eager families and friends swarm the green space.

I rise to stand and wait for Peter and Anne to slide out of the row, followed by Rhett and Tori. We mill about and stretch our legs as we wait for Maddie to make her way back to us.

"So New York City, huh?"

I smile. I've always liked Rhett, and we've gotten closer over the last few years. He's sharp, intuitive, and business savvy—I love calling him up and getting his opinion on the start-ups I consider as an angel investor. I respect the hell out of his work ethic, and I admire him even more as a husband and brother.

"New York City," I confirm with a grin. "It was ultimately Maddie's decision. I was shocked when she said she wanted to go to Columbia for law school instead of Berkeley."

Rhett smirks before leveling me with a look. "She got in to every college she applied to for undergrad, too."

I chuckle under my breath. Of course she did.

"You and Tori should come visit us this fall once we get moved in. We'd love to show you around the city and spend some time together."

Rhett nods methodically and pulls out his phone, swiping through several screens before responding.

"It looks like she'll have fall break the first week of October. I'll double check the dates with Tori, but we'd love to come visit you then."

I school my expression at his over-the-top organization. Maddie loves to call him a calendar freak to his face and behind his back. Clearly, she's not wrong. Before I can change the subject, Rhett frowns at his phone, then excuses himself to take a call.

"We're going to go find our girl!" Anne tells me, still giddy, as she and Peter head toward the stage.

Not two seconds later, Tori steps up beside me.

I tense on instinct. But just like she's proven time and time again over the last few years, she's nothing but compassionate and kind, even though we're caught in the middle of what most would consider an awkward situation.

"Are you guys all packed up?" she asks, turning to me and smiling when I meet her gaze.

"Hardly. School's been nonstop for Maddie this semester with her senior-level classes and her capstone project. I've been down in the Valley most days this month, just trying to tie up loose ends and get things ready for New York."

She nods thoughtfully, then regards me with a furrowed brow.

"Do you need help? Rhett has to get back to Virginia, but I took the whole week off work. I could stay out here for a few more days. Help you guys pack and get things ready for the move."

I shake my head and smile, insisting we'll be fine. I've already hired packers, and I planned to work from home all of next week anyway.

Her sincere generosity always surprises me. It's no wonder my brother fell for her so damn hard.

As if sensing where my thoughts have gone, Tori's expression softens. She takes in a shallow breath, then looks back toward the crowd before she speaks again.

"How is he?"

It's a loaded question.

A question I would have struggled to answer a few years ago.

But now I think the answer will surprise her.

"He's great," I reply before amending. "Or *they're* great, I should say. We're going to spend a few weeks with them this summer after we get settled in the city."

Tori nods to herself before looking back up at me.

"I'm really happy for him. And I'm even happier for *you*," she professes, wrapping her hand around my arm and squeezing it for emphasis.

"V! Dem! Maddie wants us all together for pictures," Rhett hollers from twenty feet away, stashing his phone in his pocket as he waves us over.

"After you," I insist, letting Tori walk in front of me as I crane my neck to spot my girl in the crowd.

When I find her, she beams, and I can't help but feel like all the rays of the sun are shining down on us in that moment. She runs toward me, and my arms physically ache with anticipation.

She did it.

We did it.

Against all odds, even when together seemed impossible, we somehow made our greatest dreams come true.

Maddie

Extended Epilogue: A Few More Years Later

I pull the covers tighter around myself and shiver. It's not just the late fall breeze through the open loft windows I'm feeling.

It's him.

My own personal alarm clock.

Waking me up his favorite way.

I hear him spit, and I yank the duvet off both of us.

"Hey!" I scold. He knows I'm teasing based on the way he smiles against my wanting core without looking up to meet my gaze.

"Don't do that without warning me."

That gets his attention.

"I thought you loved it when I spit on you, princess?" He's smirking like a fool—like *my* fool—no doubt waiting for my sassy response.

"I do love it, but watching is half the fun. Warn me next time so I don't miss it."

"Like this?" he challenges, locking me in his gaze, staring into my damn soul for a moment, then finally spitting with such precision it lands right on my clit.

Goddamn.

My man is good, and he knows it. I can't help the mewl that escapes me.

"Just like that," I pant, bucking my hips in encouragement before he travels back down to finish what he started.

He uses both hands to spread me open, alternating between running the flat of his tongue up my center and swirling the tip around my needy, swollen clit.

When he pushes his tongue inside me, I just about lose it. I reach down and tug on his hair, spurring him on and fucking his face.

I think I could come from his tongue-fucking alone, but then he moves up to suck on my clit, and I swear I levitate off the bed.

"Dem," I pant, because I'm so close, and he feels so good, and I don't know whether I want him to make this last all morning or make me detonate right now. "Dem," I croon again, my hips matching his rhythm as he pulls me into his mouth with greedy, desperate sucks.

My whole body tenses in anticipation before the first wave of pleasure crests and sends me toppling over the edge.

As soon as my orgasm starts, he rises to his knees, lines up his cock, and pushes in, angling his shallow thrusts so he hits my G-spot over and over again.

It's bliss.

I'm in ecstasy.

I never want this moment to end.

I don't get a break. I can barely catch my breath. One orgasm crescendos into another, and then I'm coming again, clenching him so hard he curses.

"Fuckkk, Maddie," he groans as he works himself deeper into my pulsating pussy.

Fuck, indeed.

That'll do it.

We both freeze when we hear the first whimper outside the closed bedroom door.

I roll my eyes and smirk up at my very worked up but oh-so-whipped fiancé.

The irony is that it doesn't matter how loud I am. I can pant, moan, and scream at the top of my lungs, and Hudson couldn't care less.

But the second that dog knows Dempsey's in here—giving *me* attention instead of him—the sad, pathetic puppy whimpers begin, and Dem can't stand to hear it.

Forget pussy whipped. My man is puppy whipped.

Dempsey groans again, shifting up and resting his forehead on mine.

"Just tune him out," I laugh, clenching around his dick to tempt him into finishing what he started.

"You know I can't stand to hear him whine," he whispers.

I laugh again, because I really don't have a dog in this fight—pun intended. I've already come twice. Now it's just a matter of whether Dempsey loves his cock more than his dog.

My money's on the mutt.

"What if you turned me over and fucked me so hard I can't help but scream? Would that help you tune him out?" I offer.

"You're a genius," he murmurs before kissing me, pulling out, then flipping me over and pulling me up so I'm on my hands and knees.

He smacks my ass once, and I yelp. He pushes all the way in, and I moan.

"That's it, baby girl. Let me hear you," he whispers as he hooks both hands around my hips and ruts into me from behind. I can't help but push back and meet him thrust for thrust, moaning every time his balls smack against me.

I'm screaming in pleasure in no time, no extra theatrics needed, as I gush around him and build toward my third orgasm. When his fingers dig into my skin, I know he's close. I also know he won't dare make another sound. I double down on my thrusts, squeeze around his dick, and cry out his name until I feel the first pulses of his release inside me.

We come together, a mess of pleasure, both groaning as we savor the wind down of release. Dempsey pushes gently between my shoulder blades, encouraging me to lie flat, and he covers my body with his, just the way I like, with his cock still buried deep inside me.

I clench around him appreciatively as he kisses my shoulders, runs his fingertips down my arms, and showers me with affection.

"Fuck, you're perfect," he murmurs into my hair.

I shiver again at his praise.

"I love you. I love everything about you. You're so fucking perfect for me."

I groan when he pulls out too soon for my liking, but I knew it wouldn't last long. I reach over to his side and find the T-shirt he was wearing earlier and slip it on just as he opens the door and Hudson barrels into the room.

I would have preferred to have him to myself for a few extra minutes, but I can't help but smile as he baby talks to his beloved dog.

They're both in bed with me ten seconds later, Dem sandwiched between me and the mutt we adopted last year. He kisses me, then pets him. He tells Hudson he's such a good boy, then rolls over to tell me how much he loves me. I gripe about having to change the sheets because he let the dog in bed. Again.

But when I see his smile, I can't even pretend to be mad. Witnessing him this happy—this satisfied and this loved, lying between me and the dog he always wanted—is more than I could have dreamed of for our life together.

Dempsey has never once asked me to alter the path of my life or to scale back the size of my dreams. I'm determined to spend the rest of forever making his dreams come true, too.

Craving even more Maddie and Dempsey? Catch up with them in Fielding's full-length romance book, Full Out Fiend, and sign up for my email newsletter to receive a free eBook called Hampton Holiday Collective featuring a Maddie and Dempsey holiday story set in the future!

Afterword

Thank you so much for reading Fourth Wheel! I hope you loved reading Maddie and Dempsey's story as much as I loved writing it.

The idea of pairing Maddie and Dempsey together came to me while I was writing the Hampton Hearts series. I've spent several books purposely keeping these two apart just so I could pull off that opening scene at The Oak.

If you loved this story, I have a feeling you'll love Fielding's book, Full Out Fiend. You can sign up for my email newsletter or join my Facebook Reader Group if you want to be one of the first to know about upcoming projects!

Finally, be sure to Sign up for my <u>email newsletter</u> to receive a free eBook called Hampton Holiday Collective featuring extended epilogues from all your favorite Hampton Hearts couples. Maddie and Dempsey's story is called "Haas Party of Four" and it's as spicy as it is sweet!

By Abby Millsaps

presented in order of publication

When You're Home
While You're There
When You're Home for the Holidays
When You're Gone
Rowdy Boy
Mr. Brightside
Fourth Wheel
Full Out Fiend
Hampton Holiday Collective

Too Safe: Boys of Lake Chapel Book One
Too Fast: Boys of Lake Chapel Book Two
Too Far: Boys of Lake Chapel Book Three

Acknowledgments

Thank you to all the readers, friends, mentors, and cheerleaders who supported me through this project.

My husband and daughters— thank you for your patience and support as I toiled away on a project that was anything but easy. I hope I made you proud.

Baby LouLou— Thanks for getting your shit together in the second trimester so Mommy could edit this book and stay on deadline. Much improved from your performance while I was writing Mr. Brightside. Good work, kid.

Mel— My confidant and secret keeper! Thank you for reeling me back in when I accidentally make characters too mean or have someone grinding their bare bum on their boyfriend's brother (whoopsies!). I am so grateful for your guidance, friendship, and support.

Beth— Thank you for quelling my Abbyisms and helping me make my books the best they can be! I appreciate and admire so many things about you, but above all I appreciate your friendship.

To my ARC and Promo Team— I'm grateful for your love and enthusiasm. I would not be able to do this job or create these characters without your support. Thank you for embracing Maddie and falling in love with Dempsey. Oh, and thanks for hating Fielding a little less after this book.

About The Author

Abby Millsaps is an author and storyteller who's been obsessed with writing romance since middle school. In eighth grade, she failed to qualify for the Power of the Pen State Championships because "all her submissions contained the same theme: young people falling in love." #LookAtHerNow

She's best known for writing unapologetically angsty romance that causes emotional damage for her readers. Creative spicy scenes and consent as foreplay are two hallmarks of her books. Abby prides herself in writing authentic characters while weaving mental health, chronic illness, and neurodiverse representation into the fabric of her stories.

Abby met her husband at a house party the summer before her freshman year of college. He had a secret pizza stashed in the trunk of his car that he was saving for a midnight snack—how was she supposed to resist that level of golden retriever energy and preparedness? When Abby isn't writing, she's reading, traveling, and raising her three daughters.

Connect with Abby

Website: www.authorabbymillsaps.com
Instagram: @abbymillsaps
TikTok: @authorabbymillsaps
Email: authorabbymillsaps@gmail.com
Newsletter: https://geni.us/AuthorAbbyNewsletter
Facebook Reader Group: Abby's Full Out Fiends

www.ingramcontent.com/pod-product-compliance
Lightning Source LLC
LaVergne TN
LVHW030317070526
838199LV00069B/6477